WHEN BIGFOOT ATTACKS
A Global Survey of Alleged Sasquatch/Yeti Predation
MICHAEL NEWTON

Typeset by Jonathan Downes,
Proofread by Nadia Novali
Cover by J.T. Lindroos

Layout by SPiderKaT for CFZ Communications
Using Microsoft Word 2000, Microsoft , Publisher 2000, Adobe Photoshop CS.

First published in Great Britain by CFZ Press

CFZ Press
Myrtle Cottage
Woolsery
Bideford
North Devon
EX39 5QR

ISBN: 978-1-905723-69-0

In memory of Dr. Grover Krantz (1931-2002)

Table of Contents

Author's Note

I am not a Bigfoot believer. "Belief" implies blind faith in things that lie forever in a Twilight Zone beyond all scientific proof. I *do* accept the possibility of creatures still unclassified, existing in the modern world, and I am willing to examine evidence supporting—or refuting—their existence. That said, the work in hand does not attempt to prove that any such creatures exist. Hundreds of other books pursue that goal. Some of the best—and worst—are listed in the bibliography.

Most readers of this work are probably familiar with the subject of Sasquatchery. For any novices, however, certain basic terms should be defined. They include:

- *Cryptozoology* - Coined by Dr. Bernard Heuvelmans in the late 1950s, this term describes the search for "hidden" or "unexpected" animals—i.e., any creatures unrecognised by modern science as existing in a given place or time, which nonetheless continue to surprise eyewitnesses. Those who pursue the search are dubbed *cryptozoologists*, and the beasts they seek are called *cryptids* (adopted in 1983 to replace the pejorative "monster" label).

- *Hominology* - A branch of cryptozoology named by Russian researcher Dmitri Bayanov, hominology involves the study of unclassified *hominids*—hairy bipeds of various sizes, reported within living memory from every continent on Earth except Antarctica. Whether trained in zoology or anthropology, researchers who stalk Sasquatch, Yeti and their kin are commonly described as *hominologists*.

While the research for this volume was in progress, an important source was lost, perhaps forever. Ray Crowe's International Bigfoot Society maintained an Internet website listing thousands of alleged Sasquatch encounters, broken down by state, replete with fascinating details gleaned from decades of research. While flawed by frequent duplication of entries, the IBS site was nonetheless unrivalled by any other archive readily available to researchers—until it disappeared without a trace in March 2009. That disappearance is, itself, a mystery. One well-known researcher admits to buying Crowe's physical archive, but denies control over the website. Meanwhile, Google searches for the IBS now shunt readers to another website, maintained by the Seattle-based Sasquatch Information Society, copyrighted in the name of Robert Murdock.

That individual does not respond to inquiries—at least, from me—and at press time for this volume, none of the vanished IBS files had appeared on the SIS website. While claiming 1,098 reports on file for the 50 United States—compared to Ray Crowe's 1,277 for Oregon alone—the SIS still offers next to nothing. The vast majority of its "reports," when read, say simply: "Record has not been validated or is being studied." There, at least for now, the matter rests—like the question of Bigfoot's existence—in the words of Winston Churchill, "a *riddle* wrapped in a *mystery* inside an *enigma.*"

Acknowledgements

I owe special thanks to fellow author Chad Arment; to Liz Boston, reference librarian with the Central Reference Service of Washington's Timberland Regional Library; to Jacqueline Hamm, reference librarian at the Longview (Washington) Public Library; and to Amy Scott, information services librarian with the Fort Vancouver (Washington) Regional Library District. Thanks, also, to Jon Downes at CFZ Press, and to Ray Crowe, late of the International Bigfoot Society, whose archives were invaluable while they lasted.

Introduction: Predatory Primates

I n the first half of the 5th Century B.C.E., Hanno the Carthaginian set out to circumnavigate Africa. No one knows today if he succeeded, but the brief record Hanno left of his momentous journey includes the following passage:

> [W]e sailed along the burning coast for three days and came to the gulf named the Horn of the South. At the end of it was an island like the first one, with a lake in which was another island full of savages. The greater parts of these were women. They had hairy bodies and the interpreters called them Gorillas. We pursued some of the males but we could not catch a single one because they were good climbers and they defended themselves fiercely. However, we managed to take three women. They bit and scratched their captors, whom they did not want to follow. We killed them and removed the skins to take back to Carthage. We sailed no further, being short of supplies.[1]

Modern researchers still debate the meaning of Hanno's report. Where did the brutal encounter occur? Were the creatures true gorillas or primitive humans? We may never know, but Hanno's account was only the first in a series of tales describing hairy, manlike creatures in Africa. British adventurer Andrew Battel, captured by Portuguese troops in the late 16th Century, joined the enemy's colonial army and spent many years around Mayombe, in the western Congo. His recitation of that region's fauna, first published in 1613, offered this description of a resident "monster":

> Here is a great sandy bay, two leagues to the northward of Cape Negro, which is the port of Mayombe. Sometimes the Portugals lade logwood in this bay. Here is a great river, called Banna: in the winter it hath no barre, because the generall winds cause a great sea. But when the sunne hath his south declination, then a boat may goe in; for then it is smooth because of the raine. This river is very great, and hath many ilands and people dwelling in them. The woods are so covered with baboones, monkies, apes and parrots, that it will feare any man to travaile in them alone. Here are also two kinds of monsters, which are common in these woods,

and very dangerous.

> The greatest of these two monsters is called Pongo in their language, and the lesser is called Engeco. This Pongo is in all proportion like a man; but that he is more like a giant in stature than a man; for he is very tall, and hath a man's face, hollow-eyed, with long haire upon his browes. His face and eares are without haire, and his hands also. His bodie is full of haire, but not very thicke; and it is of a dunnish colour.

> He differeth not from a man but in his legs; for they have no calfe. Hee goeth alwaies upon his legs, and carrieth his hands clasped in the nape of his necke when he goeth upon the ground. They sleepe in the trees, and build shelters for the raine. They feed upon fruit that they find in the woods, and upon nuts, for they eate no kind of flesh. They cannot speake, and have no understanding more than a beast. The people of the countrie, when they travaile in the woods, make fires where they sleepe in the night; and in the morning when they are gone, the Pongoes will come and sit about the fire till it goeth out; for they have no understanding to lay the wood together. They goe many together, and kill many negroes that travaile in the woods. Many times they fall upon the elephants which come to feed where they be, and so beate them with their clubbed fists, and pieces of wood, that they will runne roaring away from them. Those Pongoes are never taken alive because they are so strong, that ten men cannot hold one of them; but yet they take many of their young ones with poisoned arrowes. The young Pongo hangeth on his mother's belly with his hands fast clasped about her, so that when the countrie people kill any of the females they take the young one, which hangeth fast upon his mother. When they die among themselves, they cover the dead with great heaps of boughs and wood, which is commonly found in the forest.[2]

A colleague of Battel, Samuel Purchas, wrote in 1625 that Battel "told me in conference with him, that one of these Pongos tooke a Negro boy of his, which liued a moneth with them. For they hurt not those which they surprise at unawares, except they look on them, which hee auoyded. He said, their highth was like a mans, but their bignesse twice as great. I saw the Negro boy."[3]

Even after European scientists admitted the existence of gorillas, in the Eighteenth Century, they still confused the apes with chimpanzees and publicly denied that man-sized specimens existed. J.C.M. Radermacher, writing in 1780, noted that "the large species, described by Buffon and other authors as of the size of a man, is held by many to be a Chimera."[4] Only in 1847 did Thomas Savage and Jeffries Wyman finally distinguish gorillas from chimpanzees, with a study of skulls collected in Gabon. They named the new species *Troglodytes gorilla*, while chimpanzees were then known as *T. niger* (today, *Pan troglodytes*). Even then, it remained for Isidore Geoffroy-Saint-Hilaire to create the new genus *Gorilla*, in 1851.

Discovery of the western lowland gorilla (*Gorilla gorilla gorilla*) and its eastern subspecies (*G. g. graueri*) did not end the saga of man-monsters in Africa, however. Reports of even larger hairy giants continued—and were widely dismissed as pure fiction—until German explorer Robert (or Oscar, in some reports) Von Beringe shot two unrecognised specimens on 17 October 1902, in the Virunga Mountains. Another fifty-four mountain gorillas were killed for study by 1925, and today the endangered species (*G. g. berengei*) is named for its premiere assassin. Some primatologists propose yet another subspecies, the Cross River gorilla (*G. g. diehli*), but scientific opinion remains divided on the subject.[5]

Identifying gorilla species was one thing; determining their attitude toward human beings was another. In the 19th Century, British biologist Sir Richard Owen sketched a fearsome portrait of the jungle giants.

> Negroes when stealing through the shade of the tropical forest become sometimes aware of one of these frightfully formidable apes by the sudden disappearance of one of their companions, who is hoisted up into the tree, uttering, perhaps, a short, choking cry. In a few minutes he falls to the ground a strangled corpse.[6]

That far-fetched view of gorillas prevailed in popular culture through the first half of the 20th Century, with countless novels, films and "nonfiction" articles in pulp adventure magazines portraying great apes as voracious man-killers and habitual kidnappers of women. Today, by contrast, most experts describe gorillas as gentle giants, all bluff and no bite, intimidated by their smaller human kin. There is no question that gorillas have suffered greatly at human hands, with *G. g. berengei* driven to the verge of extinction in recent decades, and nearly all zoologists agree with author Roger Caras that "the chances of being injured by an unmolested specimen are slight." Caras further notes that:

> On those occasions when the gorilla actually presses home and attacks, the subject may receive a perfectly devastating sideways slap or a rending bite with enormous teeth and powerful jaws. The gorilla usually makes one punishing pass and is satisfied to move off into the thick forest near which it is almost always found. These attacks are rare, however.[7]

Rare, but not unknown. James Clarke describes the case of an African hunting guide named Rubin, who was twice attacked by a female gorilla in separate incidents, two days apart. The first assault reportedly occurred because the ape "had been spurned by the local patriarch and was in a towering rage. She suddenly saw Rubin and charged up to him. Rubin, taken completely by surprise, struck her with his panga. The female bit him. Rubin then kicked her in the stomach. The gorilla broke off the fight and dived into the undergrowth." The second incident stopped short of physical contact, when Rubin "shouted right back and the frustrated ape bowed out."[8] Author Jordi Sabater Pi documented seven gorilla attacks on humans in Spanish Guinea (now Equatorial Guinea) between the mid-1950s and January 1964. Two incidents involved gorillas wounded by hunters they mauled in self-defence; one involved a female with offspring; two were "very similar" to the foregoing cases; and two were described as unprovoked attacks.[9]

Captive gorillas may also pose a threat to man, as demonstrated by incidents at zoos in Dallas and Boston. On 27 November 1998 a thirty-three-year-old, 340-pound male gorilla named Hercules escaped from the Dallas Zoo's infirmary and invaded a nearby kitchen, where it attacked keeper Jennifer McClurg. McClurg suffered bites on her arm and torso before Hercules was tranquilised and returned to his enclosure.[10] Four tranquiliser darts were required to stop Little Joe, a 300-pound gorilla who escaped from Boston's Franklin Park Zoo on 28 September 2003, mauling a teenage zoo employee and a two-year-old child.[11] Another incident, again in Dallas, ended less happily. Jabari, a 300-pound, thirteen-year-old lowland gorilla escaped from his enclosure on 18 March 2004 and attacked a group of tourists at the zoo. Four persons were injured during the forty-minute rampage, after tranquiliser darts failed to subdue Jabari. Two of those attacked, Keisha Heard and her three-year-old son, suffered multiple bites and were briefly hospitalised. Jabari was shot and killed by police SWAT officers, when zookeepers were unable to corral him.[12] On 12 June 2009 a lowland gorilla escaped from its enclosure at Riverbanks Zoo in Columbia, South Carolina, mauled a food service employee, then immediately returned to its exhibit.[13]

Gorillas are not the only primates known for occasional clashes with humans. Roger Caras dubs chimpanzees "brash creatures as individually variable in behaviour and appearance...as men."[14] That includes sporadic outbursts of foul temper, complete with vicious biting, and while zookeepers bear the brunt of chimp fury, attacks in the wild are also reported. In March 1957, an African woman was collecting firewood near Lake Tanganyika, north of Kigoma, Tanzania, when suddenly from the bush came a chimpanzee.

> We were in the bush and the village was far. I was tying up my faggots. I
> ran away and the chimpanzee hit me twice. He was about four feet tall. I
> fell down. Then it caught the child who was on my back. I made a great
> deal of noise and other women came. Then we saw the chimpanzee eat-
> ing the child's ears, hands and head.[15]

The medical report in that case described five depressed fractures of the infant's skull caused by teeth, while the victim's scalp, hands and half of one foot were missing. A coroner's report ruled the death accidental and found that the baby had been "eaten by some animal."[16]

Nearly half a century later, in January 2004, authorities in Tanzania and Uganda reported that wild chimpanzees, struggling to survive destruction of their forest habitat, had developed a taste for human flesh. According to that report, eight children had been killed by chimps over the past seven years, with another eight seriously injured. Those who died were found with limbs and other body parts missing, apparently eaten. The most recent victim, three-month-old Jackson Alikiriza, was snatched and killed in Uganda while his mother harvested potatoes. Biologist Michael Gavin told BBC News, "They are just trying to get by. If they can't get enough food in the forest they are going to wander out in search of what's available." Dr. Frans de Wall, a professor of zoology at Emory University in Atlanta, advised reporters, "I am not sure these cases have much to do with territoriality. I think they rather have to do with predation."[17]

Tabloid headline for a recent chimpanzee attack.

Captive chimps may be equally dangerous. Consider "Moe," a young chimpanzee owned by St. James and LaDonna Davis in West Covina, California. The Davises raised Moe from infancy, and considered him "a member of the family," but ultimately they could not control him. Moe escaped from home in August 1998, at age thirty, slightly injuring two police officers before he was recaptured. In September 1999, after biting a female houseguest, Moe was removed to a wildlife sanctuary under court order.

On 3 March 2005, when the Davises visited Moe with a cake for his thirty-ninth birthday, two other chimps escaped and viciously attacked St. James, ripping out his right eye, biting off his nose, lips, and fingers before an armed attendant arrived and shot the attackers. Despite that grisly incident, the Davises continued visiting Moe until June 2007, when the chimp escaped and vanished forever into the southern California wilderness.[18]

Another horrific chimp attack occurred on 16 February 2009, when fourteen-year-old "Travis" attacked his owner in Stamford, Connecticut. Surgeons laboured for seven hours to save fifty-five-year-old Charla Nash, after Travis mauled her without provocation in a "brutal and lengthy" assault. Prior to the attack, Travis had used a key to escape from Nash's home. When police arrived on the scene, Travis stormed one of their cruisers and was shot dead by its driver. Nash suffered disfiguring wounds to her face, neck, and hands.[19]

Baboons (genera *Papio* and *Mandrillus*) which are monkeys rather than apes have a more extensive record of attacks on human beings. Roger Caras reports that "children have been stolen by them on at least a few occasions, although the motive was more likely adoption of a new baby than intended harm." In other cases, according to Caras, solitary men attacked by troops of baboons have suffered "quite appalling" damage.[20] James Clarke reports attacks by rogue mandrills (*Mandrillus sphinx*), and P.J. Pretorius describes a man-eating yellow baboon (*Papio cynocephalus*) who claimed multiple victims in Tanzania, but no details are available on either case.[21] Specific documented incidents include the following:

- **11 March 1963:** Police in the Cullinan district of South Africa shot a large male baboon after natives complained that the beast had threatened them and pelted them with stones over a two-year period. Subsequently, officers announced that in 1961 the same baboon had chased two girls, ages five and thirteen, over a 100-foot cliff to their deaths.[22]

- **10 April 1964:** A pet chacma baboon (*Papio ursinus*) escaped from its owner in Brakpan, South Africa, grabbed a one-year-old child from its stroller on the street, bit through the infant's skull, and then dropped its lifeless victim in full view of the child's hysterical mother. New legislation subsequently banned keeping baboons as pets.[23]

- **9 September 1964:** A South African shepherd, Fred Visagie, was attacked by a baboon at Rooiwal farm, in Cape Province. The monkey tore off Visagie's clothes, leaving him scratched and bruised, before it retreated. Other members of the baboon troop encircled Visagie and watched the assault without participating.[24]

- **26 September 1999:** Spokesmen for South Africa's Cape Peninsula National Park announced that three "problem" baboons had been destroyed, following a series of attacks on park visitors. Two attacks on humans were reported during September, with victims including an elderly woman and a young housewife. Park administrators blamed the incidents on tourists who "feel that they are doing [the baboons] a kindness by feeding them."[25]

- **May 2001:** Tourist Elsabie Templeton was attacked by a baboon at the Aloe Ridge Hotel in Zwartkops, South Africa. The creature tore her blouse and scratched her stomach. When Templeton reported the incident to hotel owner Alex Richter, she says, "He insinuated that I had teased the baboon. He said he wouldn't take action because the baboons were a huge draw card for foreign tourists."[26]

- **8 June 2001:** Baboons in the Kingdom of Swaziland launched a series of attacks around Maphungwane, injuring three-year-old Samkele Gamedze at her home and killing thirty-four goats on a nearby farm. A one-year-old boy was wounded at another homestead on 9 June.[27]

- **14 August 2001:** Saudi Arabian authorities announced an investigation to determine whether baboon populations in the desert country are "out of control." Farmers in the mountains around Fifa complained that 15,000 baboons had run amok, attacking homes and damaging property. Other assaults were reported from the Abha Faculty for Girls, on homes and schools around Baha, and from Taif, where a two-year-old girl was abducted and killed.[28]

- **16 November 2002:** Another guest at South Africa's Aloe Ridge Hotel, Leon de Bruin, was bitten on the thigh and buttocks by a baboon. Hotel employees described seven or eight similar incidents over the past two years, including the case of a carpenter who required ninety-six stitches to close his bite wounds.[29]

- **18 April 2003:** Four girls collecting water from a well near their village in drought-ravaged northern Kenya were attacked by a troop of some thirty baboons. Twelve-year-old Aisha Wako suffered cuts and bruises on her face, while companion Mumina Golichia escaped with torn clothing.[30]

- **15 June 2003:** A rogue baboon snatched three-month-old Neo Tukane from his bedroom, in the South African village of Madipelesa, while his mother washed clothes in an adjoining room. Hearing the baby's cries, Betty Tukane arrived in time to see her child vanish through a window in the baboon's grasp. The simian kidnapper climbed a nearby telephone pole, where it devoured the infant's brain in full view of horrified witnesses, then dropped the corpse and fled. Hunters found and killed the alleged culprit nine days later.[31]

- **January 2006:** Two separate baboon attacks on humans raised concerns in South Africa's Western Cape Province. Victims included 42-year-old Mtimkulu Manseli, mauled by a lone baboon in Alexandria, and a four-year-old boy caught in a fight between two male baboons at a picnic ground near Gordon's Bay. The first attack, at least, seemed unprovoked, and left victim Manseli with both arms slashed to the bone.[32]

- **April 2008:** Residents of Al Baha, Majarida, and Taif, Saudi Arabia, complained of repeated attacks by troops of hungry baboons, which left several persons injured. Teachers and students at Al Baha's College for Girls panicked as some 100 baboons rampaged across campus. Farmer Naif Al Shahri reported a similar raid on his farm, near Taif. "Running amok," he said, "they attack children, ransack houses and damage cars."[33]

Other primates also attack human beings. A Salvation Army missionary with forty years of service in India once told Roger Caras that monkey bites were more common in many parts of that country than snakebites.[34] Recent incidents involving various primate species include the following:

- **14 July 2000:** Police at Ishikawa, Okinawa, launched a full-scale hunt for an escaped monkey who attacked two local residents after fleeing its cage. The first incident involved only minor injuries, but the second victim was hospitalised for a bite wound that severed an artery.[35]

- **12 March 2002:** Fifty hunters scoured the neighbourhood of Suwa, Japan, seeking a rogue monkey blamed for attacks on twenty-three women. Fourteen victims were injured on March 11 and nine more the following day, most bitten on the legs while walking along public streets.[36]

- **30 March 2002:** Police recaptured an escaped monkey after it bit two persons in Seto, Japan. The animal's owner faced charges of keeping a monkey without permission.[37]

- **1 April 2003:** Dozens of monkeys invaded a girl's college at Darjeeling, in eastern India, attacking several students and shredding some 6,000 library books in a manic rampage.[38]

- **30 June 2003:** A pet monkey escaped from its cage in Paddi-Quepem, India, and attacked three local women before it was recaptured by animal control officers. The fugitive was transported to the Cotigao wildlife sanctuary.[39]

- **19 August 2004:** *Al-Anbaa,* a Sudanese newspaper, reported that "hordes of monkeys" in Kassala, near the Eritrean frontier, had attacked women and children, raiding bakeries and grocery stores for food. Authorities blamed recent deforestation for the mass assaults in two suburbs, which "start at dawn and sometimes last until dusk." Aside from raiding shops and mauling pedestrians, the hungry primates entered homes, "breaking kitchen utensils and snatching food from the children." Some reportedly were wise enough to open refrigerators and loot their contents.[40]

- **31 May 2005:** A female orang-utan attacked two visitors at Malaysia's Matang Wildlife Centre, biting both women on their legs. Victim Sibu Tong told authorities that the ape turned violent after trying to snatch a bag away from her eleven-year-old son. "As I pulled my son away," she said, "it turned on my sister and bit her leg. I quickly handed my baby to my niece and told all the children to run for safety before I rushed to help my sister. When I tried to push the orang-utan away from my sister, it attacked me."[41]

If known primates demonstrably attack human beings on occasion, is it possible that still-unclassified species do likewise? The published literature on Sasquatch, Yeti and other unknown hominids is replete with anecdotal accounts of such attacks, but no author to date has attempted a comprehensive survey of those alleged cases. *When Bigfoot Attacks* intends to close that gap in cryptozoological scholarship.

The present work is divided into nine chapters. The first examines pre-Columbian traditions of hairy "cannibal giants" reported by Native peoples throughout North America. Chapter 2 reviews "classic" cases of alleged Sasquatch attacks on humans in the United States and Canada between 1890 and 1973. Chapter 3 examines lesser-known incidents reported throughout North America, from Colonial times to the present day. Chapters 4 through 8 provide a world tour of foreign cases, including alleged hominid attacks from Latin America, Eurasia west of the Urals, Asia proper, Africa, and the islands of Oceania. Chapter 9 examines reports of human abductions, including the alleged first-person accounts of victims who survived the experience. Additional material includes comprehensive references and a selected bibliography.

For purposes of this study, an "attack" is defined as any act of unprovoked aggression against human beings, their domestic animals, dwellings or vehicles. It does *not* include staring, shouting, "stalking," "menacing," or any other reported behaviour stopping short of attempted physical contact. As humans are acquitted of assault charges without some overt gesture toward an adversary, so our giant cousins of the forest must be judged by the same standard.

Are they a threat to man in any sense?

You are the jury.

Let the trial begin.

Chapter 1.
Ancient Enemies: Myth-information?

T hey shamble through the mists of time and legend—hulking, nearly-human forms tramping primeval forests in an endless search for sustenance. They cannot rest until they feed.

But what—or who—is on the menu?

North American aborigines knew them by sight and reputation, fearsome hunters prone to dine on men and kidnap women. Long before the first pale Europeans trespassed in the New World, Native tribes described the forest-dwellers as cannibals—a term without meaning, unless both predator and prey were human beings. Native legends speak of brutal wars between tribesmen and "cannibal giants," an early form of ethnic cleansing from which only one side could emerge victorious.

But are the stories true?

Most anthropologists today believe that aboriginal Americans were spawned in Asia and approached the western hemisphere on foot, across the Bering Strait ice bridge, in prehistoric times. Some hominologists believe those trekkers were preceded or pursued by members of another race, perhaps the ancient ape *Gigantopithecus*, which may have posed stiff competition for the travellers—and may have treated them as a potential meal.

Whether or not that theory is correct, nearly identical accounts of cannibal giants are found among Native peoples throughout North America. Charting those legends on a map reveals a pattern of dispersal from coast to coast, and from the Arctic Circle to the Gulf of Mexico. Whether those tales are strictly fables or contain a germ of truth may be impossible to learn, at this remove from the events. But their consistency and sheer ubiquity throughout the continent suggests something beyond a simple campfire tale.

Our tour begins, as did the journey of our ancient ancestors, in the extreme Northwest. Native Alaskan legends speak of five different cannibal giants, or perhaps one species known by varied local names. Aleutian villagers spoke of the *Arulataq* ("bellowing man"). Around great Iliamna Lake (reputed home of giant fish, still unidentified), members of the Na-Dené tribe told stories of the deadly *Get'qun*. A few miles farther east, along the shores of Cook Inlet, Tanaina tribesmen lived in fear of the *Lenghee*, a giant that came from the north to abduct human prey. Another nemesis of the Tanaina in southern Alaska, the shaggy *Gilyuk*, likewise dined on men and marked its trails with gnawed and twisted birch saplings. That whistling terror also fancied headgear, we are told: the name *Gilyuk* translates as "big man with the little hat." Still further south, spanning Alaska's frontier with British Columbia, Tlingit shamans described the *Koosh-taa-kaa* ("land-otter man"), a hairy biped with a naked face who snatched the souls of drowning victims and those lost in the forest.[1]

The northernmost of Canada's cannibal giants was reported from the central Yukon Territory, where Natives along the Peel River knew it as *Mahoni* ("hairy man"). British Columbia, so rich in modern Sasquatch lore, also provides a wealth of cannibal giant traditions. Proceeding from the north, southward, we first meet the *Xudele,* reported by Tsetsaut tribesmen along the Portland Canal, who described it as an axe-wielding man-eater with a doglike face and up-turned nose. Nearby, dwelt the *Tenatco* ("big man"), described by Kaska storytellers as an ardent burrower. Descending through central B.C., we meet the Penutian tribe's dreaded *Gy-dem gylilix* ("man of the woods") and the Tsimsian nation's *Gydem lakhs sgyinist* ("man of the jackpines"). The *Kaigyet,* described by Carrier tribesmen, was tall and shaggy, human-faced, and impervious to arrows. Heiltsuk villagers lived in fear of the *La la.* Chipewyans fled the *Nakani* ("bush man"), while Koyukons battled the *Nakentlia* ("sneaker"), both described as nocturnal abductors of women and children, known for their foul body odour and high-pitched whistling sounds. Around Bella Coola, Salishan artists carved ceremonial masks in the likeness of the long-armed, short-legged *Snanaik,* notorious for its sharp claws and aggressive demeanour. Also represented on Kwakiutl masks and totem poles is the ferocious female *Dsonoqua* ("wild woman of the woods"). Gwich'in tribesmen vied for supremacy with the *Tinjih-rui* ("black man"). On scenic Vancouver Island, the savage *Matlox* rampaged around Nootka Sound, while Salish natives were terrorised by the *Thamekwis.* Squamish aborigines stalked and were stalked by the *Smay'il* ("wild men"). Cowichans described the *Tsamekes* ("giant") as a whistling hairy biped, seven to eight feet tall. The *Stenwyken* smelled like burnt hair and raided Okanagan Valley villages for food, when it was not kidnapping women for sex.[2]

Washington State reveals cannibal giant traditions in four areas. Along the state's border with British Columbia, legends span the international boundary, including reports of the Okanagan tribe's *Sne-nah* ("owl woman"), the Stillaguamish *Steetahl* ("wild tribe"), and the Kwakiutl *Bukwas* ("man of the woods"). The *Bukwas* hardly qualifies as giant, with an average height of only five feet, but its dark hair, bare protruding face, foul odour and nocturnal whistling otherwise conform precisely to the classic Sasquatch. The Olympic Peninsula and southern coast of Puget Sound positively teem with legends of bipedal stalkers, including the Makah tribe's *El-*

OPPOSITE: An atypical Sasquatch stones a wilderness explorer.

Millie Gaul, of the Chehalis Reserve, had a harrowing experience with the Sasquatch when one approached her home during the afternoon. Several nights later she heard a prowler, and glancing up, saw him rubbing his hand over the window pane. She screamed and the giant visitor disappeared

Every four years a strange race of giants is reported at various places in British Columbia. They are reported this year as shown on the map

Are they the LAST CAVE MEN ?

British Columbia Startled by the Appearance of "Sasquatch," a Strange Race of Hairy Giants

Entrance to one of the great caves, thought to be the home of some of the giant Sasquatch

It was near this Indian house where the first Sasquatch were reported seen years ago. The house was abandoned

Every four years great columns of fire are seen on certain mountaintops, thought to be signals from the Sasquatch. The arrow shows one of these signal fires

By Francis Dickie

IT IS peculiarly in keeping with this topsy-turvy year of violently varying weather, universal human unrest, drought, grasshopper plagues and other phenomena that there now come from various eyewitnesses the report of seeing some of the "Sasquatch," those weird hairy men reported for twenty years to dwell in the tremendous and unexplored mountain region of British Columbia, Canada.

Their reported return is particularly in keeping with this unusual year, so remarkable for the number of appearances of various startling monsters sighted from Scotland to the Caribbean, from the Pacific to the Mediterranean, the reality of which is affirmed by scores of eyewitnesses. Moreover, the statements of some of these people, in so far as certain denizens of the ocean are concerned, have been borne out, for within a short time of each other, at a dozen places on the European coast, the remains of incredible monsters of the deep have been cast up.

Of all these mysterious earthly visitants, perhaps the "Sasquatch" is the least known, by reason of the rarity of their appearance and the reluctance of those who have seen them to talk.

THE existence of a troglodyte race inhabiting the mountains of British Columbia in many of the vast caves is a tribal legend among the Chehalis Indians and those of the Seven Reservations, near Chilliwack, in the Harrison Lake district, about a hundred miles east of Vancouver. Among the Indians the race has been known for centuries by the name "Sasquatch," or hairy men.

But reports of these creatures being seen frequently at various times over a period of the last twenty years, and more frequently in recent weeks, have caused a number of people to raise the question if these strange creatures may not be more than an Indian legend of the past, and that some of the race of cavern dwellers are still living in the unexplored fastness of British Columbia.

The Sasquatch have been seen, according to the statements from both white men and Indians. The wild, hairy men have mostly been reported in the Harrison Lake district, but also as far east as the mountainous region of Yale, on the main line of the Canadian Pacific Railway.

The repeated reports of eyewitnesses of seeing one or more of the huge hairy men in recent years, and more particularly in the last month, and the mounting number of the reports of eyewitnesses now seem to point strongly that the old tribal legend, long contemporarily flouted by the white man, is true, and that at least a few of this mysterious race may still inhabit the solitudes nearby where once they were numerous. The possibility of this is further borne out when it is recalled that the remains of a giant race of men recently have been unearthed in the mountainous region of Mexico.

The chief difficulty, in fact the whole task of an investigator, in matters of such phenomena as Sasquatch or sea serpents, is, of course, the credibility of the witnesses. If unwatchful, what motive lies behind their story? In the case of the Sasquatch, the element of credence is heightened because in most cases the witnesses have been reluctant ones, some of them not revealing their stories for years.

From a careful comparison of all eyewitness statements to date, all are closely in agreement as to the following facts: The Sasquatch are gigantic men, varying from six and one-half to seven feet in height. One, and only one, witness states the nose of them to be very broad, and the arms long, reaching below the knee. All but one are agreed as to the hideousness of the face.

However, as in most instances the Sasquatch were not seen close up, it is

natural the descriptions remain very general. These people also have been close were so terror-stricken that their accounts are vague. Yet, aside from one of the most recent happenings, in only two other cases have the Sasquatch shown themselves hostile.

Tom Cedar, an Indian, was fishing in Morris Creek. Suddenly a huge rock struck the water near his canoe. Looking up, he saw a hairy-figured giant, poised to hurl another stone at him

THE fact that some of these strange people have just been reported close to civilization at this time accurately compares with dates noted by the Chehalis Indians. They point to a resident in the district. He states they bear evidence of habitation. Upon the walls are some crude drawings. In this region, according to the Indians, two large bands of Sasquatch fought a long time ago until both were brought almost to extermination.

These periodic returns to some ancient gathering place to bring these people close to what are now civilized areas.

A few days ago, a middle-aged Indian, Tom Cedar, was trout fishing from his canoe on Morris Creek, a tributary of the Harrison. He was near a rocky terraced bank. Suddenly a large rock struck the water so close to his canoe that he was drenched by the splash. Looking up, he saw with amazement a huge hairy man above him just as he threw another rock. This also barely missed the canoe. Cedar paddled rapidly upstream to the settlement.

By way of noting an odd coincidence, this particular stream, now called Morris Creek, was known as Sasksim where the white men first arrived, and it so called on old maps. Nearby are caverns which were investigated by Captain Wards, forty years a resident in the district. He states they bear evidence of habitation. Upon the walls are some crude drawings. In this region, according to the Indians, two large bands of Sasquatch fought a long time ago until both were brought almost to extermination.

THE other evidence of hostile intention of some of these creatures dates back twenty years and consists of the utterances of two Indians, Peter and Paul Williams of Chehalis. The following is a very much condensed version:

"On an evening in May," states Peter, "I was about a mile from the reserve, near the foot of the mountain, when what I at first took to be a bear rose

up in the underbrush. It was a man between six and seven feet tall, covered with hair. I turned and ran through the underbrush to my dugout. The hairy man came after me. I paddled across the stream, which is not very deep, and the man waded after. I reached the house where my wife and child were inside. I bolted the door. Presently the hairy man arrived. It was growing dark. He prowled around, grunting and growling, but after a little while went away."

About the same time Paul was chased from a creek where he was fishing. But the giant did not run after him very far, and apparently the action was only to drive the man away to get the fish he had taken.

On another occasion in the next year, Peter and another man came upon two plants so close as to distinguish a man and a woman. Though the Indians ran, they were not pursued.

Charley Victor, now living at Chilliwack, relates that he and a little group of companions, while bathing in a mountain lake year Yale, suddenly looked up to see a huge man, naked and hairy, looking down upon them from among the trees.

"His big eyes looked very kind, and I was about to speak to him when he drew back into the trees," related Charley.

Here we have the only witness who gives a favorable reaction to sight of the mysterious race.

This book place many years ago and at a point about a hundred miles from where the majority of the Sasquatch have been reported seen in recent times.

THE next account of which any fully recorded evidence is now to be seen deals with September, 1927, near the little mountain town of Agassiz, which is very near the point at which all the other Sasquatch have been reported. A party of hop-pickers were picnicking here. On their way to this a man, named Herbert Point, and a girl,

Adaline August, were walking when they saw a strange creature approaching. "He was twice as big as the average man, with hands as long they nearly touched the ground, and his nose spread all over his face. His body was covered with hair like an animal. He stopped within fifty feet of us. We ran away as fast as we could." The hitmo in quaint site accounts from a letter written by the man in answer to a query of what he had seen.

Within recent weeks Emma Paul and Millie Gaul, two other members of the Chehalis Reserve, saw one of the Sasquatch near their home on the fringe of the woods. Several nights later he was heard prowling around the house of Millie Gaul, and once rubbed his hand over the window pane.

To date, the last report was from Harrison Mills, a small hamlet on the Harrison River.

The woman, on hearing a humming noise, looked up to see a big man covered with hair on the edge of the clearing. She was frightened. Taking a backward step, she fell into one of the half-full laundry tubs at which she had been working. When she had extricated herself and looked again, the man had disappeared.

Such, in brief, are the legendary and eyewitness stories regarding the Sasquatch.

THE scientific board connected with the Museum of Vancouver is skeptical regarding the existence of any such remnant of a race that once might have roamed the forested regions.

An objection that the climate is too rigorous for a naked race, no matter how hairy, might be answered by pointing to the Fuegians, who live in a much more hospitable clime.

The eyewitness reports have always been reluctantly given. There may be many more. The chief objection among the natives to telling white foreigners is fear of ridicule. This suggestiveness is much stronger among natives than whites.

Here, for the present, the matter must rest. Perhaps further whatever may be heard in the future. Reconstructing, however, in judging the possibilities of the existence of the "Sasquatch, how many people have seen an exquisite and that remains of strange creatures have been recently washed on various shores, it is quite within the bounds of probability that but as there are unknown forces of life in the boundless depths of the ocean, equally so may there be in the enormous wilderness stretches of British Columbia wild hairy men roaming.

Copyright by Ledger Syndicate

ish-kas; the *Tsadjatko* ("giant") and *Oeh* ("cannibal woman"), both described by Quinault storytellers; and the Salish *Ke-ló-sumsh* ("giant hunters of the mountains"). Further east, native inhabitants of the Yakima Valley recall the *Wahteeta*. Finally, overlapping the Oregon border, we find tales of the *See-atco* ("giant") in the Cascade Range, the Chinook tribe's *Skookum* ("big" or "powerful"), and the Umatilla *Ste-ye-hah'* ("stick Indian"), named for its habit of poking or lobbing sticks into Native lodges after nightfall.[3]

Aside from legends shared with Washington, the state of Oregon boasts two home-grown cannibal giants. Tillamook tribesmen around Nehalem, on the northern coast, identified both male and female hominids, including the *Yi' dyi' tay* ("wild man") and his equally voracious mate, the *Xi'lgo* ("wild woman"). In south-central Oregon, Klamath and Modoc aborigines were ever wary of the *Yahyahaas*. Rounding off our tour of the Northwest, we must include the much-feared *Natliskeliguten* reported from the tri-state area of Washington, Idaho and Montana, together with the Shoshoni *Dzoavits* ("stone giant") of Idaho and Wyoming.[4]

Most of California's cannibal giant legends come from the Golden State's northern quarter; although Kawaiisu tribesmen encountered a hominid they dubbed *Miitiipi* ("bad luck") in the desolate Mojave Desert. Predators reported from more traditional settings include the Karok tribe's *Madukarahat* ("giant") of the Klamath River region, and the Pomo's *Olayome* ("rock people"), surrounding Clear Lake. Yuroks described the *Toké-mussi* in north-western California, and a towering creature known as *Oh-mah* ("wild man"). Hupa people also called their shaggy adversary *Oh-mah*, but translated it as "demon." Two cave-dwelling monsters (or, perhaps, the same one) were the Miwok *Chihalenchi* of the Sierra Nevadas and the Shoshoni *Tso'apittse* ("cannibal giant"), whose range extended north and eastward to Wyoming. Another adversary of the Miwok tribe, *Loo poo oi'yes*, whistled and howled by night, emitting foul body odour. The Yakima tribe's *Tah-tah-kle'-ah* was more refined, occasionally capable of speaking Native dialects.[5]

Cannibal giant traditions are by no means confined to the Northwest and California. Lakota tribesmen recognised two cryptic hominids within their range: the *Chiye tanka* ("big elder brother") roamed throughout Montana and the Dakotas, while the more aggressive *Rugaru* appeared only in North Dakota. Some researchers believe its name was borrowed from the French *loup-garou* ("werewolf"). Farther south, in Nebraska, Omaha tribesmen had to contend with the *Pa-snu-ta*, a kidnapper of humans whose head alone measured two feet tall. Ojibwa villagers in Minnesota knew the fierce *Misaabe*, while their Wyandot neighbours in Ontario fled the *Strendu*, a towering giant covered with scales, who prowled the shores of Lake Huron. Another Ontario predator, the Seneca *Ge-no'sgwa* ("stone giant") ranged southward into New York. Minnesota's *Misaabe*, meanwhile, reappeared in Québec to torment Natives around Grand Lake Victoria. Another Québec hominid, the *Atchen*, was unfailingly foul-tempered, but its violence paled beside that of the Algonquian *Windigo* ("winter cannibal giant"). *Windigo* legends, recorded over much of the eastern U.S. and Canada, mingled tales of a predatory Sasquatch-type creature with accounts of possessed human beings who "turned windigo" and slaughtered other humans for their flesh.[6]

The march of cannibal giants continues along North America's eastern seaboard. Three species were known to Micmac tribesmen in Canada's Maritime Provinces, including the *Gougou*, a female monster taller than a ship's mast who carried human victims in a spacious pouch; the *Gugwé*, smaller but still imposing, with a bearlike face and a whistling cry reminiscent of the gray partridge (*Perdix perdix*); and the wide-ranging *Skadegamutc*. The *Kiwáke*, described by Penobscot aborigines in Maine, was a huge beast with a shell resembling a turtle's, sprouting hair like a bear's on its head. Lenape shamans in eastern Pennsylvania and New Jersey related tales of the *Mesingw*, a shaggy hominid whose face was red and black. In southern Maryland, the Piscataway warned early British colonists about the deadly *Okee*. Cherokee natives in North Carolina and Georgia recognised two hominids, the *Kecleh-kudleh* ("hairy man") and *Tsulkalu* ("slant-eyed people"), the latter of whom arrived from western parts unknown, sometime before the 18th Century. In Florida, meanwhile, Seminole hunters were constantly on guard against the *Esti capcaki* ("tall man").[7]

Moving westward again, coming full-circle in our tour of the continent, we find more giants waiting. In Louisiana, Choctaw storytellers named their swamp-dwelling enemy *Kasheho-tapalo* ("woman call"), after the high-pitched screams it uttered, terrifying tribal hunters. Oklahoma's malodorous *Khot-sa-pohl* allegedly spoke the Kiowa language, but it valued humans chiefly as a source of protein. Ponca tribesmen in the Sooner State, likewise, dreaded the man-snatching *Mialushka*. In neighbouring Texas, Comanches had to deal with *Piamupits* ("big old giant"), while the *Karankawa* battled early Spanish settlers for a strip of coastal land between Galveston and Corpus Christi. Missionaries tried to convert the *Karankawa*, then ordered their extermination in 1688, after raids on settlements in present-day Jackson County. New Mexico's Kiowa tribesmen met the *T'oylona* ("big person") around Taos, while the Hopi confronted *So'yoko* in north-eastern Arizona.[8] The Paiutes of Nevada suffered depredations at the hands of *Numuzo'ho* ("crusher of people"), and battled a tribe of red-haired cannibal giants, described in 1883 by author Sarah Winnemucca Hopkins. She wrote:

> A small tribe of barbarians used to waylay my people, and kill and eat them. They would dig large holes in our trails at night. Our people would fall into those holes. That tribe would even eat their own dead. Yes, they would even come and dig up our dead after they were buried, and would carry them off and eat them. The Piutes called them the red-headed people-eaters.
>
> Toward the end of the war, those that were left went into a cave. My people watched at the mouth of the cave and would kill them as they came out to get food and water. My people asked them if they would be like us and not eat people like coyotes. But they would not give up. My people gathered wood and began to fill up the mouth of the cave. At last, my people set the wood on fire. At the same time they cried out to them, "Will you give up, be like men, and not eat people like beasts? Say quick—we will put out the fire."[9]

No answer came, and when the blaze burned out, all of the cannibals were dead. Author Warren Smith quotes an unnamed Paiute elder from the early 1970s, concerning his tribe's ancient foes: "They were called Siwash Indians by my people. There is some doubt that the giants were really Indians. Who ever heard of a red-headed Indian?"[10]

Our tour is complete, but what have we accomplished? First, there is no room for doubt that Native people throughout North America accepted the existence of cannibal giants. Some regarded their enemies as human or nearly so, while others mythologised the adversary, investing him with supernatural traits including hypnotic eyes, shape-shifting powers, and incredible size. Some elements of cannibal giant folklore are mundane and entirely plausible, while others clearly represent unbridled imagination.

Two possibilities exist. Either *all* Native legends of cannibal giants were plucked from thin air, with no vestige of truth to support them, or else *some* accounts must be rooted in fact—embroidered and exaggerated, beyond question, but fact nonetheless. Based on the broad range of reports, and the consistency of physical detail (stature, dark hair, big feet, foul odour, whistling calls, etc.) from coast to coast, there is no *prima facie* reason to dismiss Native reports as simple fireside tales or outright lies. And yet, assuming that some rudiment of fact supports the legends of cannibal giants, who—or *what*—on Earth were they?

One possibility, that of primitive aboriginal tribes, is circumstantially supported by references to cannibal giants who possessed coherent speech, fire, weapons, clothing, canoes and crude communal shelter. In some cases, like those of the *Karankawa* and Siwash "Indians" in Texas, Native rivals or white settlers regarded the cannibals as human, albeit a debased form of the species. History is replete with cases wherein animalistic traits have been attributed to outcast or little-known peoples. Roman historian Ctesias described a race of cave-dwelling beast-men in India, 120,000 strong, who had dog's heads and hairy tails. Marco Polo reported men with tails inhabiting Sumatra. As late as 1899, Malaysians described their Thai neighbours as cannibals with tails. Indeed, some Malaysians still call their country's Semang Negritos *orang utan* ("men of the woods"), a name properly belonging to one of the great apes.[11]

A second possible explanation for cannibal giant reports is the actual existence of a giant human race, now possibly extinct. This theory is supported not only by Native tradition and worldwide tales of giants dating from Biblical times, but also by discovery of oversized humanoid remains—skulls, skeletons and mummies—reported over five centuries from British Columbia, at least thirteen U.S. states, and a list of foreign countries including England, France, Greece, Ireland, Italy, Mexico and Switzerland. The recorded height of those specimens (or estimates, in the case of fragmentary remains) ranges from seven to seventeen feet. Individual specimens might be explained by disease, such as acromegaly or gigantism, but the official record in such cases stands at 8 feet 11.1 inches, while discoveries of multiple giants buried together makes a medical explanation less convincing. Likewise, the excavation of oversized armour, weapons and other man-made implements from "giant" graves effectively precludes the theory that all such remains belong to misidentified mammoths or other prehistoric megafauna.[12]

A third potential explanation for cannibal giant reports, supported by many cryptozoologists, is the existence of some unknown hominid whose omnivorous diet may include not only rodents, fish and fowl, but also the odd *homo sapiens.* Indeed, various authors have proposed between four and nine separate species of unrecognised primates presently living on Earth, their number including both prehistoric survivors and creatures unknown from the fossil record.[13] Some of the alleged relict survivors, notably *Homo erectus* and *Homo neanderthalensis,* were too small to pass for giants, but one species—the aforementioned *Gigantopithecus*—stood ten feet tall and weighed 1,200 pounds.[14] If it behaved, even occasionally, as some chimps, baboons and other primates have toward humans, "Giganto" must have been a formidable predator.

The possibilities posed here are not mutually exclusive. It would be strange, in fact, if there was only one solution to the riddle of ancient cannibal giants. Suppose for a moment that the giants who left their embarrassing remains at sundry points around the world coexisted not only with recognised Native peoples, but also with primitive tribes now extinct *and* with unknown primates that may have survived to the present. Why not? Multiple suspects go further toward explaining the similarities and inconsistencies of cannibal giant mythology than any one-size-fits-all solution thus far advanced.

Be that as it may, our focus in this volume is the body of reports alleging that unknown hominids—be they Sasquatch, Yeti, Kaptar or some other—pose a threat to human beings and their property. Reluctantly, we must abandon Stone Age tribes and giant specimens of *homo sapiens* to focus more precisely on the object of our mission. We resume that quest, in the next chapter, with cases commonly offered as "classic" evidence of Sasquatch aggression toward mankind.

Sasquatch meets Hollywood: *The Bloody Rage of Bigfoot.*

Chapter 2:
Classic Cases

Five published cases comprise the "classic" body of literature on Bigfoot aggression. They are examined here, together with a sixth rarely considered, but included because its final permutation claims the slaying of a Sasquatch in an act of self-defence. Our first report is vaguely dated from the early 19th Century. Its author is none other than Theodore Roosevelt, twenty-sixth president of the United States.

Bauman's Tale (18??)

Before he was an army "rough rider," assistant secretary of war, or governor of New York State, Teddy Roosevelt tried his hand at ranching in North Dakota. The blizzards of 1886-87 wiped out his cattle and his investment, but Roosevelt never lost his taste for the American frontier, as a big-game hunter and author. One of his books—*The Wilderness Hunter,* published in 1893—contains the first widely-known account of apparent Bigfoot predation on humans.

In that account, quoted below, Roosevelt presents a story personally told to him by an aged frontiersman, describing undated events from the raconteur's youth. Said events allegedly occurred somewhere in the Bitterroot Range, part of the Rocky Mountains marking the present-day border between Idaho and Montana. Bigfoot researcher Bobbie Short says that Roosevelt began writing *The Wilderness Hunter* in 1890, around the time of Idaho's admission to the Union as a full-fledged state. Rugged "mountain men" in the mould of Jim Bridger, Jedediah Smith, and "Liver Eating" Johnson scoured the Rockies for furs between 1810 and the early 1840s, the presumed parameters of Bauman's tale.[1]

Roosevelt's story is best told in full.

> Frontiersmen are not, as a rule, apt to be very superstitious. They lead lives too hard and practical, and have too little imagination in things spiritual and supernatural. I have heard but few ghost stories while living on the frontier, and those few were of a perfectly commonplace and conventional type.

THEODORE ROOSEVELT IN HUNTING COSTUME.

But I once listened to a goblin story, which rather impressed me. A grizzled, weather-beaten old mountain hunter, named Bauman, who was born and had passed all of his life on the frontier. He must have believed what he said, for he could hardly repress a shudder at certain points of the tale; but he was of German ancestry, and in childhood had doubtless been saturated with all kinds of ghost and goblin lore, so that many fearsome superstitions were latent in his mind; besides, he knew well the stories told by the Indian medicine-men in their winter camps, of the snow-walkers, and the spectres, and the formless evil beings that haunt the forest depths, and dog and waylay the lonely wanderer who after nightfall passes through the regions where they lurk; and it may be that when overcome by the horror of the fate that befell his friend, and when oppressed by the awful dread of the unknown, he grew to attribute, both at the time and still more in remembrance, weird and elfin traits to what was merely some abnormally wicked and cunning wild beast; but whether this was so or not, no man can say.

When the event occurred, Bauman was still a young man, and was trapping with a partner among the mountains dividing the forks of the Salmon

from the head of Wisdom River. Not having had much luck, he and his partner determined to go up into a particularly wild and lonely pass through which ran a small stream said to contain many beavers. The pass had an evil reputation because the year before a solitary hunter who had wandered into it was slain, seemingly by a wild beast, the half eaten remains being afterwards found by some mining prospectors who had passed his camp only the night before.

The memory of this event, however, weighed very lightly with the two trappers, who were as adventurous and hardy as others of their kind. They took their two lean mountain ponies to the foot of the pass where they left them in an open beaver meadow, the rocky timber-clad ground being from there onward impracticable for horses. They then struck out on foot through the vast, gloomy forest, and in about four hours reached a little open glade where they concluded to camp, as signs of game were plenty.

There was still an hour or two of daylight left, and after building a brush lean-to and throwing down and opening their packs, they started upstream. The country was very dense and hard to travel through, as there was much down timber, although here and there the sombre woodland was broken by small glades of mountain grass. At dusk they again reached camp. The glade in which it was pitched was not many yards wide, the tall, close-set pines and firs rising round it like a wall. On one side was a little stream, beyond which rose the steep mountains slope, covered with the unbroken growth of evergreen forest.

They were surprised to find that during their absence something, apparently a bear, had visited camp, and had rummaged about among their things, scattering the contents of their packs, and in sheer wantonness destroying their lean-to. The footprints of the beast were quite plain, but at first they paid no particular heed to them, busying themselves with rebuilding the lean-to, laying out their beds and stores and lighting the fire.

While Bauman was making ready supper, it being already dark, his companion began to examine the tracks more closely, and soon took a brand from the fire to follow them up, where the intruder had walked along a game trail after leaving the camp. When the brand flickered out, he returned and took another, repeating his inspection of the footprints very closely. Coming back to the fire, he stood by it a minute or two, peering out into the darkness, and suddenly remarked, "Bauman, that bear has been walking on two legs." Bauman laughed at this, but his partner insisted that he was right, and upon again examining the tracks with a torch, they certainly did seem to be made by but two paws or feet. However, it was too dark to make sure. After discussing whether the footprints could possibly be those of a human being, and coming to the conclusion that they could not be, the two men rolled up in their blankets, and went to sleep under the lean-to.

At midnight Bauman was awakened by some noise, and sat up in his blankets. As he did so his nostrils were struck by a strong, wild-beast odour, and he caught the loom of a great body in the darkness at the mouth of the lean-to. Grasping his rifle, he fired at the vague, threatening shadow, but must have missed, for immediately afterwards he heard the smashing of the under wood as the thing, whatever it was, rushed off into the impenetrable blackness of the forest and the night.

After this the two men slept but little, sitting up by the rekindled fire, but they heard nothing more. In the morning they started out to look at the few traps they had set the previous evening and put out new ones. By an unspoken agreement they kept together all day, and returned to camp towards evening.

On nearing it they saw, hardly to their astonishment, that the lean-to had again been torn down. The visitor of the preceding day had returned, and in wanton malice had tossed about their camp kit and bedding, and destroyed the shanty. The ground was marked up by its tracks, and on leaving the camp it had gone along the soft earth by the brook. The footprints were as plain as if on snow, and, after a careful scrutiny of the trail, it certainly did seem as if, whatever the thing was, it had walked off on but two legs.

The men, thoroughly uneasy, gathered a great heap of dead logs and kept up a roaring fire throughout the night, one or the other sitting on guard most of the time. About midnight the thing came down through the forest opposite, across the brook, and stayed there on the hillside for nearly an hour. They could hear the branches crackle as it moved about, and several times it uttered a harsh, grating, long-drawn moan, a peculiarly sinister sound. Yet it did not venture near the fire.

In the morning the two trappers, after discussing the strange events of the last 36 hours, decided that they would shoulder their packs and leave the valley that afternoon. They were the more ready to do this because in spite of seeing a good deal of game sign they had caught very little fur. However it was necessary first to go along the line of their traps and gather them, and this they started out to do. All the morning they kept together, picking up trap after trap, each one empty. On first leaving camp they had the disagreeable sensation of being followed. In the dense spruce thickets they occasionally heard a branch snap after they had passed; and now and then there were slight rustling noises among the small pines to one side of them.

At noon they were back within a couple of miles of camp. In the high, bright sunlight their fears seemed absurd to the two armed men, accustomed as they were, through long years of lonely wandering in the wilderness, to face every kind of danger from man, brute or element. There were still three beaver traps to collect from a little pond in a wide ravine nearby. Bauman volunteered to gather these and bring them in, while his companion went ahead to camp and made ready the packs.

On reaching the pond Bauman found three beavers in the traps, one of which had been pulled loose and carried into a beaver house. He took several hours in securing and preparing the beaver, and when he started homewards he marked, with some uneasiness, how low the sun was getting. As he hurried toward camp, under the tall trees, the silence and desolation of the forest weighted on him. His feet made no sound on the pine needles and the slanting sunrays, striking through among the straight trunks, made a gray twilight in which objects at a distance glimmered indistinctly. There was nothing to break the gloomy stillness which, when there is no breeze, always broods over these sombre primeval forests.

At last he came to the edge of the little glade where the camp lay and shouted as he approached it, but got no answer. The campfire had gone out, though the thin blue smoke was still curling upwards.

Near it lay the packs wrapped and arranged. At first Bauman could see nobody; nor did he receive an answer to his call. Stepping forward he again shouted, and as he did so his eye fell on the body of his friend, stretched beside the trunk of a great fallen spruce. Rushing towards it the horrified trapper found that the body was still warm, but that the neck was broken, while there were four great fang marks in the throat.

The footprints of the unknown beast-creature, printed deep in the soft soil, told the whole story.

The unfortunate man, having finished his packing, had sat down on the spruce log with his face to the fire, and his back to the dense woods, to wait for his companion. While thus waiting, his monstrous assailant, which must have been lurking in the woods, waiting for a chance to catch one of the adventurers unprepared, came silently up from behind, walking with long noiseless steps and seemingly still on two legs. Evidently unheard, it reached the man, and broke his neck by wrenching his head back with its fore paws, while it buried its teeth in his throat. It had not eaten the body, but apparently had romped and gambolled around it in uncouth, ferocious glee, occasionally rolling over and over it; and had then fled back into the soundless depths of the woods.

Bauman, utterly unnerved and believing that the creature with which he had to deal was something either half human or half devil, some great goblin-beast, abandoned everything but his rifle and struck off at speed down the pass, not halting until he reached the beaver meadows where the hobbled ponies were still grazing. Mounting, he rode onwards through the night, until beyond reach of pursuit.[2]

Fact or fiction?

Early frontiersmen were notorious weavers of "tall tales," often verging on comic absurdity, but Bauman seems to have told his strange story straight-faced. Roosevelt, despite some misgivings, was "rather impressed." Beyond that, we can say no more.

Chetco River (1890)

We owe our next report to naturalist-author Ivan Sanderson, who offered it for public scrutiny in his classic work *Abominable Snowmen: Legend Come to Life* (1961). According to Sanderson, the supposed events occurred somewhere along the Chetco River, which drains a rugged coastal section of south-western Oregon, near the Californian border. The Chetco is some fifty-five miles long, descending steeply from 3,700 feet elevation toward the Pacific Ocean. Today, all but its lower five miles lie within the Siskiyou National Forest.[3]

According to Sanderson, the events he describes occurred in 1890. After a setup noting the anxiety of local residents, provoked by "really gigantic" humanoid footprints found along the coast, Sanderson moves fifty miles inland to a mining camp, whose occupants suffered "unpleasant noises" and nocturnal movement of large objects. The miners blamed bears, until Bigfoot-type tracks were found in the camp. A futile search was organised, then abandoned. Soon afterward, a miner was "chased into camp by something very large, the looks of which he did not wait to investigate."[4] Sentries were posted in pairs, but they soon came to grief. According to Sanderson:

> One couple going to relieve a watch found their two companions dead and really grossly mutilated. They had in fact been literally smashed and apparently by being picked up and slammed repeatedly onto the ground so that they looked as if they had fallen off a high cliff onto rocks. The account particularly specifies that there was nothing anywhere near off which they could have fallen. The wretched men had emptied their rifles and there was both spoor and a large blood-trail leading off into the bush.[5]

Furious miners followed the trail, but found nothing—except a fresh lava flow, which Sanderson rightly describes as "astonishing." The trail ends there for us, as well, with no further information available. Despite his reference to "the account," Sanderson provides no source for his story, and long-time Sasquatch researcher John Green had found no supporting documentation by 1978.[6] So it remains, today.

"Headless Valley" (1905-1960)

Our third classic case comes from Canada's Mackenzie Mountains, in the Dencho Region of the Northwest Territories, where the Nahanni National Park Reserve lies 311 miles west of Yellowknife. Translations of *Nahanni* from the native Dene language vary, alternately rendered as "spirit" or "people over there, far away." Our specific point of interest is the valley of the South Nahanni River, flowing from the Mackenzies eastward, through the Selwyn Mountains, to feed the Liard River.[7]

No one can say precisely when the Nahanni Valley acquired its evil reputation, variously known as "Deadman's Valley," "Headless Valley," and "the Valley of Missing Men."[8] Its first confirmed mention in print appeared in *Time* magazine, on 20 January 1947, with an article quoting John Buchan, 1st Baron Tweedsmuir, who served as Canada's governor general from November 1935 until his death in February 1940. Buchan, according to *Time,* said that the "valley was full of gold and some said it was hot as hell owing to the warm springs....It had a wicked name too, for at least a dozen folks went in and never came out....Indians said it was the home of devils."[9]

That piece dated the origin of the Nahanni's legend from "40 years ago," with the unsolved decapitation of two brothers named MacLeod. Thereafter, *Time*'s unnamed reporter wrote: "Prospector Martin Jorgensen, who went in after gold in 1910, was also found dead. The bones of another prospector, Yukon Fisher, were discovered near a creek in 1928. Three trappers vanished in the valley. In 1945 woodsman Walter J. Tully came on the body of an Ontario miner, Ernest Savard, in his sleeping bag, his head all but severed." The final tally, *Time* declared, was thirteen dead or missing.[10]

If that were not mysterious enough, surviving prospectors described the valley as "a lush almost tropical country where the river never froze even when the temperature sank to 50 below in the surrounding mountains. Great herds of fat deer and caribou, they said, cropped the green pastures." In December 1946, *Vancouver Sun* columnist Jack Scott satirised the region as a "bodyless valley where ripe bananas hang from the boughs of pine trees [and] dusky native girls swim about in the deep, warm pools." Professor Alan Cameron, exploring for the University of Alberta, penetrated the valley in 1936, crediting its balmy climate to hot springs and warm winds called *chinooks*. Ten years later, prospectors Frank Henderson and John Patterson left the valley with thirty ounces of gold, found "coarse and free on the bottom of a creek and strung out in quartz along the cliffs."[11]

As *Time's* report went to press, *Vancouver Sun* editor Pierre Burton and four companions— including Constable Jim Reid of the Royal Canadian Mounted Police—were en route to Headless Valley, hoping to improve the paper's circulation with front-line reports from the land of mystery. As the *Sun* reported on 16 February, they found an abandoned prospector's cabin, complete with a pinup photo of actress Rita Hayworth which they confiscated "for historic value," and left without solving the valley's riddle.[12]

From that point onward, like J.R.R. Tolkien's *Lord of the Rings,* the Nahanni legend grew in the telling. A pulp men's magazine, *Adventure,* published a short piece on the valley from Canadian author Bruce Wright in early 1951, then another decade passed before Ivan Sanderson revisited the subject in *Abominable Snowmen.* Sanderson recapped the story by quoting from an undated, anonymous column in *Doubt,* a journal published between 1931 and 1959 by the Fortean Society of New York City.[13] Regrettably, he did not cite the column in his bibliography, which rendered it untraceable at press time for this work. The passage read:

> This valley, number one legend of the Northlands, has as its background, stories of tropical growth, hot springs, head-hunting mountain-men, caves, pre-historic monsters, wailing winds, and lost gold minds. Actual fact certifies the hot springs, the wailing winds, and some person or persons who delight in lopping off prospectors' heads. As for the prehistoric monsters, Indians have returned from the Nahanni country with fairly accurate drawings of mastodons burned on raw hide. The more recent history began some 40 years ago (circa 1910) when the two MacLeod brothers of Fort Simpson were found dead in the valley, and reportedly decapitated. Already the Indians shunned the place because of its "mammoth grizzlies" and "evil spirits wailing in the canyons."

Canadian police records show that Joe Muholland of Minnesota, Bill Espler of Winnipeg, Phil Powers and the MacLeod brothers of Ft. Simpson, Martin Jorgenson, Yukon Fischer [*sic*], Annie La Ferte, one O'Brien, Edwin Hall, Andy Hays, an unidentified prospector and Ernest Savard have perished in the strange valley since 1910. In 1945 the body of Savard was found in his sleeping bag, head nearly severed from his shoulders. Savard had previously brought rich ore samples out of the Nahanni. In 1946 prospector John Patterson disappeared in the valley. His partner, Frank Henderson, was to have met him there, but never found him.[14]

Sanderson then asserts that the Nahanni's phantom head-hunters "are alleged locally...to be ABSMs [Abominable Snowmen] of the *Sasquatch* type and with all its characteristics." He is the first author to mention Sasquatch in connection with the tales of Headless Valley, and his allusion to "reports in the form of private letters" offers no further documentation.[15]

Enter Frank Graves Jr., a mechanic-turned adventurer who literally found his way to Headless

Valley via Sanderson. In 1962, while working as a stock-boy at Chilton Books, in Philadelphia, Graves read *Abominable Snowmen* and approached Sanderson—who doubled as a Chilton editor—for advice on the best way to crack the Nahanni. That scheme fell through, but Sanderson referred Graves to Minnesotan Michael Eliseuson, then planning a Nahanni trek for the American Expeditionary Society.[16]

In fact, it seems that two separate parties explored Headless Valley during 1965. One expedition—dubbed the "Ross River group," for its jumping-off point—was described after the fact as "five friends' summer of discovery." The friends in question—Robert Henry, Bruce Tannehill, Marc Wermager, Rollie White, and David Wolfe—spent sixty days in the region, during August and September, emerging with 5,000 feet of 16mm film but no reports of monsters.[17]

The Eliseuson party arrived while the Ross River group was still present, and three of its members—Eliseuson, Frank Graves, and George Boyum—autographed Dave Wolfe's travel diary as a memento of their meeting. The team's other members were Minnesotans Wayne Engrebretson and Bruce Shorer, plus an individual identified by Canadian website editor Al Robinson of Ottawa as "Ivan T. Saunders from back East (interested in Big-Foot)." Clearly, that refers to Ivan Terrence *Sanderson,* but Sanderson, in turn, later described the Eliseuson expedition without naming himself as a member. Specifically, he wrote that Frank Graves "joined up with another gang I had been helping, out in Minnesota, led by one Michael Eliseuson....He also got them all out in one piece, which was quite a feat in itself." Author Loren Coleman compounded the confusion, four decades later, claiming that Graves explored Headless Valley "in the 1940s."[18]

Upon returning to the States, Graves submitted an article to Sanderson, who published it, with some parenthetical notes, under the title "The Valley Without a Head." Tireless researcher Chad Arment reprinted the piece in 2004, and while he could provide no provenance, the best guess for a date is sometime during 1965-67, perhaps in the quarterly journal *Pursuit,* published by Sanderson's Society for the Investigation of the Unexplained (SITU).[19]

While presented as a first-person account, the Graves article includes two introductory paragraphs lifted verbatim from the *Doubt* column Sanderson quoted in *Abominable Snowmen.* Omitting any mention of companions beyond an unnamed "Indian friend," Graves then proceeded to detail his adventure, including tales of overflights by Russian aircraft, discovery of sixteen-inch humanoid footprints, sightings of super-sized eagles and ravens, and an encounter with "an enormous white thing" resembling "a gigantic dog...twenty times the size of any wolf I had ever heard of," which "stood straight up on rather long legs." (Loren Coleman, reportedly working from notes left by Graves in SITU's archives, later changed that description to fit a beast "3.5 feet high at the shoulders with a wide head and short legs, covered in a shaggy white coat.") Graves ended his account with sketchy plans to revisit the Nahanni and enjoy "a lifetime of wondrous things to look into...and a real chance to discover something worthwhile."[20]

By the late 1960s, Headless Valley was firmly established as a part of Bigfoot lore. In 1969, author "Eric Norman"—a pseudonym shared by pulp writers Warren Smith and Brad

Steiger—briefly summarised the valley's reputation, adding the new claim that "[o]ften, search parties have found the deep indentations of giant, human-like footprints around the decapitated skeletons." A year later, writing under his own name, Smith published a somewhat longer recitation of the Nahanni head-hunters, quoting an unnamed prospector found near death in 1906, who described his assailants as "monkey-men" prone to communication through "whistles and howling like crazed monsters." Neither report cited any verifiable source.[21]

In 2005, author Dick North suggested a possible suspect for some of the Nahanni slayings. Albert Johnson, also known as Arthur Nelson, was a solitary trapper in the Northwest Territories whose dispute with neighbours during 1931 touched off the "Arctic Circle War"—and, half a century later inspired the film *Death Hunt,* starring Charles Bronson and Lee Marvin. Most Canadians remember Johnson/Nelson for his shootouts with Mounties and civilian vigilantes, ending with his own death on 17 February 1932, but author North also explores some tantalising theories linking the elusive "Mad Trapper" to Headless Valley.[22]

Alas, it all leads nowhere. After briefly recapping the Nahanni Valley's mysterious deaths from 1908 onward—and suggesting that decapitated victims may have been killed for their gold teeth, with heads removed to conceal the motive—North admits that "Nelson" did not arrive in the district until 1927, months after Yukon Fisher (née Charles Taylor) was slain. Furthermore, he left the Nahanni in May 1931, before victim Phillip Powers vanished. Nelson might conceivably have killed three victims lost in 1929, but none of them was ever found, and two remain nameless.[23] We must acquit him, then, for lack of evidence.

Authors Gary Mangiacopra and Dwight Smith recapped the history of Headless Valley in January 2006, with an article in Chad Arment's *North American BioFortean Review.* While providing the first cohesive timeline of events, listing twenty-three persons killed or vanished in Headless Valley between 1905 and 1960, they finally draw no conclusions and name no suspects, human or otherwise.[24]

Rachel Wills, writing on the Internet in June 2009, added a new twist with vague reference to "a fierce tribe, the Naha, [that] had vanished [from the Nahanni Valley] years earlier without explanation."[25] Further research reveals that "[t]he Naha were the Dene tribe who claimed the Mackenzie Mountains as their territory. They were nomadic within their territory, using different parts of the mountains and valleys according to the season. And they were fierce warriors, unhesitating in their attack upon anyone who camped within their boundaries and sometimes beyond....In some versions of the story, the Naha were tracked down and killed, in others the warriors simply disappeared."[26]

Could the "lost" Naha tribe have survived into modern times, still wreaking vengeance on trespassers? Another Hollywood film, *Last of the Dogmen,* explored a similar theme in 1995, surmising that a band of Cheyenne warriors from the 1860s still existed in Montana's Oxbow

OPPOSITE: *Sasquatch* terrorizes hapless humans.

LANCE HENRIKSEN ANDREA ROTH

SASQUATCH

They found
the missing link
...and it's not
friendly

DVD
VIDEO

BASED ON A TRUE STORY

Quadrangle, but no more evidence supports that theory with regard to Headless Valley than the groundless claims linking its murders to Bigfoot.

Ape Canyon (1924)

No tale of Sasquatch mayhem against humans is more widely known, or more grossly distorted, than the supposed events occurring near Washington's Mount St. Helens in July 1924. Stripped to its basics, the story claims that a party of prospectors working a claim on the Muddy River, some eight miles from Spirit Lake, fought a pitched battle with "the fabled 'mountain devils' or mountain gorillas of Mount St. Helens" on 10 July. Portland's *Oregonian* broke the story on 13 July, naming the human combatants as Fred Beck, Gabe Lefever, John Peterson, Marion Smith, and Smith's son Roy.[27]

According to that article, the miners glimpsed a party of four huge "apes" and found large tracks around their cabin several times before battle was joined. Finally:

Smith met with one of the animals and fired at it with a revolver, he said. Thursday [10 July] Fred Beck, it is said, shot one, the body falling over a precipice. That night the animals bombarded the cabin where the men were stopping with showers of rocks, many of them large ones, knocking chunks out of the log cabin, according to the prospectors. Many of the rocks

Fred Beck in 1967
OPPOSITE: The covers of Beck's booklet

fell through a hole in the roof and two of the rocks struck Beck, one of them rendering him unconscious for nearly two hours.[28]

On 14 July the *Oregonian* reported that officers from the Spirit Lake ranger station had examined the prospectors' cabin, counting some 200 stones strewn around and inside it, plus some "queer four-toed footprints." One Ranger Huffman told the *Oregonian* that seventy YMCA members had camped within a mile of the supposed battleground on the night in question, but heard nothing. When asked if the youths might be responsible, Huffman replied, "They were all in camp that night and the day these fellows claim to have had their fight. Wait 'till you see the cabin. Boys could never have pulled that job."[29]

Still, Huffman suspected a hoax. He subsequently told *Oregonian* reporter L.H. Gregory,

> "Old Man Smith, who started this ape stampede, absolutely believes it. If ever a man was 'wild-eyed' it was Smith when he came down here from the cabin with the story of having been attacked by apes. Something happened up there, but I can't imagine what though. It wasn't apes. Another funny thing is that you can't shake the stories of the other men with Smith. Oh there's a mystery about it. The mystery to me is who put up the

job on Smith and his companions and how in the world they did it."[30]

Bigfoot researcher Peter Byrne interviewed Fred Beck in 1960, deeming him "to be honest and to be telling a true account of something that actually happened." A year later, Byrne went looking for the cabin's ruins but failed to find them. During that expedition, a local resident opined that Beck's party was probably stoned "by young boys, out for a lark." Another source told Byrne "that it was well known that a local man had been responsible for the footprints in Ape Canyon in 1924."[31]

Fred Beck resurfaced in September 1967, dictating his story to son Ronald for private publication. Padded with Native American legends and newspaper clippings on Bigfoot, Beck's long-delayed story nonetheless contained some surprises, beginning with a statement that "I hope this book does not discourage too much those interested souls who are looking and trying to solve the mystery of the abominable snowmen. If someone captured one, I would have to swallow most of the content of this book, for I am about to make a bold statement: No one will ever capture one, and no one will ever kill one—in other words, present to the world a living one in a cage, or find a dead body of one to be examined by science. I know there are stories that some have been captured but got away. So will they always get away."[32]

Why? Because Fred Beck regarded the "apes" of Mount St. Helens as "spiritual beings," insisting that "events leading up to the ape episode were filled with the psychic element." In fact, Beck's life from childhood onward allegedly included bouts of clairvoyance and close encounters with ethereal entities. Of Ape Canyon, he wrote: "Our time spent in Mt. St. Helens was a series of psychic experiences. The method we found our mine was psychic." On his party's fourth trip to the region, during 1922, "[a] spiritual being, a large Indian dressed in buckskin, appeared to us and talked to us." Two other "Masters," a man and woman, also helped direct the miners in their quest for gold, though false starts caused dissension in the party. As to Bigfoot, Beck believed "these beings were present and observing us, but they had not yet appeared in physical form."[33]

Beck's meetings with the "Masters" allegedly continued long after the battle of Ape Canyon. "Since that day in 1924," he said, four decades later, "I have went on and progressed and have learned much, and now I can look back and put the puzzle together from the reservoir of knowledge I have learned." Concerning Bigfoot, while Beck never asked the Masters anything specific, he concluded that "[t]he Abominable Snowmen are from a lower plane. When the condition and vibration is at a certain frequency, they can easily, for a time, appear in a very solid body. They are not animal spirits, but also lack the intelligence of a human consciousness. When reading of evolution we have read many times conjecture about the missing link between man and the Anthropoid Ape. The Snowmen are a missing link in consciousness, neither animal nor human. They are very close to our dimension, and yet are a part of one lower. Could they be the missing link man has been so long searching for?"[34]

So much for the sole surviving eyewitness of the events at Ape Canyon. Ranger Huffman's skepticism, and the stories told to Peter Byrne in 1961, were partially corroborated in April 1982 by Vancouver resident Rant Mullens. An eighty-six-year-old retired logger, Mullens told reporters that he and an uncle, George Ross, were returning from a fishing trip in July 1924, when they "decided to throw a scare into some miners in the area." As Mullens explained, "George was always playing jokes, so he and I rolled some rocks down over the edge. Then we got out of there fast. When we heard that the miners were telling hairy ape stories, we both had a good laugh. We never told anyone the true story." Later, in 1928, he and Ross "thought we would have a little fun" by carving giant wooden feet and leaving tracks around their current logging site.[35]

But is the Mullens story true or yet another hoax? Assuming that Mullens and Ross *did* perpetrate a potentially fatal "joke" by dropping boulders onto total strangers, knocking one of them unconscious, what were the creatures seen—and supposedly shot—by Beck's party before the pranksters arrived? Who or what left giant footprints around Ape Canyon four years before Mullens whittled his first pair of wooden feet?

The prospect of a hoax within a hoax was raised by British authors Colin and Janet Bord in 2006. They suggest that Mullens fabricated his role in the Ape Canyon skirmish as part of a long-running feud with one Raymond Wallace, yet another notorious hoaxer whose family claims that he "invented Bigfoot."[36] Clearly, neither man could claim that honor, but their childish game of one-upmanship raises the possibility that Mullens lied in 1982, for purposes of self-aggrandizement.

Once again, the case against Bigfoot remains unproved.

"Jim Carter" (1950)

We are not finished with Ape Canyon, yet. In 1973, Bigfoot researchers Don Hunter and René Dahinden published *Sasquatch,* revised and re-released as *Sasquatch/Bigfoot* in 1993. The book's first chapter relates the sad case of "a well-known Seattle mountaineer named Jim Carter," who vanished from a twenty-member climbing party near Ape Canyon in May 1950. According to Hunter and Dahinden, Carter left his party as it was descending Mount St. Helens, near a landmark called Dog's Head, at an altitude of 8,000 feet.[37] From there:

Carter's ski tracks indicated he had raced down the mountain, as one searcher described it in a story in the Oregon *Journal,* "taking chances that no skier of his calibre would take unless something was terribly wrong or he was being pursued." The speaker was Bob Lee, a Portland mountaineer, who is a member of the exclusive international Alpine Club and who has led and advised U.S. expeditions to the Himalayas.

In his wild descent, Carter jumped several gaping crevices before going right off a steep canyon wall. Neither he nor his equipment was ever found....

Lee said that both he and Dr. Otto Trent, the surgeon for the Seattle Mountain Rescue Council, came to the same conclusion: "The apes got him."[38]

Dramatic stuff, indeed ... but how does it withstand examination? According to the Bigfoot Field Researchers Organization, Hunter and Dahinden lifted their description of the incident more-or-less verbatim from an article written by James Halpin for *Seattle Magazine,* published on 15 August 1971.[39] Researcher Bobbie Short dates the Halpin article from 1970, but traces the story further back, to an article published in Washington's *Longview Times,* sometime during August 1963.[40]

As for the *Oregon Journal,* it was Portland's afternoon daily newspaper from 1902 to 1982, when it ceased publication, but inquiries to local libraries failed to unearth the article quoted in *Sasquatch.*[41] Likewise, I found no other trace of Bob Lee or Dr. Trent ... but all is not lost.

A climber *did* vanish on Mount St. Helens, around 3:00 P.M. on 21 May 1950. The *Longview Daily News* and Vancouver *Columbian* of 22 May described the missing person as "a Seattle youth," eighteen-year-old *Joe* Carter, whose disappearance prompted a turnout by the Longview ski patrol. One day later, the papers revised their descriptions of Carter, identifying him as a thirty-two-year-old employee of Seattle's Boeing aircraft factory. On 24 May the papers noted that Carter had "a serious diabetic disorder," and was climbing without insulin when he vanished.[42]

On 24 May the hunt for Carter shifted from Spirit Lake to the Lewis River, where searchers led by Don Bascom found tracks "believed to be the last trace of the missing man. They lost the tracks on top of a steep cliff, where Carter evidently had crossed the muddy river to the south side." Searchers announced their pessimism on 26 May, then regrouped on 28 May, after tracks made by ski poles were found near Pine Creek. According to searcher Hugh Monge of Longview, "It appeared that two ski poles had been tied together and used as a cane." Don Bascom's party found more tracks at the base of Muddy Glacier on 30 May, but the fruitless search was called off on 5 June.[43]

And there matters rested until 1963, when the *Longview Times* injected Bigfoot into Carter's story, garbling his name in the process. Nothing in the original newspaper coverage suggests that Carter was pursued by anyone or anything, or that he skied off a cliff and vanished before touching down. In fact, the evidence of bound ski poles used as a cane, plus other tracks found six days after the Lewis River discovery, refute that story absolutely. Whatever fate befell Joe Carter, we cannot accuse Bigfoot.

The Iceman Goeth (1967-70)

Most readers of this book will have some knowledge of the so-called "Minnesota Iceman" and the controversy it inspired, spanning four decades, but a brief recap of the events is useful here.

During 1967 and '68, Minnesota showman Frank Hansen toured the American carnival circuit with an exhibit billed as "The Missing Link." Those who paid to see it found an apelike figure in a block of ice, within a glass casket. In early December 1968, one Terry Cullen—described in various accounts as a zoologist or herpetologist, either from Milwaukee or the University of

---

OPPOSITE: A combo-pack of *Bigfoot Terror.*

BIGFOOT TERROR

DVD

4 BLOOD-FREEZING FEATURES

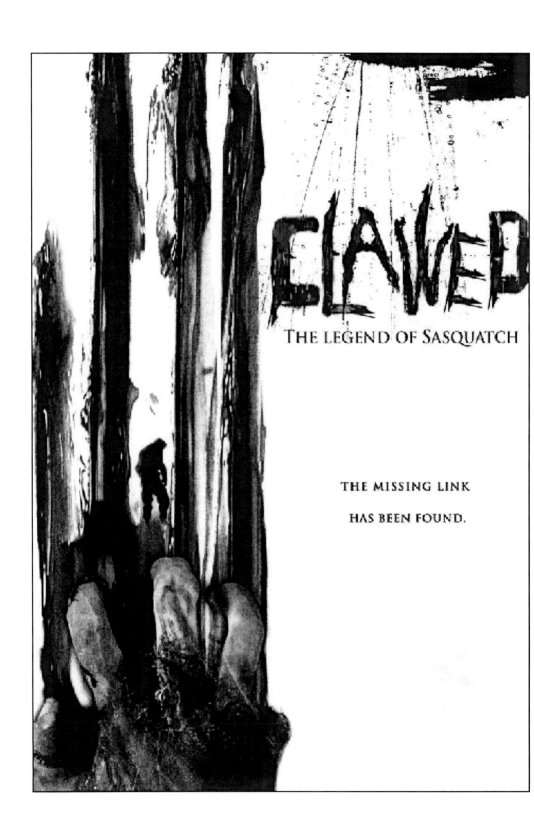

CLAWED

THE LEGEND OF SASQUATCH

THE MISSING LINK

HAS BEEN FOUND.

Minnesota—saw the exhibit at Chicago's International Livestock Exposition. Intrigued, he contacted Ivan Sanderson, who at the time was entertaining houseguest Bernard Heuvelmans, the "Father of Cryptozoology."[44]

Soon, Sanderson and Heuvelmans traced Hansen to his Altura, Minnesota, farm. Visiting Hansen on 16-18 December 1968, the scientists performed as thorough an examination as they could, without thawing the block of ice that surrounded their subject. Hansen requested that they keep their findings quiet, but both researchers ignored him. Heuvelmans, writing for the *Bulletin of the Royal Institute of Natural Sciences of Belgium* in February 1969, dubbed the Iceman *Homo pongoides* ("apelike man"). Sanderson wrote an account of the case for *Argosy* magazine in May 1969, followed by a more scholarly piece for the Italian journal *Genus,* later in the year. In 1974, Heuvelmans teamed with Russian Yeti researcher Boris Porshnev to publish a book which cited the Iceman as proof of surviving relict Neanderthals (*Homo neanderthalensis*).[45]

Frank Hansen, meanwhile, constantly revised his stories of the Iceman's provenance. In December 1968 he told Sanderson and Heuvelmans that the carcass was found by Chinese fishermen, floating at sea in a three-ton block of ice, and was housed at a refrigeration plant in Hong Kong until purchased by a still-unidentified American millionaire. That buyer, Hansen claimed, had met him at the Arizona State Fair in 1967, offering the Iceman as a touring exhibit in exchange for a share of the proceeds. Hansen changed his story in January 1969, contacting Heuvelmans and Sanderson to say that they had seen a replica constructed by craftsmen in April 1967. Neither scientist believed him.[46]

On 21 April 1969, Hansen staged a press conference at his farm to unveil the new replica Iceman, insisting that the model was the same object viewed by Heuvelmans and Sanderson four months earlier. While both authors rejected that claim, citing an odour of rotting meat that surrounded the Iceman they saw in December, mainstream scientists dismissed the incident as a hoax from day one. Matters went from bad to worse as several different firms claimed credit for manufacturing the exhibit.[47]

Two months later, on 30 June 1969, the now-defunct *National Bulletin* tabloid newspaper struck a new note with an article titled "I Was Raped by the Abominable Snowman." Supposed author "Helen Westring" claimed that she was deer-hunting near Bemidji, Minnesota, when the randy Iceman attacked and ravished her, provoking her to kill the beast in self-defence.[48] There is no more reason to believe the article, on balance, than the countless other Bigfoot stories fabricated by the *Weekly World News* and similar tabloids, but subsequent events suggest that it may have planted a notion in Frank Hansen's mind.

In July 1970, thirteen months after the *National Bulletin's* hoax piece was printed and promptly forgotten, Hansen's latest story on the Iceman surfaced in *Saga,* one of many American "men's magazines" specialising in stories of crime and adventure. While maintaining that he had obtained the Iceman carcass "through pure chance and random circumstance," Hansen

OPPOSITE: Sasquatch victims are *Clawed* for your viewing pleasure.

discarded his former account of a creature found floating at sea, recasting himself as a hero of sorts.[49]

Hansen's final tale is simply told. While serving as a U.S. Air Force Captain in Minnesota, in autumn 1960, Hansen went deer-hunting with three fellow officers at Whiteface Reservoir, sixty miles north of Duluth. On their second day of hunting, Hansen separated from his friends and found a doe, but someone else fired at the deer before he could shoot. Following the animal's blood trail, Hansen met no other hunters, but found three apelike creatures devouring the now-lifeless doe. As Hansen "froze in horror," one of the beasts rushed toward him, "screeching and screaming."[50] As Hansen described the event for *Saga*:

> I cannot remember aiming my rifle nor do I recall pulling the trigger, but a bullet must have slammed into the beast's body. As blood spurted from his face the huge creature staggered, seemingly stunned by this unexpected happening....I have absolutely no recollection of ever seeing the other two creatures again. They seemed to have vanished into "thin air."... I have no recollection of time and perhaps my mind blanked out. When I regained composure there was only the natural silence of the swamp.[51]

Having run some distance in a daze, Hansen fired several shots that attracted a pair of strangers. They, in turn, drove him back to the point where his three friends were waiting for Hansen, beside their vehicle. Hansen kept his story to himself, fearing that Air Force psychiatrists might judge him insane, or that he might have shot a human prankster dressed in an ape suit. He returned to the shooting scene on 2 December, found the hairy corpse partly covered in new-fallen snow, and drove it back to the Duluth air base, where Hansen placed it in a home freezer, overriding his wife's shrill objections.[52]

From that point on, the story follows its familiar route, from carnival exhibits to exposure by Sanderson and Heuvelmans, sparking renewed fears of prosecution and Hansen's substitution of a dummy corpse. He closes with a plea for amnesty, writing:

> There will be many skeptics that will brand this story a complete fabrication. Possibly it is. I am not under oath and, should the situation dictate, I will deny every word of it. But then no one can be completely certain unless my conditions of amnesty are met. In the meantime I will continue to exhibit a "hairy specimen" that I have publicly acknowledged to be a "fabricated illusion" and leave the final judgment to viewers. If one should detect a rotting odour coming from a corner of the coffin, it is only your imagination. A new seal has been placed under the glass and the coffin is absolutely air-tight.[53]

True or false? Interviews granted by Hansen in July 1989 and April 2002 failed to cast further light on the subject, and no sideshow sightings of the Iceman have been reported for several decades. Today, the only thing that may be said with any certainty is that Frank Hansen has no credibility.

Chapter 3.
North America: Big Feet, Big Trouble

Our first stumbling block in assessment of Bigfoot attack claims from North America is the fact that no comprehensive, reliable database of alleged Sasquatch sightings exists. The sources that attempt to tabulate such incidents include:

- Author John Green's claim of 1,677 Bigfoot sightings and track-finds for the United States and Canada by 1978.[1]
- Rick Berry's 1993 tabulation of 1,050 Sasquatch encounters from fourteen eastern U.S. states (although his text describes only 996 cases, including several duplicates).[2]
- Christopher Murphy's citation of 2,557 reports for the U.S. and Canada as of 2006. Strangely, his work includes a map cribbed from Green, with statistics indicating that ten American states (including Oregon and California, in the heart of Bigfoot country) had logged no new sightings in twenty-eight years.[3]
- Ray Crowe's International Bigfoot Society (IBS), whose website, prior to vanishing without a trace in March 2009, claimed more than 4,000 Bigfoot encounters. Sadly, many of those reports were duplicates—281 for Oregon alone—while others were irrelevant accounts of Chupacabra sightings, "giant chicken tracks," a town populated by cannibals, and so on.[4]
- A claim of 2,408 U.S. reports logged by the Sasquatch Information Society (SIS) through October 2009, the vast majority of which include no information beyond notations that the "record has not been validated or is being studied."[5]
- The Bigfoot Field Researchers Organization (BFRO) claim of 3,869 reports from the U.S. and Canada through November 2009, padded by listing of various general media reports as "sightings."[6]
- A tabulation of 2,416 reports from the United States, collected by researcher Autumn Williams through November 2009.[7]

From those sources and others cited in the endnotes, I have collected all reports of Sasquatch aggression toward humans, their animals and property that were accessible by press time for this work. The following pages compile and discuss those reports by nature of the incidents: alleged homicides; nonfatal assaults on humans; attacks on animals; claims of home invasions; aggression toward vehicles; and incidents of objects thrown at humans—a total of 456 reported incidents in all.

Fatal Attractions

Many Native American tribes greeted early European settlers with tales of forest-dwelling cannibal giants, but no substantive documentation exists for those legends. Elimination of prehistoric imponderables leaves twenty reports of alleged or suspected Sasquatch homicides from North America besides the classic cases already discussed in Chapter 2.

Our first report comes from the Okefenokee Swamp, where a nine-man hunting party met a towering biped called "the Man Mountain" in March 1829. When the gun smoke cleared, five men supposedly lay dead, their heads ripped off, while four shaken survivors measured the thirteen-foot corpse of their slayer. Reported as a "matter of fact" by newspapers in Maryland and Georgia, the events remain unsubstantiated.[8]

The next case, dated vaguely from "the 1800s," refers to a "wildman" terrorising prospectors at Thompson Flats, in Oregon's Curry County. As summarised by researcher Stan Sweet: "In the old days, after all the miners had been run off by the wildman, one brave miner decided to stay....Some time later they found him at his sluice box with his head bashed in by a bloody rock, which was still lying nearby." While the tale provides no further information, we know that prospecting began around Thompson Flat in 1852, and that Curry County was created in December 1855. The unnamed miner's death remains unverified.[9]

Next comes the perplexing tale of Deadman's Hole, in San Diego County, California. According to authors Warren Smith and "Eric Norman" (a pen name shared by Smith and colleague Brad Steiger), three mysterious deaths occurred at the site: a prospector in 1858, a second victim in 1888, and William Blair in 1922, all strangled by "extraordinarily large, strong fingers." Later that year, hunters Charles (or Frank) Cox and Edward Dean supposedly shot "a gorilla" at Deadman's Hole and thus solved the mystery.[10]

The truth of Deadman's Hole is rather different. John Green reports that local researcher Patrick Householder documented two deaths "from the 1880s," one victim being stabbed, the other shot. And while Green claims those slayings were "traditionally blamed on a sasquatch-type creature," the "monster" legend actually stems from a journalistic hoax published in the *San Diego Union* on April Fool's Day 1888. That story describes hunters Cox and Dean killing a ravenous beast with a human face and exploring its cave filled with human remains. In fact, Householder's research notwithstanding, it seems the whole tale is a sham.[11]

Another case first reported by "Eric Norman," then repeated on the IBS website, involves the Burgoine brothers of Grizzly Lake. While Norman gives no further geographical details—and seventeen Grizzly Lakes exist in six western U.S. states—the IBS narrows it down to Lewis County, Washington. Sadly, while the Evergreen State claims two Grizzly Lakes, they are found in Skamania and Snohomish Counties, respectively.[12]

From that shaky start, we read of the three brothers mining copper, sometime in the 1860s. First one sibling vanishes while wintering alone in their isolated cabin, then a second disappears the next year, leaving a journal entry that describes "strange hairy monsters" prowling outside. The lone survivor's fate is unrecorded, and in the absence of any corroboration, we may safely assume that the story is fiction.[13]

Fast-forward to 1920 and the tale of Albert Petka, attacked by a "bushman" who boarded his boat at Nulato, Alaska, on the Yukon River. Petka's dogs reportedly frightened the creature away, but his injuries proved fatal. As in the foregoing cases, documentation remains elusive.[14]

In 1994 ex-sheriff's deputy Fred Bradshaw relayed another chilling tale to Ray Crowe. His story describes two unnamed men from Quinault, Washington, found dead in 1927 with "their rifles twisted and distorted, and with all their bones crushed and broken like they had been repeatedly smashed against the ground." Bradshaw recalled seeing a police file on the double-slaying, but found that it had been discarded in the meantime. On balance, the story sounds like a transplanted version of Ivan Sanderson's report from the Chetco River in 1890 (see Chapter 2).[15]

And with repetition in mind, we next consider the 1943 story of John Mire (or McQuire), AKA "The Dutchman," fatally injured by "a hair-covered man" at DeWilde's Camp, near Ruby, Alaska (Yukon-Koyukuk County), before his dogs routed the beast. John Green notes the story's "strangely coincidental" resemblance to Albert Petka's case from 1920, but concludes that "there is certainly nothing impossible in the incidents described."[16] And nothing, we must add, to prove that they occurred.

Green's next vague report comes from Portlock, Alaska. As reported in the *Anchorage Daily News* on April 15, 1973:

> [S]ometime in the beginning years of World War II, rumours began to seep along the Kenai Peninsula that things were not right in Portlock. Men from the cannery town would go up into the hills to hunt the Dall sheep and bear, and never return. Worse yet, the stories ran, sometimes their mutilated bodies would be swept down into the lagoon, torn and dismembered in a way that bears could not, or would not, do.
>
> Tales were told of villagers tracking moose over soft ground. They would find giant, man-like tracks over 18 inches in length, closing upon those of the moose, the signs of a short struggle where the grass had been matted down, then only the deeper tracks of the manlike animal departing toward the high, fog-shrouded mountains with their steep valleys and hidden glaciers.[17]

Portlock's inhabitants packed up and left *en masse* in 1949, leaving a ghost town that remains uninhabited today. As to the alleged Sasquatch victims, their number and names, no record survives.[18]

Green's last report of a Bigfoot fatality, again from Alaska, first appeared in an unspecified 1956 issue of *Sports Afield,* under the by-line of one Russell Annabel, described by biographer Jeff Davis as "one of the most colourful and controversial characters ever to set foot in Alaska." For what it may be worth, Annabel related the story of an Indian called Stickman, abducted by "Gilyuk the shaggy cannibal giant" from Tyone Lake "sometime about the 1940s." Only Stickman's red flannel underwear remained, his corpse allegedly consumed.[19]

Our next story may fairly be dismissed out of hand, since it came from notorious hoaxer Ray Wallace, reported four decades after the fact, but I present it here for the sake of preserving a comprehensive record. According to Wallace, a Native American soldier came home on furlough to Del Norte County, California, in February 1954, and vanished while panning for gold on Blue Creek. A "whole army of 50 men" allegedly spent two weeks searching for the unnamed miner and found nothing—presumably including no evidence of the implied Sasquatch abduction.[20]

IBS researcher Larry Lund reported another confused and undocumented case from Yacolt, Washington, in March 1996. According to Ray Crowe: "Larry said that the original homesteader family was found murdered back in the late 1800s. In the 1960s a county sheriff was dispatched to the house after the report of a light was noted. Thinking he'd nab some teenage pranksters, he found a burning oil-lamp, and the house was full of human (tested) blood spatters. No body was found."[21] And again, true or false, nothing suggests Bigfoot's involvement.

IBS researcher Harry Oakes presents the next case, based on his interview with an unnamed sheriff's deputy in Clallam County, Washington. The story involves an anonymous woman attacked by Sasquatch and "ripped into three pieces" while her boyfriend watched, sometime during 1964 or '65, at some unspecified site in the Olympic Mountains. Oakes believed the report, but Ray Crowe notes that Harry met his informant in a bar, adding: "not for sure it wasn't the alcohol talking...or maybe it loosened his tongue just enough...and it was the truth."[22] No record of the crime has been revealed thus far.

A third-hand tale from "about 1965" first appeared in *The Bigfoot Bulletin,* published by George Haas and his San Francisco Bay Area Bigfoot Research Organization. The *Bulletin's* issue for 31 October 1970 (Halloween) included a letter from Private Nick Campbell at Fort Ord, California, relating a conversation with two National Guardsmen from Texas. According to them, "a giant, hairy creature" had "reportedly killed a couple of people" near Longview, Texas. A local minister, Rev. Royal Jacobs, also told Campbell that he (Jacobs) had joined a Bigfoot-hunting posse some years earlier, and that he'd seen "the body of a person the creature had torn apart."[23]

IBS correspondent Jackson Moore relayed a story of trucker and ex-paratrooper Bob Foreacre, who allegedly vanished without a trace while helping Moore search for Bigfoot tracks in San Diego County, California, sometime during 1970. Foreacre left their camp at 10 P.M., date unknown, and never returned. His remains had not been found when Moore told the story to

Bigfoot tackles cops and robbers.

ABOMINABLE

SOME THINGS ARE BETTER LEFT UNFOUND

Ray Crowe in 1993—nor had any evidence been found connecting Bigfoot to Foreacre's disappearance.[24]

Rich Grumley, founder of the now-defunct California Bigfoot Organization, told Ray Crowe another tale of Sasquatch homicide in 1993, repeating some of it to researcher Bobbie Short in 1999. Pared to its essence, the tale recalls Grumley's interview with an unnamed California poacher, sometime during 1980-81. The informant claimed that he was hunting game illegally in Inyo County, sometime in "the mid-to-late 1970s," when he was caught and detained by forest rangers. Before releasing him, the nameless officers allegedly cautioned that Bigfoot "had killed several people" in the area. Duly frightened, despite a complete lack of proof, the poacher never returned.[25]

Ray Crowe published another undated tale from the 1970s, based on a phone call from "someone in the TV industry" who relayed details of an interview conducted with an unnamed state trooper in Bend, Oregon. As summarised by Crowe, the policeman "commented on four hunters being killed in the Bend area in the 1970s. The rifle had been found twisted out of shape. Also there was a report from the Forest Service of a Sasquatch footprint of large size [that] had been found in a lava bed near Bend, [where] the lava had been fresh at the time. The Forest Service people said also that a large-breasted female [Sasquatch] had been seen in the Bend area."[26]

What are we to make of such a hodgepodge? Where is the police report confirming the deaths? Were four men hunting with a single rifle? How could Bigfoot survive a stroll through "fresh" lava? Indeed, where was such lava found, when Oregon's last volcanic eruption occurred in 1860?[27]

Before his death in 2000, Grumley relayed another startling case from Oregon's Mount Jefferson Wilderness. There, he claimed, several unnamed girls from Las Vegas were hiking with an equally anonymous male guide, sometime in 1976 or '77, when "something big"—nine or ten feet tall "at least"—attacked their party. The guide fired several shots from a .30-30 rifle before he was seized and "torn apart." The girls escaped to summon forest rangers, who scoured the region in vain. As usual, no official record of the incident exists.[28]

Kentucky resident Jan Thompson presents our next case in a collection of "guardian tales," advertised on her Internet website as "real horror stories from real people." A self-described witness to various monstrous encounters, Thompson dates this story from the early 1980s, when she worked the night shift at a service station abutting Land Between the Lakes, a 170,000-acre recreation area straddling the Kentucky-Tennessee border. On the unspecified night in question, two policemen arrived at the station, "shaken beyond description," and spilled the story of a tourist family—three in all—slaughtered in their motor home at a nearby campground. Bloody handprints and "hand paintings" marked the trailer's walls. An unnamed coroner allegedly concluded that the victims had been mutilated by four "piercing, well-

OPPOSITE: Sasquatch displays an *Abominable* appetite for human flesh.

defined claws, and...by some keen, mordantly long incisors." A "clump of long, grey and brown hairs" was carried off for lab analysis, results unknown. Official records of the case, predictably, are nonexistent.[29]

From 1995, we have the vague suggestion of a Sasquatch homicide cast in language designed to foster suspicion. Ray Crowe reports that veteran Bigfoot-hunter Peter Byrne visited Oregon's Cathedral Ridge on 24 September, after an unnamed hiker saw "something move in the brush," then found a large footprint. "Coincidentally," another anonymous hiker allegedly vanished at the same place on 25 September. Records of Portland Mountain Rescue confirm the disappearance of a climber on Cathedral Ridge sometime in 1995, but supply no further details.[30]

Finally, in September 1997, an even more suspicious tale emerged, once again from hoaxer Ray Wallace. On 15 September a Native American named Tuffy Dowd allegedly wrote to Wallace, briefly describing a series of violent incidents attributed to Bigfoot in Del Norte County, California. Aside from stealing cattle and kidnapping women, Sasquatch was also blamed for stoning two unnamed miners to death at their claim on Blue Creek. Based on its source, the dearth of details, and the total absence of corroboration, the tale inspires no confidence.[31]

Near Misses

Claims of Sasquatch assaults upon humans far outnumber alleged homicides. Research conducted for this volume uncovered forty-four North American cases, listed chronologically below insofar as available information permits.

- 28 February 1856: A correspondent for Shreveport, Louisiana's *Caddo Gazette* reported that a hairy "wild man" recently had dragged a mounted hunter from his horse, thereafter "biting large pieces out of his shoulder and various parts of his body. The monster then tore off saddle and bridle from the horse and destroyed them, and holding the horse by the mane broke a short piece of sapling, and mounting the animal, started at full speed across the plains in the direction of the mountains, guiding the horse with his club." Those startling events allegedly occurred near the untraceable town of "Parailifta," Arkansas.[32]

- 23 January 1869: The *Minnesota Weekly Record* related a tale from Gallipolis, Ohio, where a "gigantic" wildman rushed a carriage occupied by a father and daughter, dragging the man from his seat and grappling fiercely with him until the girl lobbed a stone at the beast and thus drove it away.[33]

- September 1883: Another carriage assault was reported from Illinois, where a "wildman, naked as Adam" charged a buggy driven by the wife of Dr. John Saltenberger, three miles outside Centreville. Mrs. Saltenberger defended herself with a whip, putting the beast (or man) to flight.[34]

- 26 May 1897: A "gorilla-like" biped surprised Bob Forner and Charles Lukins while they were cutting timber outside Rome, Ohio. Both men wrestled with the beast and compelled it to retreat.[35]

- January 1902: An eight-foot, hairy "wildman" terrified skaters at Chesterfield, Idaho, "flourishing a huge club and giving vent to a series of wild yells." Afterward, searchers found footprints "over twenty inches in length and about seven inches wide."[36]

- November 1922: Sometime before the fifth, a "big baboon, thought to have escaped from a rum-running ship," attacked young William Ellinger of Babylon, on New York's Long Island, tearing his clothes. Hunters who glimpsed the creature at an abandoned house proved too slow to capture or kill it.[37]

- March 1923: An "ape man" terrorised females in Council Bluffs, Iowa, rushing from behind them to grab their skirts and legs. Various press reports counted six, twelve, and fourteen victims within a three-week period, claiming that the mauler always struck "within fifteen minutes of midnight," invariably fleeing when its victims screamed.[38]

- Autumn 1939: Somewhere in New Jersey's Berkshire valley, a nocturnal hunting party met a "huge, hairy man-like creature" that killed several hounds and "threw a man who got too close to it," then ran into a nearby swamp.[39]

- October 1943: While hunting near Oregon's Mount Ashland, Bill Cole and O.R. Edwards chose separate trails. Edwards soon glimpsed a seven-foot "manlike creature covered with brown hair," cradling in its arms "what looked like a man." Though fearing that the beast had kidnapped Cole, Edwards returned to their car and awaited his friend's return. Cole reappeared a half-hour later, unscathed, and neither man mentioned the incident for years afterward. Interviewed by a friend of Ivan Sanderson in the 1960s, Cole admitted colliding with Bigfoot, but "didn't think that the animal had carried him."[40]

- April 1944: Nurse Shirley Elkins met her future husband when he visited a hospital in Paintsville, Kentucky, seeking treatment for multiple injuries sustained in a fall. A year later he confessed that a six-foot apelike creature with a bushy tail had attacked him as he (the victim) was trolling for catfish.[41]

- 1 August 1955: While cutting grass along Georgia's Kinchafoonee Creek, Joseph Whaley said he was accosted by a six-foot hairy biped with "tusk-like teeth and pointed ears." As it approached, Whaley swung his scythe, slashing the creature's chest and arms. The beast pursued him to his Jeep, ripping his shirt, scratching his arm and shoulder before Whaley escaped.[42]

- 14 or 21 August 1955: During a Sunday swim in the Ohio River, near Dogtown, Indiana, Mrs. Darwin Johnson felt "a large furry hand with claws" grab her knee, pulling her underwater. She kicked free and made her way to shore, reporting that her leg was scratched and bore "a green stain with a palm outline [that] could be seen for several days." Despite its anomalous nature, the tale remains associated with Bigfoot in various publications.[43]

- May 1956: A hairy nine-foot prowler with eyes "as big as light bulbs" grabbed farmhands Otto Collins and Philip Williams at a ranch near Marshall, Michigan, tucking one beneath each arm and carrying them a short distance before it dropped them and fled.[44]

- 1960: While camping near Lost Lake, on the eastern face of Oregon's Mount Hood,

The tabloid treatment, courtesy of *Weekly World News.*

Gary Carr and a friend woke screaming in their pup tent when "a hairy hand" grabbed each boy's hair. The prowler fled, unseen.[45]

- August 1963: The *Longview* (Washington) *Times* reported that authorities had evacuated a group of hysterical Boy Scouts from the neighbourhood of Mount St. Helens, after the youths were "attacked by the 'ape men.'" A formal report of the incident, promised by scouting officials in Olympia, never materialised.[46]

- 1965: John Becker, a resident of Frederick, Maryland, told state police that a six-foot hairy biped had attacked him in his backyard, near Gambrill State Park. No further details are available.[47]

- July 1966: Several teenagers reported seeing "an ape in a tree," outside Fontana, California. The beast allegedly grabbed one boy, tearing his clothes and inflicting several scratches.[48]

- Summer 1966: Another arboreal creature, this one an albino, leaped from its tree to maul a youth near Yakima, Washington. The victim was reportedly found lying "shocked and clutching white hairs."[49]

- 9 July 1967: Trucker "James P." was asleep in his cab, near Brooksville, Florida, when an "8 foot tall, hairy, gorilla like creature" opened the door and grabbed his feet. He managed to reach the truck's horn and thus put the monster to flight.[50]

- 22 April 1968: An eight-foot biped attacked William Schwark and a friend in Cleveland, Ohio, knocking Schwark down a slope, leaving him with the now-familiar torn clothes and scratched shoulder.[51]

- August 1968: KXOK radio in Kinloch, Missouri, reported that a hairy beast had snatched a four-year-old boy from his family's yard, then dropped him when the child's grandmother screamed. The woman thought it was a bear, while the boy chose a model of a gorilla as the abductor's likeness.[52]

- 1968: Washington resident Art Gilbert told Ray Crowe that an unnamed friend of Gilbert's was "picked up by a Bigfoot and thrown down," near the town of Orchards.[53]

- 7 November 1969: While sleeping in the rear bed of his pickup truck at Lake Worth, Texas, Charles Buchanan claimed that he was lifted—sleeping bag and all—by a beast resembling "a cross between a human being and a gorilla or an ape." The creature instantly dropped Buchanan and left, apparently satisfied, after Buchanan handed it a bag of leftover fried chicken.[54]

- 29 August 1970: While searching for trespassers on her land at Wilsonville, Oregon, a young woman armed with a shotgun met Bigfoot. Before she could fire, the beast grabbed her arm and tossed her into patch of thistles.[55]

- 1970: Sasquatch allegedly roused another Florida trucker from sleep in his cab, outside Brooksville, reaching through an open window to grab the dozing victim. In this case, the trucker's cries supposedly lured local dogs to save him, driving the manbeast away.[56]

- 6 June 1973: A "musty-odoured, red-eyed, human-sized creature or monster" harassed campers on the outskirts of Edwardsville, Illinois, ripping one youth's shirt and scratching his chest.[57]

MY 8 HRS OF HELL WITH BIGFOOT

MOUNTAIN CLIMBER'S OWN STORY

700lbs of savage fury was trying to tear me apart

16 **DEAD MAN FOUND**

A "survivor's" story.

- 15 June 1974: Horseman "F.M." was riding through woodlands twenty miles west of Douglasville, Georgia, when a screaming, green-eyed biped charged from the forest to clutch his saddle. F.M. escaped and later found deep scratches on the saddle's leather.[58]
- August 1973: A resident of Edgewood, Maryland, told friends he was attacked by Bigfoot near his home, defending himself with a flashlight.[59]
- October 1974: While hunting raccoons at night, four residents of Auglaize County, Ohio, flushed a hairy biped from cover near Saint Marys. The creature knocked one man down while fleeing from the party's dogs.[60]

- 24 October 1976: Teenage witness "Joseph" met Florida's "skunk ape" around midnight, in woods south of Orlando. Grabbing a stick, he hit the nine-to-ten-foot creature on one side of its head, then fled toward his waiting Jeep. The angry beast reached in through the passenger's side, scratching Joseph's arm before the reckless youth escaped.[61]

- August 1977: Brian Jones and "two Ritchie boys" saw a red-eyed creature peering through a window of their house in Stilwell, Oklahoma. Rushing outside, Jones collided with an eight-foot malodorous biped, which lifted him off the ground, then dropped him and fled, ducking gunshots from the Ritchies.[62]

- 3 October 1977: Donnie Hall, a security guard residing in Opa-Locka, Florida, reported a skunk ape attack at his workplace. The ten-foot biped allegedly ripped off Hall's shirt, then escaped under fire from Hall's pistol.[63]

- 5 October 1977: The *Orlando Sentinel* reported a hitchhiker's claim that he was attacked by a six-foot "skunk ape" outside Belleview, Florida, two or three days earlier.[64]

- Early winter 1977: Jackie Tharp of Williams, Indiana, reported that Bigfoot had grabbed her arm, then let go when she screamed. Searchers found thirteen-inch humanoid footprints. Geography confuses the case, since Indiana has two towns called Williams, in Adams and Lawrence Counties.[65]

- 1977: An unnamed farmer residing near Otis, Oregon, responded to a ruckus in his chicken coop and met "a large white Bigfoot" which slapped him down before it fled, running on two legs.[66]

- 22 October 1978: The supermarket tabloid paper *Modern People* reported that Albert Permella had been "brutally attacked by a smelly 8-foot tall creature resembling the feared Bigfoot monster," while fishing at an unnamed creek near Yakima, Washington. Permella, who proved untraceable during research for this book, was "bruised and shaken," but otherwise unharmed by his "gigantic, hideous looking" assailant.[67] On balance, the story smacks of fabrication in the vein of many others published by the competing *Weekly World News*.

- October 1979: While not exactly an assault, this tale collected by Peter Byrne describes Sasquatch approaching and touching a small boy in the yard of his Hood River, Oregon, home. The beast then stepped over a fence and disappeared into the forest, before men in the house could reach their guns.[68]

- 10 September 1980: Kentucky paranormal researcher Bart Nunnelly reports that on this date, Bigfoot chased an unnamed woman around her car at a shopping mall in Maysville. No further details are available.[69]

- November 1981: According to the Gulf Coast Bigfoot Research Organization (GCBRO), Sasquatch assaulted a nocturnal hunter in Ohio's Hanover Township, frightening the man so badly that he swore off hunting for two decades thereafter.[70]

- Late 1980s: Ray Crowe reports that "two little Indian boys" were fishing for salmon somewhere in Skamania County, Washington, when Sasquatch waded into the Columbia River and rocked their boat, then retreated.[71]

- Autumn 1991: Correspondent Richard Holzmeyer told Ray Crowe that Bigfoot attacked two unnamed "college boys" on David Hill Road, west of Forest Grove, Oregon, tossing one youth into a briar patch.[72]

- 1999: An unnamed resident of "Bughurry Hollow," allegedly located in McDowell County, West Virginia, responded to noise from his yard and met a tall black creature which "grabbed [him] and threw [him] down like a limp rag." Upon recovering, he found four of his dogs dead, the fifth injured.[73]

- 15 October 2000: Our next anonymous tale portrays a witness walking his dog somewhere in "the north woods of Minnesota." Two simian creatures attack without warning, first seizing the man, then dropping him to dismember his pet.[74]

- Undated: John Green reports two more incidents of Sasquatch hauling sleepy truckers from their cabs—one in eastern Florida, the other in Texas—but offers no details, stating simply that the victims "suffered nothing worse than being pulled out on the ground."[75]

What's for Dinner?

As this book went to press, North American reports of violent interaction between Sasquatch and other animals spanned 223 years, from 1785 through to 2008. In broad terms, the reports include claims of Bigfoot attacking livestock, domestic pets, and wild animals. Some cases indicate predation; others suggest self-defence, while some appear motiveless. Reports may also be divided into those where large bipeds were seen; those presenting suggestive evidence, such as oversized humanoid footprints; and others where Bigfoot is blamed or suspected for no apparent reason.

Seventy-three reports claim Sasquatch attacks on various species of livestock, including twenty cases involving cattle, sixteen involving barnyard fowl, seven incidents with horses, seven more with sheep, six involving pigs, two with goats, one involving rabbits, and fourteen wherein multiple species were killed or injured without apparent preference.

Of those seventy-three cases, thirty-five include eyewitness descriptions of unknown bipedal predators, fifteen claim discovery of large humanoid tracks (two in conjunction with sightings), three refer to strange vocalisations by unseen creatures, and two describe foul odours often associated with Bigfoot. Eighteen cases offer no evidence of Sasquatch involvement beyond suspicion, rumours, native legends, or unrelated sightings in the general vicinity at other times.

Two of the most intriguing cases claim that hairy predators were killed by farmers defending their property. The first tale, reported from "somewhere in Georgia," describes a biped seven or eight feet tall slain at Little Mountain, then paraded through "the town" in a pickup truck before it was buried beneath heavy stones. Unfortunately, Georgia has three Little Mountains (in Lumpkin, Rabun and Towns Counties), plus a Little Mountain Creek (Harris County) and a Little Mountain Ridge (Chattooga County). Inquiries to the respective county newspapers and libraries produced no information to corroborate the story.[76]

The other alleged Sasquatch slaying occurred in Pemiscot County, Missouri, sometime in the late 1940s. Hunters tracked "something like a gorilla" to Nigger Wool Swamp (now Ne-growool Swamp) and riddled it with bullets. This time no parade was held, and no details of the body's disposition are available. While questions linger, John Green is undoubtedly correct in stating that the documented slaying of an apeman—much less *two*—should have been front-page news throughout America, and probably worldwide.[77]

Added confusion arises thanks to a report filed from untraceable "Piney Ridge," Missouri, where hunters allegedly pursued a Sasquatch fond of killing goats and sheep in 1947. Colin and Janet Bord suggest that this case may duplicate the incident from Nigger Wool Swamp, but John Green clearly separates the two events. And, in fact, the creature stalked at Piney Ridge escaped its trackers, after killing several of their hounds and overturning their Jeep. Again, geography defeats our efforts to learn more: the only Piney Ridge known in the Show-Me State today is a juvenile psychiatric facility located in Waynesville. Meanwhile, Missouri boasts sixteen locations named *Pine* Ridge, scattered over eleven counties.[78]

Bigfoot's alleged interaction with livestock ranges from simple harassment to full-scale dismemberment. One "wild man," seen at Lancaster, Pennsylvania, in December 1858 was described as "sucking the cows," whatever that may mean. The most unusual cases involve five incidents, all reported from the Pacific Northwest, where slaughtered animals were found in trees. They include a horse "tied up in [a] tree" on the Colville Indian Reservation, in Washington's Okanogan County, sometime in the 1950s; fifteen to twenty sheep found hanging from trees in Union County, Oregon, in 1979; a dismembered goat found near Welches, Oregon, in February 1994; a hog found near Estacada, Oregon, in April or May 1995, with a fourteen-inch humanoid footprint nearby; and a cow discovered in Clackamas County, Oregon, date unknown.[79]

Some cases of alleged Bigfoot predation on livestock offer alternative explanations. Police blamed a cult for the mutilation of Jeff Schafer's cattle in Clark County, Washington, during 1989. A farmer in Chelsea, Oklahoma, blamed "a tall black man with long shaggy clothes" for stealing his chickens August 1996, while GCBRO analysts concluded that the "long stringy clothes...was bigfoot hair." A rancher in Nevada County, California, collected hair at the site where his chickens vanished, and despite his conviction that "no cat could have done this," the hair was identified as a cougar's.[80]

Reported attacks on domestic pets are less common, but forty-six cases were found spanning 115 years, from 1891 to 2006. Thirty of those cases included eyewitness testimony, although two referred to Bigfoot sightings "some time" before the events in question. Large footprints were found in three cases, including one with "three toed/clawed tracks" atypical of Sasquatch or any known primate. Two other cases included reports of strange vocalisations attributed to Bigfoot.[81]

Eighty-five percent of all attacks on pets involve dogs, including cases where canines are the apparent aggressors, either defending their turf or dispatched against Bigfoot by hunters. The remaining cases include one predator that favoured cats, one that killed only rabbits, and five in which multiple species were slain (including a pet deer and a peacock). Authorities blamed a bear for one attack (in 1912), and a wolverine for another (date unrecorded), but some re-

Bigfoot joins Al-Qaeda...

searchers dismiss those solutions in favour of blaming Sasquatch. On balance, there is no logical reason why Bigfoot—if it exists—should not kill small domestic animals, either for food or in self-defence, if attacked.

Finally, large omnivores may be expected to prey on other wild animals. And, in fact, we have ninety-three reports on file alleging Sasquatch predation on various wildlife species (excluding claims of Bigfoot fishing or dining on insects, shellfish, and rodents). Fifty-three of those cases involve deer or elk: forty-one with claims of Bigfoot killing or pursuing live animals, plus eleven stories of carcasses stolen from hunters. Other tales include eight reports of Sasquatch eating road kill; five describing theft of fish from fishermen; four each involving bears and rabbits; three each involving beavers, ducks, and coyotes; one each involving feral hogs, raccoons, porcupines, wild horses, and wild turkeys; and five referring to unspecified "animals."

The cases reviewed include forty-two sightings of large unknown bipeds, twelve cases with

Shocking Mafia reality TV show – WINNER COMMITS MURDER!

WEEKLY WORLD® NEWS

THE WORLD'S ONLY RELIABLE NEWSPAPER

5 WAYS TO TELL IF YOUR PETS ARE REINCARNATED PEOPLE

BIGFOOT vs. ALIENS!

Battle captured on home video – EYEWITNESS TELLS ALL!

APRIL 17, 2006

$2.99 US / $3.95 CANADA

16>

7 25274 51030 6

Bat Boy rampage in N.Y.

...and captures alien invaders!

humanoid footprints reported, and six involving "Bigfoot-type" sounds. In the remaining thirty-two incidents, Sasquatch predation is inferred from previous regional sightings or the "suspicious" condition of carcasses found in the wild.

And, in fact, something strange *does* appear to be happening with wild animal remains in America's woodlands. Four reports describe mutilated deer remains found in trees, while another claims that six-point antlers were left "in trade" for stolen deer entrails. Stranger still are the reports of multiple carcasses cached—or even artfully arranged—in various locations. The list includes an Oklahoma "deer kill stash" discovered in October 1971; three deer found with Bigfoot tracks in Ohio, in November 1992; multiple deer with legs "broken and twisted," again from Ohio, in December 1992; an Ohio Bigfoot sighting near a cave filled with dismembered deer, in summer 1993; four more deer found in Ohio, in October 1994; mutilated deer carcasses found stacked in an Illinois forest; unspecified animal carcasses found "in [a] possible display arrangement" near Coshocton, Ohio, in April 2001; and a Minnesota report from the following month, of "stripped carcasses of three beavers [with] the skeletons...stacked all facing the same way." The most dramatic incident, filed by witness Tuklo Nashoba from an unspecified location in south-eastern Oklahoma, describes "a Bigfoot Super Highway" strewn with "literally thousands of bones from dead animals."[82]

As with the livestock kills, our most intriguing case—and by far the oldest—describes the capture of a predatory "wild man." On 4 January 1785 *The Times* of London told its readers:

> There is lately arrived in France from America, a wild man, who was caught in the woods, 200 miles back from the Lake of the Woods [in present-day Minnesota], by a party of Indians; they had seen him several times, but he was so swift of foot that they could by no means get up with him. He is nearly seven feet high, covered with hair, but has little appearance of understanding and is remarkably sullen and intractable. When he was taken, half a bear was found lying beside him, which he had just killed.[83]

And there, sadly, the story ends.

Sasquatch Calling

Many tales describe Bigfoot-type creatures approaching human dwellings. Sightings of unknown bipeds on residential property are too numerous—and frequently too vague—for analysis here, but eighty-seven reports logged since 1904 claim direct contact with homes, including several forced entries. In thirty-seven cases apelike voyeurs peered through windows, then departed—one after telling a startled resident, "Somebody shot me and I don't like it!"[84] Of the remaining cases, twenty-five describe dwellings struck or shaken; eleven claim attempted entry; eight describe actual entry (of seven homes and one barn); one has Sasquatch walking on a roof; and seven report theft of objects (generally food) from porches or outbuildings. Eleven of the eighty-nine cases claim damage to homes.

Aside from window-peeping incidents, reports considered here include twenty eyewitness sightings, fifteen cases with unusual sounds, four reports of large footprints, two descriptions of "Bigfoot-type" odours, and two discoveries of unidentified hair (one in conjunction with tracks). Reports of physical damage, ranging from torn window screens to houses "trashed," may also be considered evidence.

Actual home invasions are our primary concern. Cases on file include the following:

- February 1925: A malodorous, "very hairy" creature entered a rural home in Forrest County, Mississippi, glimpsed by three children while their parents slept. No physical evidence was found.[85]
- July 1958: A child claimed that a six-foot biped with red eyes located "on the side of his head like a rabbit" entered a farmhouse somewhere in southern Illinois. Again, no evidence remained. [86]
- 1961-63: Residents of Klamath County, Oregon, found their summer cabin raided during three consecutive summers, with the door "hanging in splinters...and the inside in shambles," furniture toppled, and cans of food "squeezed open." Several "large piles of hardened faeces" lay in one corner, while dust on the floor "showed the unmistakable imprint of 18-inch bare feet."[87]
- 1964: Another child woke from sleep to see "a huge dark object" prowling through her home in La Follette, Tennessee. Parents and siblings slept through the alleged invasion, later dismissing it as a nightmare.[88]
- 1965: According to Bigfoot researcher Ray Crowe, one Ken Hinkle "saw a Bigfoot enter a Yoder [Oregon] area house, nobody home, apparently messed it up, and left."[89]
- October 1977: A security guard in Apopka, Florida, suffered scratches from a ten-foot hairy beast that tried to break down his door.[90]
- 1979: Residents of Welches, Oregon, returned from a shopping expedition to find a window of their home broken and the house ransacked, with traces of unidentified long hair on the floor. One child subsequently claimed sightings of a "beautiful" bipedal beast in the neighborhood.[91]
- Summer 1989: Bigfoot researcher Ray Crowe reported a home invasion near Goat Mountain in Clackamas County, Oregon. Citing an unnamed witness, Crowe said "the screen door [was] torn off, folded in half, and something had gone out the opposite door. Nothing was taken, and the place wasn't torn up."[92]

Three other reports describe large hairy arms thrust through windows: at Marietta, Washington, in October 1967; at a rural home near Hudson, Michigan, in spring 1977 or 1978; and in Otero County, New Mexico, in July 2004.[93]

Driven to Distraction
Since the first alleged attacks on horse-drawn carriages in 1869 and 1883, reports of Bigfoot's strange love-hate relationship with human vehicles have multiplied. Research conducted for this work uncovered seventy-three specific cases, and it seems likely that others may exist.

Six witnesses describe Sasquatch running beside their cars, peering through windows at speeds ranging from ten to seventy miles per hour, but most reports depict more aggressive conduct. Fifty-three describe large creatures striking, rocking, tipping or shoving vehicles; seven report assaults on occupants of cars or trucks; three claim that hairy bipeds leapt onto cars; while three more report objects thrown at vehicles. The majority of vehicles attacked (77 percent) were parked when the incidents occurred, but some creatures seem willing to charge moving cars. In one aberrant case, a "good Samaritan" Sasquatch allegedly pulled a car from a roadside ditch in Lane County, Oregon.[94]

Forty-three of the cases considered here include eyewitness sightings of large bipedal beasts. Six other witnesses described a musky stench familiar from many reports, while two more heard distinctive vocalisations. Twelve-inch-wide muddy handprints found on two vehicles in 2001—one in Montezuma County, Colorado; the other in Lane County, Oregon—remain unexplained.[95]

Beyond assaults on sleeping truckers, noted previously, two reports describe Sasquatch attacks on occupants of moving vehicles. On 13 August 1965 Christine van Acker was driving near Monroe, Michigan, with her mother, Ruth Owens, when a Bigfoot rushed their car. Mrs. Owens saw a "huge hairy hand" grab Christine's head and slam her face into the door post, whereupon their car swerved off the road. Workers from a nearby farm heard Mrs. Owens screaming and rushed to the scene, finding her hysterical and Christina unconscious, with a livid bruise on her face. Subsequent searches of the neighbourhood revealed no monster.[96]
One year later, on 27 August 1966, Jerri Mendenhall and another teenage girl were driving outside Fontana, California, in search of an apelike creature reported by multiple witnesses since July. As luck would have it, the monster found them, charging their car and lunging through a window at Jerri, inflicting scratches which she later displayed to police.[97]

The most famous vehicle "attack" on record is the case of Charles Wetzel, logged from Riverside, California, on 8 November 1958. Wetzel was crossing the Santa Ana River when a creature with a "scarecrowish head" and skin covered in scales "like leaves" threw itself across the hood of his car, scrabbling at the windshield, then tumbled free. Whatever it was, the beast bore no apparent resemblance to Bigfoot. Skeptics suggest that Wetzel struck a low-flying vulture or other large bird.[98]

Getting Stoned
Apes and monkeys of various species routinely throw objects at each other and at trespassers in their domain. Projectiles include their own faeces, along with sticks, stones, nuts and fruit. In March 2009 a chimpanzee called Santino, lodged at Sweden's Furuvik Zoo, stockpiled chunks of concrete from the floor of his cage for use as ammunition against human visitors.[99]

It comes as no surprise, therefore, to learn that ninety-three reports since 1864 describe Sasquatch pelting humans, their homes and vehicles with various items. Rocks are the most common missiles, reported in sixty-five cases. Some are huge boulders, weighing an estimated 200 to 300 pounds, while smaller stones sometime descend in showers of prolonged duration. Eleven cases involve sizeable logs; four involve sticks or tree limbs; three claim showers of sticks *and* stones; three more involve pine cones; another three describe pelting with snowballs; while one beast lobbed a coffee can and another hurled a nondescript "object."

In terms of evidence, the cases reviewed for this chapter include twenty-seven eyewitness sightings, twenty-one reports of Bigfoot-style vocalisations; four cases where humanoid tracks were discovered, and four more with reports of "typical" Sasquatch odours.

On balance, the creatures that delight in pelting humans seem to mean no harm. Our tally here excludes the Ape Canyon incident described in Chapter 2 and the alleged stoning death of two Blue Creek miners noted earlier in this chapter—both of which seem likely to be hoaxes—and the final score includes only three casualties. Sometime in 1961, nonagenarian Florence Cooper regaled local Boy Scouts with her tales of travelling to California in a covered wagon, settling near Yreka. During their childhood, Cooper's future husband allegedly suffered a broken arm when Bigfoot hurled a rock at him, but details and documentation remain elusive.[100]

Fast-forward to June 1994, when victim "Denise" claims an invisible tormentor pelted her with stones the size of "giant pumpkins" at Multnomah Falls, Oregon. One rock allegedly crushed her foot, causing her to lose consciousness. Twenty-six months later, in August 1996, "fire fighter Larry" was reportedly engaged in battling a wildfire near Oakridge, Oregon, when someone or something hurled a rock that struck him in the back. More followed, but the barrage ceased when Larry cried out in protest. While relating Denise's story, IBS investigator Rip Lyttle also referred to "an Australian tourist...killed at Crater Lake N[ational] P[ark] just a year ago"—i.e., in 1993. Lyttle implies a connection to Bigfoot rock-throwing, but a survey of deaths recorded at the park between 1872 and 1997 reveals none in 1993. Neither were any of those lost over 125 years Australians, although German tourist Kerstin Hadelka died in a fall at the park on 16 September 1992.[101]

Ferocious Footage

Next to witnessing a Bigfoot rampage in the flesh, the best proof would be catching one on film. But do such films exist?

Fictional cinematic portrayals of hairy bipeds run amok span more than half a century, including *The Snow Creature* (1954), *Man Beast* (1956), *The Abominable Snowman* (1957), *Half Human* (1958), *The Legend of Boggy Creek* (1972), *Shriek of the Mutilated* (1974), *The Beauties and the Beast* (1974), *Creature from Black Lake* (1976), *Snowbeast* (1977), *Night of the Demon* (1980), *The Barbaric Beast of Boggy Creek* (1985), *Sasquatch* (2002), *Clawed* (2005), *Sasquatch Mountain* (2006), *Abominable* (2006), and *Sasquatch Assault* (2009).

But what about the real thing?

First on the scene with supposed evidence of hominid aggression was the History Channel's *MonsterQuest* series, investigating claims of various cryptids worldwide. The show's second episode, aired on 7 November 2007, was provocatively titled "Sasquatch Attack." It focused on alleged Bigfoot invasions of a remote hunting cabin in northern Ontario, Canada, where a crude trap constructed by hammering nails through a board apparently wounded some unknown intruder. A follow-up episode—"Sasquatch Attack II," aired on 12 November 2008—subjected bloodstains from the trap to DNA analysis, with test results suggesting that the intruder may be "a nonhuman primate."[102]

Between those *MonsterQuest* broadcasts, the Animal Planet network weighed in with a competing series called *Lost Tapes,* consisting of videotapes allegedly recovered from cameras owned by victims of lethal cryptid attacks. Amidst fatal maulings by sea serpents, giant raptors, living dinosaurs, the Mongolian death worm and *El Chupacabra,* the series presented three episodes depicting supposed attacks by hairy hominids.

The first case—Episode No. 2 of Season 1, titled "Bigfoot"—premiered on 30 October 2008. It purports to tell the story of a game warden whose life is threatened by a homicidal poacher, until a man-eating Sasquatch arrives to save the day and devour the villain.

Next up—Episode No. 4 of Season 1, "Swamp Creature," aired on 6 January 2009—follows a college professor and her nephew in pursuit of a Louisiana bayou-dwelling beast, left famished for human flesh in the wake of Hurricane Katrina. Finally (at least, so far), Episode No. 3 of Season 2 aired on 6 October 2009. Titled "Swamp Creature," it depicts a hunting party's disastrous meeting with a murderous monster in the Arkansas backcountry.[103]

Although presented in the you-are-there mockumentary style popularised by *The Blair Witch Project* (1999), later played for laughs on TV's *FreakyLinks* (2000-01), *Lost Tapes* is clearly an exercise in fiction. Any attempt to trace the "victims" named on air through media or law enforcement channels swiftly demonstrates that none of the events portrayed are factual.

Which brings us to the "Gable film."

Sometime in 2007, a brief clip of herky-jerky videotape depicting a supposed cryptid attack surfaced on the Internet. Researcher Loren Coleman traced the clip to one Steve Cook, a Michigan disc jockey and proprietor of a website devoted to the Wolverine State's legendary "dogman," said to be a hybrid of sorts between Bigfoot and a Hollywood werewolf. Cook, in turn, claimed that he had acquired the original film—supposedly shot on an 8mm movie camera by someone named Gable, sometime in the 1970s—at a Michigan estate sale in 2004.[104]

As for the blurry beast depicted in the film itself, seen lurching toward the camera on all fours, it bears no resemblance to Sasquatch. Various bloggers have cast their anonymous votes for a bear, gorilla, or wolfman.

Lifelong Sasquatch tracker Autumn Williams has pursued the film through local contacts and interviews with spokesmen for Michigan's Department of Natural Resources, and discovered apparent "new footage" in July 2009, without fully accepting Loren Coleman's conviction that the films constitute a hoax.[105]

On March 24 2010, *The History Channel* broadcast the final episode in the series *Monster Quest*. This debunked the "Gable Film", and included an interview with the perpetrator.

And there, at least for now, the matter rests. If Bigfoot/Sasquatch does exist somewhere in North America, there is no *prima facie* reason to assume that it should be less dangerous than any other beast of comparable size. Bears, cougars, moose, and even deer have killed and maimed humans at various times—as have domestic cattle, dogs, horses, and pigs. Whether Sasquatch considers mankind a food source, a potential threat, or simply an annoying curiosty, close contact may prove hazardous.

In Bigfoot's defence, the case remains unproven.

mapinguari
a festa

com as bandas
Rebossa
NegroLéo Trio

a performance
A Carioca
com Leleco Basil

DJs
Lencinho
Millena

Exposição

às 20h
5 merréis

12
março
Lapa

Brasil Mestiço . Av Mem de Sá, 61

Chapter 4.
Latin America: Tropical Terrors

Crossing the Rio Grande into Mexico, we must bypass most of that republic's thirty-one states before we encounter the first tales of predatory bipeds in the far southeastern corner of the country. Even then, the initial reports from Chiapas are disappointing.

Ivan Sanderson, in 1961, reported that man-sized hairy creatures known as *Cax-vinic, Salvaje,* or *fantasma humano* was "not *quite* but *very* well-known in the forests" of Mexico's southernmost state. Correspondent Cal Brown described the beast's cries to Sanderson, writing, "I don't think I have ever heard anything so disturbing—not frightening but more dreadful and haunting, and full of threat I couldn't imagine." Nonetheless, no stories of attacks on humans were forthcoming. Geologist Wendell Skousen told Sanderson, "Several persons reported they were chased by it down the mountain, although with the fear they have of whatever it is, they probably just caught a glimpse of it and ran all the way down the mountain at top speed."[1]

To the northeast, in Yucatán, two aberrant creatures appear more aggressive. The first is said to be a kind of hairy pygmy, ranging in height from thirty to forty-eight inches. Variously known as *Ahlu't, Aluche, A'lus, Alux, Barux* or *Kat,* the little people lob stones at humans, shove them out of hammocks as they sleep, and sometimes infect them with fevers. Given the claims that they wear hats, while carrying machetes and shotguns, they may represent an unknown forest-dwelling tribe and hardly fall into the Bigfoot-Yeti realm.[2]

Stranger still is the Yucatán "wolfwoman," reported from the state capital of Mérida on 2 February 2004. Journalist Martin Morita told the story as follows in Mexico City's *Reforma* newspaper:

> MERIDA, Mexico—Over 100 residents of the Texn Palomeque commissariat of the municipality of Hunucma, backed by 10 police officers of said entity, went after an alleged "paranormal being" dubbed "the Wolf-

Cashing in on the *Mapinguari*.

woman," whose escapades have caused fear among residents of this and other Yucatan communities.

Armed with rifles, shotguns, pistols and equipped with lanterns, the locals organised themselves by groups and plunged into the wilderness in order to put an end to this "being," described by eyewitnesses as hairy, standing approximately a meter and a half, walking on two legs and with glowing red eyes.

The alleged wolfwoman has slain hundreds of farm birds in this commissariat and has also been seen in communities within other municipalities, such as Umn, Halach, and Sisal.

Tadeo Cauich, one of the municipal police officers of Hunucma who accompanied the hunters, said that the matter has already turned into a legend and that there is a great amount of fear in the locality, to the extent that residents of Texn Paloqueme and other neighbouring commissariats no longer go out at night, fearful of encountering the strange being.

Residents of Texn did not have the luck to find the "wolfwoman," although some say the creature was seen running toward Umn.

But it isn't just the wolfwoman who has the hairs of the locals standing on end, since other municipalities and communities claim having seen other supernatural beings, as occurred in Opichn, an eastern locality, where there was talk of the "Huay kekn"—a devil hound, in the Mayan language—responsible for the deaths of dozens of pigs, dogs and cats in that area. The presence of the notorious "Chupacabras" has even been reported in Merida, the state capital.

Apparitions and attacks by these phenomena have increased in recent weeks and new accounts emerge every day from those who swear having seen or been victims of such attacks.[3]

Again, nothing links Bigfoot or any equivalent beast to the reported incidents.

A more traditional monster allegedly inhabits the state of Quintana Roo, sprawling over 19,387 square miles of the eastern Yucatán Peninsula. As we shall see, the creature—dubbed *Sisemité* and known by at least fifteen other regional names—has been reported from a vast range extending southward through much of Central America.[4]

El Sisemité

Widely reported from southeastern Mexico through Guatemala, Belize, Honduras and Nicaragua, *El Sisemité* is also known in various locales as *Chichimeque, Chichimicli, Chichinité, Itacayo, Li Queck, Simichi, Siguanaba, Sirpi, Sissimito, Suinta* ("spirit of the mountains"), and

U tcur witsir ("guardian hill spirit"). More specific to our interest is the Mayan name *Qetcux*, which translates as "abductor."[5]

Descriptions of *El Sisemité* are fairly consistent throughout its range, summarised in September 1915 by the University of Pennsylvania's *Museum Journal.* According to that article:

> There is a monster that lives in the forest. He is taller than the tallest man and in appearance he is between a man and a monkey. His body is so well protected by a mass of matted hair that a bullet cannot harm him. His tracks have been seen on the mountains, but it is impossible to follow his trail because he can reverse his feet and thus baffle the most successful hunter....If a Sisemite captures a man he rends the body and crushes the bones between his teeth in great enjoyment of the flesh and blood. If he captures a woman, she is carried to his cave, where she is kept a prisoner....He sometimes steals children in the belief that from these he may acquire the gift of human speech.[6]

Despite that fearsome reputation, only one specific case of *Sisemité* violence exists. According to Ivan Sanderson, Miguel Huzul, a resident of Cobán, Guatemala, filed a criminal complaint sometime in the early 1940s, charging that his son-in-law "was delinquent in having permitted his daughter to be seized by a creature of the mountains to which he gave a name that was apparently too much for the recording officer and which he therefore put down as 'a sort of gorilla or man' as far as it could be deciphered and transliterated." By the time Sanderson reported that case in 1961, his copy of the police report had been lost. Sanderson noted that "No action was taken because the father was disbelieved, while it was rather nicely pointed out that if all that is said about the *Sisimete* is true, the young man could not be accused of cowardice and/or delinquency."[7]

Central America and the Caribbean

Several other tales of aggressive Bigfoot-type creatures have also emerged from Central America. In 1898, while exploring Honduras, Edward Jonathan Hoyt allegedly killed a five-foot-tall apelike creature with red eyes "like balls of fire," when he woke to find it crawling over the foot of his bunk.[8] Humans aside, no New World primate recognised by science attains that size.

No date is offered for the next report, received by Ivan Sanderson from a New Jersey resident named A. Haworth. According to Haworth, an unnamed "friend from El Salvador told him of a hairy human-shaped creature that killed cattle on his uncle's farm near the Honduras border."[9] Sadly, no further details are available.

Finally, from southern Panama, we have the tale of an American prospector named Shea who allegedly shot and killed a menacing manlike creature in 1920, in the Serrania del Sapo mountains of Darién Province, near Piñas Bay.[10] The beast was not preserved for scientific study, but since modern Piñas Bay is a popular tourist attraction, we may assume that Bigfoot predation is not a recurring problem.

A final matter, from the Bahamas, may best be consigned to the realm of legend. Initially reported by British zoologist and oceanographer John Stanley Gardiner in 1886, the story concerns hairy bipeds known as *Yeho,* said to sport bear-like claws on backwards-pointing feet reminiscent of *El Sisemité'*s. Known as nocturnal prowlers, confined to Andros and Long Island, male *Yehos* reportedly snatched human females and impregnated them, producing shaggy offspring. A century after Gardiner's first report of the creatures, French cryptozoologist Michel Raynal dismissed them as mythical, spawned by folk memories of real-life gorillas among imported Africans.[11]

South America

There is clearly room enough for monsters in South America, a sprawling continent of 6,890,000 square miles. In 2009 an estimated 385,742,554 persons inhabited the continent, for an average of 21.4 per square mile, but that statistic is grossly misleading. The sparsely-populated Amazon Basin comprises nearly half of South America (3,178,876 square miles), while the rugged Andes Mountains account for another 2,175,000 square miles. Some 12.5 percent of the continent's population is confined to ten teeming cities: São Paulo, Brazil (with 11,037,593); Bogotá, Colombia (7,259,597); Lima, Peru (7,605,742); Rio de Janeiro, Brazil (6,186,710); Santiago, Chile (4,987,600); Caracas, Venezuela (3,276,000); Buenos Aires, Argentina (3,059,728); Maracaibo, Venezuela (2,063,670); Santa Cruz, Bolivia (1,545,161); and Montevideo, Uruguay (1,269,648)[12]

That said, the fact that monsters might be found in South America does not mean that they are, much less that they are known to prey on humans. The late John Keel, writing in 1970, declared that "[b]etween 1952-65 there were eighteen documented cases of people in Argentina, Venezuela, and Brazil being attacked and injured by unidentified hairy creatures in human form." Sadly, Keel cited no sources and briefly detailed only one case, discussed below in the section on Argentina.[13]

Mono Grande

Tales of a large, sometimes aggressive primate are ubiquitous across the breadth of northern South America. Through Colombia and Venezuela, southward into eastern Ecuador and the Madidi region of Bolivia, the man-sized hairy beast is variously known as *Mono grande* ("big monkey"), *Mono rey* ("king monkey"), *Mohan* or *Mojan, Muan,* and *Tigre mono* ("tiger monkey"). Across its range, the beast is said to wield tree limbs as weapons, to stone native huts, and to snatch tribal women as mates.[14]

In 1920, while exploring the Serranía del Perijá mountains which form Colombia's natural boundary with Venezuela, members of a party led by Swiss geologist François de Loys allegedly met two large, menacing monkeys that hurled excrement at the hikers, then rushed them while brandishing tree limbs as bludgeons. Gunfire dropped the larger of the pair, a female, while her mate escaped into the forest. Afterward, De Loys and company propped the corpse upright on a wooden crate and snapped a photograph that remains a subject of heated debate to this day.[15]

Ivan Sanderson deemed the creature an "obvious" spider monkey (genus *Ateles*), while dubbing the photo "an outright hoax, and an obnoxious one at that, being a deliberate deception." Bernard Heuvelmans disagreed, stating that "it is hard to deny that Loys's monkey has a more massive body and thicker limbs than the ordinary spider-monkeys." Furthermore, Heuvelmans opined that de Loys "would hardly have gone to the trouble at such a critical moment of his explorations to photograph such a common animal." Swiss anthropologist George Montadon christened the beast *Ameranthropoides loysi* in 1929, while Scottish anatomist and anthropologist Arthur Keith preferred *Ateles loysi*. In 1996 cryptozoologists Loren Coleman and Michel Raynal denounced Montadon's classification *Ameranthropoides loysi* as a racist fraud, penned to support Montadon's theory that South American aborigines evolved from native monkeys and were thus inferior to whites.[16]

Whatever de Loys photographed in 1920, the *Mono rey* remains elusive and reports of its attacks on livestock or humans—including a report that large apes armed with clubs killed one member of a three-man party in April 1968, in Brazil's Serra Pacaraimã mountain range—are still unsupported by factual documentation. British author Simon Chapman joined an expedition to identify the *Mono grande* in 1997, but found only rumours and legends, including an undocumented claim that a live specimen was once displayed at Bolivia's Santa Cruz Zoo.[17]

Salvaje and *Vasitri*

Whether the *Mono grande* is alone in prowling its vast range remains a subject of debate. At least one other manlike beast is said to occupy the jungles of Colombia and Venezuela, snatching human females when its mood swings toward romance and procreation. In the Arauca Department of eastern Colombia, across Venezuela's Guiana Highlands and in the Orinoco Basin, it is known as *Salvaje* ("savage"). On the Upper Orinoco tribesmen call it *Vasitri* and *Maipuran* (both meaning "big devil"). Other regional names include *Achi, Conerre, Paudacota yege,* and *Vasuri.* [18]

Bernard Heuvelmans cites vague claims that *Vasitris* sometimes dine on human flesh, while offering two reports from the early 1950s that describe hundreds of cattle slain by something that ripped out their tongues, on ranches along Brazil's *Rio Araguaia and around Ybitimi, Paraguay. While sightings of man-sized monkeys persist from the region, and one report claims that a five-foot-tall Salvaje* was slain by a native hunter on the Orinoco River in 1990, documentation for killings or abductions of humans remain as ephemeral as those offered for the *Mono grande.*[19]

Our sole report with any details dates from autumn 1954 and carries us into the realm of UFOlogy. According to that tale, Gustavo Gonzales and Jose Ponce left home in the Caracas suburb of Petare, Venezuela, at 2:00 A.M. on November 28, intending to gather produce for sale in Caracas later that day. En route to a local warehouse, they observed a luminous sphere floating six feet off the pavement, blocking their path. Gonzales stopped his truck and stepped out to observe the orb more closely, whereupon a three-foot-tall hairy troll attacked him from the shadows, biting and clawing. Gonzales fought back with a knife, which glanced off his assailant's hide "as if it had struck steel." A second hairy dwarf leapt from the sphere, blinded Gonzales with light from "a metallic tube," then both beasts ran back to their craft, climbed aboard, and escaped in a flash.[20]

Whether that tale is true or a flight of utter fantasy, it clearly shares nothing in common with the other tales of shaggy manlike creatures roaming South America's forests. Nor, quite obviously, does it help support a charge of *Salvaje/Vasitri* aggression toward humans.

Didi Do It?

From the Guianas—present-day Guyana, Suriname, and French Guiana—tales have long emerged describing tailless simian bipeds, averaging five feet in height, variously known as *Didi, Dai-dai, Didi-aguiri, Dru-di-di, Massikruman,* and *Quato.* Published sightings span a period of 120 years, from 1868 to 1987.[21]

Didis are described as shy ... but only to a point. In 1931 Italian anthropologist Nello Beccari emerged from the jungles of then-British Guiana with tales of "fabulous hairy men called *didi,* which all the Indians fear, although they have never seen them." According to Beccari, that fear was inspired by the fact that "the *di-di* lived in pairs and that it was extremely dangerous to kill one of them, for the other would inevitably revenge its mate by coming at night and strangling the murderer in his hammock." George Eberhart adds that the *Didi* is said to hurl sticks and mud on occasion, when angered. On a more sinister note, some natives claim the beasts are "able to mate successfully with humans."[22] Happily for those involved, none of the published sightings by explorers include any acts of aggression by *Didis* glimpsed during rain forest rambles.

Mato Grosso Mysteries

Brazil is the fifth largest country on Earth, encompassing 3,287,597 square miles. Forty percent of the vast Amazon Basin lies within Brazil proper, including the state of Mato Gross ("thick woods," in Portuguese), which comprises eleven percent of Brazil's total area.[23] Small wonder, then, that Brazil offers multiple monsters for our consideration.

First in line is a puzzling creature variously known as *Caá-pora* ("mountain lord"), *Caipora, Caypoté, Coropira, Corubira, Curupira* ("small body"), *Kaaguerre, Kaapore, Korupira, Kurupi, Kurú-piré,* or *Yurupari.* In some accounts it is a small hairy biped, no more than four feet tall, with certain human traits that include smoking pipes and riding bareback on deer or wild pigs. Less amusing to the natives are its habits of abducting children and occasionally raping human females.[24]

A very different description of the same creature appears on an Internet website called "The Spiders Den" [*sic*], presented by an anonymous scribe. It reads [with grammar uncorrected]:

> The Kuru-pira is a guardian species of the Deana people in Brazil, also known as a boraro because of its distinctive call. He has red eyes that glow like burning emebers and jaguar like fangs. His ears stand erect and his form is a of a tall human with a hairy chest and large gentitals. He has no knee joints and has difficulty getting up when he falls. The Kuru-pira can be immediately recognized by his oversized feet that face the wrong way. His heels are in the front and his toes toward the back, it is fasioned to deceive they point in the direction that the creature had just come

from leading victims directly into his path as they try to avoid him.

When a Kuru-pira attacks a victim he emits a distinctive boraro growl. His roar is similar to that of a jaguar only slightly more prolonged and considerably louder. He may kill his victims by two methods, either instnatly with his urine which is said to be leathal, or by holding a person tightly untill they are crsuehd. Once dead the Kuru-pira makes a small hole in the skull of the victim and sucks out blood and flesh.

After a Kuru-pira feeds upon its victim it closes the hole made in the head and a demon spirit pocesses the empty shell of a body and the "man" no longer who or what he use to be, lives with the wild animals. The Kuru-pira is a protecter of the forest and animals, and one becomes in danger if they take from the forest more then they can cary or eat.[25]

No source is offered for these claims, which diverge so widely from other accounts of the *Curupira,* and in the absence of documentation there is no apparent reason to take them seriously.

In 1914, a decade before his mysterious disappearance in Brazil, explorer Percy Fawcett reported an encounter with tribe of hairy, apelike bipeds in Mato Grosso. Known as *Maricoxi* or *Morocoxo,* the creatures also possessed some strikingly human attributes. According to Fawcett:

As we stood looking from right to left, trying to decide which direction was the more promising, two savages appeared about a hundred yards to the south, moving at a trot and talking rapidly. On catching sight of us they stopped dead and hurriedly fixed arrows to their bows, while I shouted to them in the Maxubi tongue. We could not see them clearly for the shadows dappling their bodies, but it seemed to me they were large, hairy men, with exceptionally long arms, and with foreheads sloping back from pronounced eye ridges, men of a very primitive kind, in fact, and stark naked. Suddenly they turned and made off into the undergrowth, and we, knowing it was useless to follow, started up the north leg of the trail.

It was not long before sundown, when, dim and muffled through the trees, came the unmistakable sound of a horn. We halted and listened intently. Again we heard the horn call, answered from other directions till several horns were braying at once. In the subdued light of evening, beneath the high vault of branches in this forest untrodden by civilised man, the sound was as eerie as the opening notes of some fantastic opera. We knew the savages made it, and that those savages were now on our trail. Soon we could hear shouts and jabbering to the accompaniment of the rough horn calls—a barbarous, merciless din, in marked contrast to the stealth of the ordinary savage. Darkness, still distant above the treetops, was settling rapidly down here in the depths of the wood, so we looked about us for a camping site which offered some measure of safety from attack, and finally took refuge in a tacuara thicket. Here the naked savages would not dare to follow because of the wicked, inch-long thorns. As we slung our hammocks inside the natural stockade we could hear the savages jabbering excitedly all around, but not daring to enter. Then, as the last light went, they left us, and we heard no more of them.

Next morning there were no savages in our vicinity, and we met with none when, after following another well-defined trail, we came to a clearing where there was a plantation of mandioca and papaws. Brilliantly coloured toucans croaked in the palms as they picked at the fruit, and as no danger threatened we helped ourselves freely. We camped here, and at dusk held a concert in our hammocks, Costin with a harmonica, Manley with a comb, and myself with a flageolet. Perhaps it was foolish of us to advertise our presence in this way; but we were not molested, and no savage appeared.

In the morning we went on, and within a quarter of a mile came to a sort of palm-leaf sentry-box, then another. Then all of a sudden we reached open forest. The undergrowth fell away, disclosing between the tree boles a village of primitive shelters, where squatted some of the most villainous savages I have ever seen. Some were engaged in making arrows, others just idled—great apelike brutes who looked as if they had scarcely evolved beyond the level of beasts.

I whistled, and an enormous creature, hairy as a dog, leapt to his feet in the nearest shelter, fitted an arrow to his bow in a flash, and came up dancing from one leg to the other till he was only four yards away. Emitting grunts that sounded like "Eugh! Eugh! Eugh!" he remained there dancing, and suddenly the whole forest around us was alive with these hideous ape-men, all grunting "Eugh! Eugh! Eugh!" and dancing from leg to leg in the same way as they strung arrows to their bows. It looked like a very delicate situation for us, and I wondered if it was the end. I made friendly overtures in Maxubi, but they paid no attention. It was as though human speech were beyond their powers of comprehension.

The creature in front of me ceased his dance, stood for a moment perfectly still, and then drew his bowstring back till it was level with his ear, at the same time raising the barbed point of the six-foot arrow to the height of my chest. I looked straight into the pig-like eyes half hidden under the overhanging brows, and knew that he was not going to loose that arrow yet. As deliberately as he had raised it, he now lowered the bow, and commenced once more the slow dance, and the "Eugh! Eugh! Eugh!"

A second time he raised the arrow at me and drew the bow back, and again I knew he would not shoot. It was just as the Maxubis told me it would be. Again he lowered the bow and continued his dance. Then for the third time he halted and began to bring up the arrow's point. I knew he meant business this time, and drew out a Mauser pistol I had on my hip. It was a big, clumsy thing, of a calibre unsuitable to forest use, but I had brought it because by clipping the wooden holster to the pistol-butt it became a carbine, and was lighter to carry than a true rifle. It used .38 black powder shells, which made a din out of all proportion to their size. I never raised it; I just pulled the trigger and banged it off into the ground at the ape-man's feet.

The effect was instantaneous. A look of complete amazement came into the hideous face, and the little eyes opened wide. He dropped his bow and arrow and sprang away as quickly as a cat to vanish behind a tree. Then the arrows began to fly. We shot off a few rounds into the branches, hoping the noise would scare the savages into a more recep- tive frame of mind, but they seemed in no way disposed to accept us, and before anyone was hurt we gave it up as hopeless and retreated down the trail till the camp was out of sight. We were not followed, but the clamour in the village continued for a long time as we struck off northwards, and we fancied we still heard the "Eugh! Eugh! Eugh!" of the enraged braves.[26]

Fifty-five years after Fawcett's encounter, author "Eric Norman" reported a rampage by "primitive Indian giants" in Xingu National Park, a preserve for indigenous peoples in north-eastern Mato Grosso, created by President Jânio da Silva Quadros in April 1961. Citing an untraceable Reuters dispatch from July 1966, Norman claims that jungle villagers fought pitched battles with "giant jungle warriors," afterward displaying huge captured weapons to members of the Brazilian Air Force. Norman also says that Brazil's Indian Protection Service planned an expedition to investigate the raids, but no further news was forthcoming.[27]

Brazil's second-most famous cryptid (after the giant anaconda, or *sucuriju gigante*) is the *Mapinguari* or *Mapinguary,* also known throughout its wide range as *Capé-lobo* ("wolf's cape"), *Juma, Kubê-rop, Mão de pilão* ("pestle hand") , *Ow-ow, Pé de Garrafa* ("bottle foot"), and *Pelobo.* Witnesses generally describe a creature five to six feet tall on its hind legs, with a simian face and long hair. Some reports include a horn on the creature's forehead or a second mouth on its belly. As with *El Sisemité* and the *Yeho,* some stories refer to backwards-pointing feet. Others claim the beast has no feet at all, leaving small round impressions that explain its "bottle foot" nickname.[28]

Given such widely divergent descriptions, we might expect disagreement concerning the *Mapinguari's* identity, and such in fact is the case. Authors Loren Coleman and Patrick Huyghe consider the creature an unknown pongid, ignoring its bottle-like tracks to present a sketch of a hairy biped with normal ape feet (including an opposed great toe). Bernard Heuvelmans sus-pected "a powerful great ape ... like the one shot by Loys in Venezuela," while Ivan Sanderson cast his vote for a Sasquatch-type cryptid. Meanwhile, having pursued the beast since 1988, ornithologist David Oren believes the *Mapinguari* may be a relict *Mylodon*—a prehistoric ground sloth known to have survived in Patagonia until 10,000 years ago.[29]

The first specific tale of *Mapinguari* malevolence dates from 1930, when a hunter named Inoncêncio met a howling bipedal creature along the Urubú River in Amazonas. As Inoncêncio described the encounter:

> It remained where it stood, looking perhaps suspiciously at the place where I was. Then it roared again as before. I could wait no longer and fired without even troubling to take proper aim. There was a savage roar and then a noise of crashing bushes. I was alarmed to see the animal rush growling towards me and I fired a second bullet. The terrifying creature was hit and gave an incredibly swift leap and hid near the old *samaumeira* [a tree, *Bombax globosum*]. From behind this barricade it gave threatening growls so fiercely that the tree to which it was clinging seemed to shake. I had previously been on jaguar-hunts and taken an active part in them, and I know how savage this cat is when it is run down and at bay. But the roars of the animal that attacked me that night were more terrible and deafening than a jaguar's. I loaded my gun again and, fearing another attack, fired in the direction of the roaring. The black shape roared again more loudly, but retreated and disappeared into the depths of the forest. From time to time, I could still hear its growl of pain until at last it ceased. Dawn was just breaking.[30]

Daylight revealed no trace of the *Mapinguari* but flattened, bloodstained shrubbery and "a sour penetrating smell." Bernard Heuvelmans heard "the ring of truth" in Inoncêncio's tale, but even if we deem it accurate in every detail we may still dispute his definition of an "attack." The beast's behaviour as described resembles the classic threat displays of male gorillas, which rarely culminate in violence. Even when wounded and enraged the *mapinguari* made no effort to harm its tormentor.[31]

Mapinguari sightings spread into northern Argentina during the early 21st Century. In 2001 an anonymous couple claimed that a six-foot-six hairy biped with "razor-sharp claws and bare buttocks" had attacked them near Rosario de la Frontera, 300 miles northwest of Buenos Aires in Salta Province. Around the same time, José Exequiel Alvarez—a volunteer fire chief who doubled as head of the Juan Carlos Rivas Archaeological and Paleontological Group—made plaster casts of large footprints found near the skeletal remains of a colt. Veterinarian Luis Calderon opined that the colt had been devoured by some unspecified predator "with sharp teeth and powerful jaws." Before year's end, rancher Rogelio Martinez sighted a similar ape-like beast and blamed it for "regular livestock depredations" on his property.[32]

The mystery might have been solved when witnesses Hugo Rodas and Raul Torres found "something very unusual" near El Duraznito. As described by José Alvarez, "A large unknown animal lay by the roadside, apparently run over by a vehicle. They got out of their car to take a look, turned it around using a stick, and were astonished. They had never seen anything like it. It had amazing claws, was like a human, measured 1.5 meters in length, [and] had a bearlike snout with enormous fangs and genitals identical to those of a male human." Tragi-

:ally—some might say suspiciously—the carcass was neither preserved nor photographed for posterity.[33]

Ecuadorian Enigmas

Something strange is also happening in Ecuador, where George Eberhart cites reports of a "giant hominid" with long hair and prominent eyes. His description of the creature's behaviour is terse but disturbing: "Bloodthirsty. Lives in villages. Has knowledge of wells and masonry. Wears animal skins. Rapes women and kills men. Openly practices sodomy."[34]

Those ill-mannered rustics may be related to another bipedal cryptid reported from southern Ecuador and neighbouring Peru. Variously known as *Camuenate* ("father of the monkeys"), *Isnachi* ("strong man"), *Maemi, Majero,* and *Maquisapa maman* ("mother of the spider monkeys"), this creature seems to be a mountain dweller, four feet tall on average, with long fangs in a snout like a mandrill's. Its appearance in troops of fifteen to twenty might suggest communal living, but no reports exist of it attacking humans or wearing clothes. Descriptions of a six-inch tail likewise suggest a different species than the larger vicious predators.[35]

Yet another peculiar primate was described from Peru in the 16th Century, when Spanish conquistadors paused in their slaughter of native tribesmen to record their mythology. George Eberhart notes that the beasts, called *Tarma,* were reputed "to mate with Indians and give birth to hybrids." That turn of phrase implies participation by male *Homo sapiens*—a suggestion that mirrors the tale of captive apewoman "Zana" in Abkhazia—but no further information is available.[36]

Argentinean Apemen

Long before the Mapinguari surfaced in Argentina, reports of giants were recorded from the southern region known as Patagonia. Venetian scholar Antonio Pigafetta was one of 240 men who sailed with Ferdinand Magellan to circumnavigate the globe in 1519, and also one of eighteen who returned alive to Spain in 1522. His memoir of that journey, published as *Relazione del primo viaggio intorno al mondo* (*Report on the First Voyage Around the World*), describes Magellan's encounter with giant natives at Port San Julian. The first "was so tall that our heads barely came up to his waist," while "[h]is voice was as deep as a bull's bellowing." Magellan allegedly captured two giants, but both died in transit and were cast overboard. Pigafetta further claimed that Magellan had dubbed the giants "*Patagão*," an unexplained term that apparently gave Patagonia its name. [37]

A half-century later, in 1578, Sir Francis Drake anchored at Port San Julian, where—according to ship's chaplain Francis Fletcher—hostile giants stormed Drake's camp, killing two seamen before they were repulsed.[38]

Two more reports emerged from the 1590s. Sir Thomas Cavendish (or Candish) sailed for South America aboard the *Lester,* in August 1591, and crewman Anthonie Knivet reported seeing twelve-foot-tall corpses in Patagonia. Englishman William Adams left Holland on one of five Dutch ships dispatched to circumnavigate the world in 1598. He ultimately reached Japan, and died there battling the Portuguese, but not before he wrote of a skirmish between his crewmen and "unnaturally tall natives" along the coast of Tierra del Fuego.[39] Much later in May 1766, Commodore John Byron returned to England from a trip around the world begun in June 1764, aboard HMS *Dolphin*. Crewmen spread tales of nine-foot-tall natives in Patagonia, reported first in the *Gentleman's Magazine* on 9 May, but when formal report of the voyage appeared in 1773 the tribesmen had shrunk to an average six feet six inches.[40]

Based on that correction, most modern skeptics dismiss all reports of Patagonian giants as hoaxes or tongue-in-cheek "travelers' tales." Some more charitable critics claim that Commodore Byron and others met Tehuelche tribesmen, indigenous to Patagonia and the southern pampas region of Argentina, some 5,000 of whom survived in 2001.[41] Whether or not they clashed with European intruders, they are not giants—and in fairness to Bigfoot, none of the tales recorded between the sixteenth and eighteenth centuries describe Patagonia's oversized dwellers as apelike in any respect.

Early exploration aside, scattered reports of vaguely Bigfoot-type attacks persist from Argentina. One allegedly occurred on 28 July 1962, at Bajada Grande, a northwestern suburb of Paraná, the capital of Entre Ríos Province. On the afternoon in question, an unnamed motorcyclist was ambushed by "something with a round head, white hair and three eyes," which grabbed his collar, "then turned away and left." No other witnesses confirmed the incident, and the creature has not reappeared.[42] Two years later, truck driver Alberto Kalbermatter was passing along a rural road outside Resistencia, capital city of Chaco Province, when a more conventional nine-foot-tall creature covered in long black hair, with "a human-like face," stepped in front of his vehicle and uttered a frightening cry. Kalbermatter fled, nearly flattening the creature in his haste. Fortean author John Keel reports that a UFO was seen in the same vicinity several days earlier, but he provides no further details.[43]

Authors Loren Coleman and Patrick Huyghe provide our last sighting—or, rather, a spate of sightings, occurring between 31 May and 2 June 1985. They name five witnesses and allude to "others," all describing a creature (or creatures) which Coleman and Huyghe call a freshwater merbeing, known collectively to locals as "Negroes-of-the-water." Less than three feet tall, boasting webbed fingers and toes, one of the beasts allegedly tried to kidnap a five-year-old child on its first appearance, frightening other witnesses two nights later, without actual contact or menacing gestures.[44]

A problem arises in trying to pinpoint the location of those incidents. Coleman and Huyghe say that the sightings occurred in "Roque Sáenz Peña, Argentina," but no such town exists per se. Instead, there are *four* geographic locations named for Roque Sáenz Peña Lahitte, who served as Argentina's president from 12 October 1910 until his death on 9 August 1914. They include Presidente Roque Sáenz Peña, a residential neighbourhood in Buenos Aires; a Buenos Aires suburb called Sáenz Peña; a town named Presidente Roque Sáenz Peña in Chaco Province; and a Presidente Roque Sáenz Peña Department (equivalent to a county) in Córdoba Province. Additionally, we find the Roque Sáenz Peña Hospital in Rosario (Santa Fe Province), and Presidencia Roque Sáenz Peña at Resistencia, in Chaco Province.[45] Barring receipt of further details, no determination can be offered of the strange report's validity.

Chapter 5.
Eurasia: Continental Carnivores

Accounts of predatory hominids in Europe and the Near East date from the earliest recorded history to modern times. While some can be explained today through twenty-twenty hindsight, with interpretation of mythology aided by archival research and insights from forensic psychiatry, others continue to inspire debate. We start here with the broad strokes, then proceed with more specific cases, moving eastward from the island states of Europe and across the continent to end our journey in the Middle East.

In Search of Manimals

As in the Western Hemisphere, all nations and societies throughout Eurasia spawned ancient tales of hairy bipeds who were often cast as adversaries of mankind. Some dined on humans or their livestock; others had a talent for seduction that eclipsed their brutish form.

Ogres and trolls supply the earliest examples of such creatures, ranging from Iceland and the Faroe Islands across Scandinavia, then southward into Europe through the Balkans. Generally speaking, ogres were giants, while trolls were often smaller, but they shared a taste for human flesh, and none were sympathetic to the human race. Denmark's Grendel, slain by Beowulf, is probably the best-remembered ogre, thanks to various translations of the epic poem penned in Old English around C.E. 1000.[1]

Altogether different in form and habit were the fauns and satyrs of Greece, described as libidinous entities, exclusively male, who were human in form from the waist up, while below they had the hind quarters and cloven hooves of goats to match the curved horns on their heads. Prone to seducing young women they met in fields and forests, satyrs prefigure the menacing Goatman reported from Prince George's County, Maryland, since 1957, and from Texas in the 1980s.[2]

Another predatory race, the Cercopes, were known to Greek and Roman authors during ancient times. Traditionally, they inhabited the wastes of Lydia in Greece, and the neighbourhood of Ephesus in Asia Minor (near modern Selçuk, in Turkey's İzmir Province). The Cercopes were bestial humanoids with tails, who preyed on travelers and met their match in Hercules. After defeating them in battle, Hercules delivered the Cercopes to Zeus, who transformed them into apes and stranded them on the island of Pithicusae—"Island of the Apes," now Ischia, located in the Tyrrhenian Sea near the Gulf of Naples.[3]

Throughout the Middle Ages, Europe was beset by tales of "wildmen," variously known as *wudéwásá* ("wood man") in Old English, *gruagach* in Irish, *skogsrå* in Swedish, *homo silvestris* in Latin, *callicantzari* in Greek, *wildeman* in German, *zruty* in Slovak, and by sundry other names. Throughout their range, wildmen were generally described as naked, hairy humanoids, often of normal stature, though some tales portray both giants and stunted troll-like figures. Generally viewed as adversaries of mankind, they are depicted in ancient woodcuts as battling armed knights—sometimes sporting swords and armor of their own—or being hunted with hounds. As late as 1691, a young Swede was convicted of bedding a female *skogsrå* and sentenced to death for bestiality.[4]

During the same years, European peasants lived in fear of werewolves, shape shifting cannibals empowered by black magic to adopt the form of wolves or other predators. Fueled by the Inquisition's witch-hunt hysteria, French authorities held their first recorded werewolf trial in 1521, condemning more than 30,000 defendants by 1630. Many suspects confessed under torture, and while most are now regarded as innocent victims of religious hysteria, some accused of multiple murders and acts of cannibalism may have been early serial killers.[5]

Suspected lycanthropes were not the only casualties, however. In Scotland, residents of Hynish, on the Isle of Tiree, complained of a human-wolf hybrid called the "hound eater," which slaughtered their dogs by day and night.[6] Swedish cleric and author Olaus Magnus, in his *History of the Northern Peoples* (1555), described the residents of Lithuania, Livonia and Prussia suffering livestock losses to wolves and werewolves alike. According to pseudonymous author "Eric Norman," Magnus wrote:

> These werewolves besieged isolated farms, broke into homes, and devoured every living thing. Their favorite haunt is a ruined castle near Courtland [in western Latvia], which place all humans are afraid to approach. It is said that this is the place of the werewolves and no man dares go near....They are equally ferocious with their own kind and the weaker ones are slain by their fellows.[7]

Europe's most notorious predator, the Beast of Gévaudan, was almost certainly a quadruped, possibly an imported exotic. Its depredations ceased in 1765, with 113 persons dead and forty-nine injured, but similar outbreaks claimed at least twenty-one victims around Vivarais during 1809-13, while more attacks occurred in Indre between 1875 and 1879.[8]

Germany suffered a similar problem with werewolves, according to 19th-Century author J.D.H. Temme. At Greifswald, in the north-eastern state of Mecklenburg-Vorpommern, a "frightfully large number" of lycanthropes prowled the streets after nightfall, attacking people at random, until students from the local university wiped them out. In 1831, at Zarnow in Pomerania, townsfolk stalked a beast that caused "great harm to humans and cattle," killing at

Medieval woodcut depicting European *wudéwásá*.

least one child, and found themselves confronted by "a large strange man" in lieu of the wolf they expected.[9]

Part of European werewolf mythology, at least, seems to stem from the berserkers, Viking warriors who donned animal skins and ran amok in battle, crazed with bloodlust. Somewhere in the distant past, those fighters may have drawn their inspiration from Norse legends of savage apemen from the underworld who raided outlying homes and small villages—a myth later combined with *Beowulf* to inspire Michael Crichton's best-selling novel *Eaters of the Dead* (1976), filmed in 1999 as *The 13th Warrior*. That story posits that the predatory "wendol" or "mist-monsters" were relict Neandertals.[10]

While such tales are expected from ancient legends and medieval witch-hunting authors, reports of predatory primates still emerge from Eurasia on occasion. Despite a teeming population of 181 persons per square mile in Europe and 114 per square mile in the Near East, reports of harrowing encounters with large hairy bipeds still emerge from time to time.

The United Kingdom

With 59,644,600 persons occupying 88,782 square miles of land—and no indigenous apes except the Barbary macaque colony on Gibraltar—the countries of England, Scotland, and Wales seem uniquely disqualified to support a population of primates hostile to humans. Nonetheless, hairy wildmen may be found among the carvings at Canterbury Cathedral, and Plate 201 of Queen Mary's Salter (dating from the 14th Century) depicts a shaggy biped surrounded by three hunting dogs.

More recently, on 21 January 1879, a labourer driving a wagon filled with furniture along the Shropshire Union Canal from Renton, Staffordshire, to Woodcock, Shropshire, claimed that "a strange black creature with great white eyes" leapt from the shrubbery onto his horse's back. The driver lashed out with his whip, which passed through the apelike thing's body, suggesting a spectral nature. The horse broke free and fled "with the ghost still clinging to its back," but was later found unharmed aside from fright. A policeman consulted by the driver explained: "Oh, I know what that was. That was the Man-Monkey, sir, as does come again at that bridge ever since the man was drowned in the Cut."[11]

We might dismiss a ghost-ape without serious consideration, if it were not for the modern investigative efforts of Fortean author Nick Redfern. His pursuit of the Man-Monkey through archives and personal interviews disclosed other sightings in the same vicinity, including incidents from 1943, 1972-73, 1982, and 1993-94. The creature(s) seen on those occasions physically attacked no one, but crashed through bushes, uttered evil-sounding cries, and generally did their best to terrorise the neighbourhood.[12]

In January 2003, following reports of a Sasquatch-type creature at Bolam Lake Country Park, Northumberland, Jonathan Downes led a team from the Centre for Fortean Zoology—Richard

OPPOSITE: A typical European wildman image of the Middle Ages.

Freeman, John Fuller, and Graham Inglis—to investigate. They saw the beast on 18 January, but it managed to elude them.

Downes described "a dark, man-shaped object approximately seven-and-a-half feet tall. It had a barrel chest and thick muscular arms and legs. I had a very clear sighting but I saw no glowing eyes and wasn't able to tell whether or not it was covered in hair."[13]

The next closest thing to a menacing Bigfoot within the UK is Scotland's "Big Grey Man" of Ben MacDhui (or Macdui). Ben MacDhui is the tallest of the Cairngorms, at 4,295 feet, and the UK's second-highest mountain, after Ben Nevis (also found in Scotland). Today, the Cairngorm Ski Centre draws tourists, while the summit is accessible by foot or bicycle.[14]
It was not always so.

Professor Norman Collie logged the first known encounter with Ben MacDhui's bipedal cryptid in 1891, although he kept it to himself for more than three decades. At that, there was not much to tell: a sound of heavy footprints trailing Collie through a snowstorm that prevented him from glimpsing his pursuer. "I was seized with terror and took to my heels," Collie said, "staggering blindly among the boulders for four or five miles nearly down to Rothiemurchus Forest." As a result, he declared that there was "something very queer about the top of Ben MacDhui," and never returned to the spot.[15]

After Professor Collie, various other witnesses reported glimpses of a "giant figure" on the mountain, or—more commonly—a sound of being followed at a distance. None claims that the creature has attacked, if in fact it exists, and author Ron Halliday suggests a prosaic explanation for the incidents. Hysteria aside, the frozen snow on mountain peaks, when walked upon, may produce an audible "double footfall" effect as it cracks and collapses. Likewise, a visual illusion dubbed a "Brocken spectre" may present an image of a (nonexistent) giant figure when the sun shines from behind a hiker who looks down from a height into fog or mist.[16]

Whether or not the Big Grey Man exists, in fact, nothing suggests that he has ever harmed a living soul.

The Pain in Spain

The Spanish autonomous communities of Aragon and Catalonia, abutting the Pyrenees Mountains, have long produced tales of large, hairy, cave-dwelling wildmen variously known as *basajaun* ("forest lord") or *mono careto* ("ugly ape"). While folklore portrays the creatures as generally benevolent, guardians of shepherds' flocks, some twentieth-century reports paint a different picture.[17]

On or about 15 May 1979, for example, a group of labourers in Huesca allegedly met a *basajaun* at a site 143 miles west of Barcelona. The six-foot-tall creature rose from its seat on a log and approached them, making "animal noises," then hurled a tree trunk at the working party,

OPPOSITE ABOVE: A Medieval knight battles a wildman.
OPPOSITE BELOW: battle royal between humans and wildmen.

whereupon they fled.[18]

Fourteen years later, in June 1993, two separate incidents were reported from Catalonia. The first, according to reporter Sergio de la Rubia-Muñoz, involved a group of speleologists camped at the ruins of an old church near Collada de Vallgrasa, in the Catalan Pyrenees. During the night they heard "strange noises resembling those of an enraged cat" and saw "a frightened, weird, shaggy creature" flee the church ruins, running on two legs.[19]

While that night-prowler was timid, the same cannot be said for two hairy bipeds who "pounced on" a couple of palaeontologists soon thereafter, in a forest between Farga de Bebié and Ripoll, Catalonia. The humans fled, but apparently claimed no injuries. Like the cavers from Collada de Vallgrasa, they remain anonymous today.[20]

One final allegation of hominid violence comes from Spanish author Miguel Aracil, related in his book *Misterios Ocultos* (Barcelona: Protusa, 1997) and translated by Fortean investigator Scott Corrales. According to Aracil, woodsmen working around the Pyrenean region of Peña Montesa on some unknown date were attacked by "a bizarre, hairy creature with semi-human features," which "went on to indulge itself a vandalistic frenzy, shattering vehicles and heavy forestry equipment and even hurling tree trunks against humans, according to one account." The tree-hurling incident, coupled with Aracil's reference to a peaceful sighting "many years later," suggests that the rampage is an exaggerated retelling of the account from May 1979.[21]

On balance, while the Spanish stories are intriguing, none can be substantiated. As an indictment against Bigfoot, they must be dismissed for lack of evidence.

Russia: Apes at Large?

There is no shortage of apeman reports from the former Soviet Union, now the Russian Federation, coupled with the former Soviet Socialist Republics of Azerbaijan, Kazakhstan, Tajikistan, Turkmenistan, and Uzbekistan. A vast territory sprawling from Eastern Europe across the Caucasus Mountains to the Pamirs and on through Siberia, the late USSR has produced a wealth of Bigfoot-Yeti sightings, with legends of violent interaction spanning some 2,600 years. It has also produced the only reports of hairy hominids employed as soldiers in combat.

The first such claim comes down to us from the Avesta, the primary texts of Zoroastrianism, composed under Persia's Achaemenid Empire, circa 550–330 B.C.E. According to mythology recorded there, subhuman creatures called *paré* ("malevolent sprites") were drafted into combat units fielded against Persia's enemies. Details are vague, to say the least, and no other evidence exists to support those accounts.[22]

Nonetheless, that legend—and an event reported to Moscow in the 1920s—may have inspired a Russian plot more outlandish than any conceived by Ian Fleming in his James Bond novels. In 1925, Major General Mikhail Stephanovitch Topilski led a company of Soviet soldiers against anti-communist guerrillas based in the Pamirs, a mountain range in Central Asia formed by the junction of the Himalayas, Tian Shan, Karakoram, Kunlun, and Hindu Kush ranges. After storming a particular cave, location uncertain, the soldiers captured one opponent who told them that his unit had suffered attacks by apelike creatures and had killed one. In fact, Topilski's men allegedly retrieved its body from the cave. As Topilski described it:

> At first glance I thought the body was that of an ape. It was covered with hair all over. But I knew there were no apes in the Pamirs. Also, the body itself looked very much like that of a man. We tried pulling the hair, to see if it was just a hide used for disguise, but found that it was the creature's own natural hair. We turned the body over several times on its back and its front, and measured it.
>
> The body belonged to a male creature 165-170 cm tall, elderly or even old, judging by the greyish colour of the hair in several places. The chest was covered with brownish hair and the belly with greyish hair. The hair was longer but sparser on the chest and close-cropped and thick on the belly. In general the hair was very thick, without any under fur. There was least hair on the buttocks, from which fact our doctor deduced that the creature sat like a human being. There was most hair on the hips. The knees were completely bare of hair and had callous growths on them. The whole foot including the sole was quite hairless and was covered by hard brown skin. The hair got thinner near the hand, and the palms had none at all but only callous skin.
>
> The colour of the face was dark, and the creature had neither beard nor moustache. The temples were bald and the back of the head was covered by thick, matted hair. The dead creature lay with its eyes open and its teeth bared. The eyes were dark and the teeth were large and even and shaped like human teeth. The forehead was slanting and the eyebrows were very powerful. The protruding jawbones made the face resemble the Mongol type of face. The nose was flat, with a deeply sunk bridge. The ears were hairless and looked a little more pointed than a human being's with a longer lobe. The lower jaw was very massive. The creature had a very powerful chest and well developed muscles ... The arms were of normal length, the hands were slightly wider and the feet much wider and shorter than man's.[23]

Back in Moscow, Josef Stalin had assumed command of the Soviet Union following Vladimir Lenin's death in January 1924. Delivery of Major General Topilski's report apparently gave Stalin the idea of creating invincible soldiers from ape-human hybrids, but the thought was not original to the "man of steel." In fact, Dr. Ilya Ivanovich Ivanov—a specialist in artificial insemination and the interspecific hybridisation of animals—had proposed creation of such manimals in 1910, in an address to the World Congress of Zoologists in Graz, Austria.[24]

The notion seemed bizarre, but shocked reactions failed to deter Ivanov. In 1924, now working at the Pasteur Institute in Paris, he secured permission to use the institute's experimental primate station in Kindia, French Guinea, for hybridisation trials. Strapped for funds, Ivanov sent pleas to Anatoliy Vasilievich Lunacharsky—Russia's People's Commissar on Education

and Science—and to other Soviet officials. The begging paid off in September 1925, when Nikolai Petrovich Gorbunov, head of the USSR's Department of Scientific Institutions, allocated $10,000 for Ivanov's research through the Russian Academy of Sciences—a move requiring approval from Stalin and his Politburo. Stalin's stated goal: development of "living war machines," strong and savage, insensible to pain, indifferent to diet and living conditions.[25]

Ivanov reached Kindia in March 1926, but left a month later, disgruntled to learn that the facility had no sexually mature chimpanzees. Back in France, he negotiated with Matteo Mathieu Maurice Alfassa, colonial governor of French Guinea, to conduct his experiments at the botanical gardens in Conakry (Guinea's capital and largest city). Arriving there with son Ilya Jr. in November 1926, Ivanov supervised the capture of adult chimpanzees from the wild, which were then caged at Conakry. On 28 February 1927 he artificially inseminated two female chimpanzees with human sperm, following up with a third specimen on 25 June. None of the three conceived, and the third died in France, after the Ivanovs decamped from Africa with thirteen chimps in July 1927.[26]

Berserkers depicted in animal masks.

The twelve survivors were packed off to Sukhumi—capital of Abkhazia, on the Black Sea—for further experiments at a new Russian-run primate station, while Ivanov sought permission to inseminate human females with chimpanzee sperm in French Guinea. Colonial officials drew the line at that blasphemy, and while Ivanov lobbied for his new scheme at Sukhumi, two years passed before Nikolai Gorbunov came to his rescue again, securing support from the Society of Materialist Biologists, affiliated with Moscow's Communist Academy. In spring 1929 the SMB established a commission to promote Ivanov's experiments at Sukhumi, mandating recruitment of five female volunteers. That draft was still incomplete in June, when Sukhumi's only post pubescent male ape—an orang-utan—dropped dead. Fresh chimps, Ivanov learned, were unavailable until summer 1930. Frustrated, Ivanov sought to obtain male chimps from a Cuban heiress, but the story leaked to reporters and sparked international ridicule.[27]

It was the end for Ivanov, although he did not share the drastic fate of many who fell out of Stalin's favour. Politically denounced in spring 1930 and formally arrested on 13 December of that year, he was spared the firing squad or exile to Siberia, dispatched instead to spend five years working at the Kazakh Veterinary-Zoologist Institute in Alma-Ata (now Almaty), the capital of Kazakhstan. A stroke killed Ivanov on 20 March 1932. Renowned physiologist/psychologist Ivan Petrovich Pavlov wrote his obituary.[28]

No evidence suggests that Soviet "humanzee" experiments outlived Ivanov, but Russian soldiers still encountered hairy hominids from time to time. In December 1941, Lieutenant Colonel Vasghen Sergeyevich Karapetyan of the Soviet Army Medical Corps reported a humanoid encounter from the Caucasus Mountains of the Dagestan Autonomous Soviet Socialist Republic. The creature had been caged by locals, Karapetyan was told, on suspicion of being a German spy in disguise. Karapetyan later wrote:

> I entered a shed with two members of the local authorities. When I asked why I had to examine the man in a cold shed and not in a warm room, I was told that the prisoner could not be kept in a warm room. He had sweated in the house so profusely that they had had to keep him in the shed. I can still see the creature as it stood before me, a male, naked and barefooted. And it was doubtlessly a man, because its entire shape was human. The chest, back, and shoulders, however, were covered with shaggy hair of a dark brown colour. This fur of his was much like that of a bear, and 2 to 3 centimeters [one inch] long. The fur was thinner and softer below the chest. His wrists were crude and sparsely covered with hair. The palms of his hands and soles of his feet were free of hair. But the hair on his head reached to his shoulders partly covering his forehead. The hair on his head, moreover, felt very rough to the hand. He had no beard or moustache, though his face was completely covered with a light growth of hair. The hair around his mouth was also short and sparse. The man stood absolutely straight with his arms hanging, and his height was above

the average—about 180 cm [nearly six feet]. He stood before me like a giant, his mighty chest thrust forward. His fingers were thick, strong and exceptionally large. On the whole, he was considerably bigger than any of the local inhabitants. His eyes told me nothing. They were dull and empty—the eyes of an animal. And he seemed to me like an animal and nothing more.[29]

Karapetyan pronounced the apeman innocent of espionage and never saw it again, but a subsequent report from Dagestan's Ministry of the Interior (now unavailable) allegedly confirmed its capture near Buynask. Most published accounts claim that the beast was shot by a military firing squad, either following conviction of desertion from the army or simply because no one knew what else to do with it.[30]

Six years later, during 1947, a member of the Azerbaijani militia named Ramazan claimed that a hairy apelike creature—locally known as *gulebaney* ("wild man")—had leapt upon him near his home and dragged him to a tree where its female counterpart stood waiting. The creatures examined Ramazan from head to toe, then got into a hooting argument and shoving match before releasing him unharmed, near dawn. No further details are available, beyond the fact that "Ramazan" was also once the name of a village in the Absheron Rayon of eastern Azerbaijan, although it no longer exists.[31]

A possibly related creature, called *gul* or *golub-yavan*, was once believed to exercise hypnotic powers over humans in the Pamir Mountains of Tajikistan, but the only report of hostile activity dates from 1939, when an unnamed villager from Imeni Kalinina claimed he had wrestled with one and was knocked unconscious. A similar—if not identical—beast, the *nasnas* ("wild man"), supposedly kidnapped and ravaged humans in the mountainous Vakhan (or Wakhan) district between Tajikistan and northeastern Afghanistan, while villagers returned the favour by killing and eating the apemen.[32] Once again, corroboration is nonexistent.

Our last report from Russian soil—and from Eurasia—dates from late August and early September 1988. According to the tale, several teenagers embarked on a fishing expedition to Lake Lovozero, located on the Kola Peninsula in northern Russia's Murmansk Oblast. Their vacation was spoiled by a simian creature seven to eight feet tall, covered in grey hair, which harassed them in their cabin and chased them around the countryside at various times, over several days. The teens dubbed it "Afonya," the title of a 1975 Russian film about an alcoholic plumber, and reported the sightings to local authorities. Russian author Dmitri Bayanov says that investigators glimpsed the beast in 1988, and lured it with recorded primate calls the following summer, drawing it close enough to photograph several footprints.[32]

On balance, while reports of human conflict with hairy bipeds in Eurasia span a much longer period of time than any from the Western Hemisphere, they remain insubstantial, with supporting evidence elusive. Even if *all* of the stories reported are taken as fact, it appears that wildmen of Europe and the Near East have been victims as often as predators. Nothing on file to date suggests a threat to *Homo sapiens* from Bigfoot-type creatures.

OPPOSITE: Karapetyan's sketch of a Russian wildman.

Paul du Chaillu kills his *Kooloo-kamba.*

Chapter 6.
Africa: Hearts of Darkness

Africa lays claim to half the world's great apes (Family *Hominidae*). Chimpanzees and gorillas got their start here, as did several strains of proto-humans: *Homo ergaster, H. gautengensis, H. habilis, H. rhodesiensis, H. rudolfensis*, and *H. sapiens idaltu*.[1] As we saw in the introduction to this volume, reports of hairy African wildmen or "monsters" began with reports from Hanno the Carthaginian, circa 480 B.C.E., and continued through the 17th Century C.E. European naturalists recognised African apes by the mid-late 18th Century, but still dismissed reports of man-sized primates as chimerical. The lowland (now western) gorilla was not formally described until 1847—and even then, more mysteries remained.

From German East Africa—now Burundi, Rwanda and Tanzania—reports of even larger apes continued to emerge. Again, they were dismissed as fantasy, until Captain Robert von Beringe shot two specimens during October 1902. One carcass was preserved and sent to Berlin's Zoological Museum, where Professor Paul Matschie classified it as a new species—the mountain gorilla—and named it *Gorilla beringei* in 1903. Matschie identified another subspecies of western gorilla—the Cross River gorilla (*Gorilla gorilla diehli*) in 1904, and formally named the eastern lowland gorilla (*G. beringei graueri*) in 1914.[2]

Africa, it seemed on the eve of World War I, had no shortage of man-sized apes, after all. Today, despite 2008's surprise discovery of a previously unknown *G. gorilla* colony in the Republic of Congo, all known species are endangered. Africa's endless warfare, habitat destruction, and the "bushmeat" trade keep mankind's closest living relatives forever perched on the brink of extinction. Despite the best efforts of conservationists and governments addicted to the tourist trade, the damage may be irreversible.

Still, Africa—Earth's second-largest continent at 11,668,598 square miles, and the second most-populous, with one billion inhabitants—has some wild places left. The Congo Basin, sprawling over all or part of ten nations, comprises 1,428,577 square miles of rainforest and wetlands. Aside from mountain gorillas and fifty percent of Africa's surviving wild elephants, the Congo Basin harbours 1,000 known species of birds, 400 species of mammals, 280 species of reptiles, 216 species of amphibians, 900 species of butterflies, and 10,000 species of plants (including 3,000 species found nowhere else on the planet).[3] Some cryptozoologists suspect that it may also be the last refuge of relict living dinosaurs.

It comes as no surprise, then, that reports of cryptic hominids persist from parts of Africa, or that those tales include occasional claims of attacks on humans. Our pursuit of those tales begins in Sierra Leone and proceeds southward from there, in search of hairy predators.

Monkey Madness

While Africa's initial tales of violent hominids focused on man-sized apes, the continent's west coast offers a different kind of "monster" altogether. The *Engbéré* of Sierra Leone, also known as *Engbé* in nearby Côte d'Ivoire, is said to be a small biped, three to four feet tall, with a penchant for kidnapping humans. Its victims are borne away to villages deep in the rainforest, from which they never return.[4]

While a tribe of pygmies might appear to be the most logical suspects, assuming that such events ever occurred, *Engbé* is the Ubangi term for a well-known primate species, the moustached monkey or moustached guenon, (*Cercopithecus cephus*). Included on the International Union for Conservation of Nature's "Red List" of threatened species, *Cercopithecus cephus*—with three recognised subspecies—ranges from the Sanaga River in Cameroon south and eastward to the Congo River, and south of the lower Congo into the north-western corner of Angola. Its official native range does not include Sierra Leone or Côte d'Ivoire.[5]

Leaving that obstacle aside, how does the moustached monkey measure up as a potential kidnapper? One of the smaller guenons, an average male adult measures fifty-nine inches from its head to the tip of its twenty-eight-inch tail, tipping the scales at 9.5 pounds. The species is diurnal and arboreal, living in groups of four to thirty-five individuals, feeding primarily on fruit, seeds, leaves, and insect. The closest it comes to predation is raiding birds' nests, where eggs and fledglings may be devoured.[6]

All in all, hardly a candidate for man-snatching.

The Tano Giant

Things sound more promising in Ghana, where a night-prowling cryptid larger than a man is said to abduct women and children along the upper Tano River. Author Louis Bowler introduced Western readers to the beast in 1911, writing:

> Far away in the primeval forests of the Upper Tano, in the Gold Coast Colony, a strange tale is told by the natives of a wild man of the woods, which would appear from the description given to be a white ape of extraordinary stature and human instinct. The natives who live in the village near to the haunts of this freak of nature are terrified out of their wits. They barricade their doors at night, and place broiled plantains and cassava on the jungle paths leading into the village to propitiate him and appease his hunger. They declare he comes to the village at night, and only runs when fire is thrown at him. The women especially are almost

scared to death, and go in a body to their plantain farms. It appears that two women while gathering plantains were confronted by this creature. One he seized and flung over his shoulder carrying her off; the other ran screaming with fright back to the village. No trace of the other woman has been found. Several children have been taken by this creature, their mutilated bodies being found with the whole of their bowels devoured.

The hunters and women who have seen this animal describe him as "past all man" in size; his arms they describe as thick as a man's body; his skin "all the same as a white man," with black hairs growing thereon. The hands have four fingers but no thumb, the head is flat, and, as they describe it, "left small for big monkey head," meaning that it was very near or like a large monkey's head. They say the mouth "was all the same as monkey with big teeth sticking out, and he carries a skin of a bush cow," which the natives say "he carries for cloth when small cold, catch him," meaning he wraps himself up in it when feeling cold. A hunter tried to shoot him, but he smashed the gun and broke both the hunter's arms. Many other incidents are related of this terror of the Upper Plains.[7]

Ivan Sanderson speculated that the creature might be a relict specimen of *Plesianthropus*, writing: "understand that it is believed that the thumb of *Plesianthropus* was exceptionally small for the size of its hand, and was placed very high up on that hand. Is it possible that it might have been carried pressed against the side of the palm and so not be apparent?"[8] In fact, however, the fossil specimen dubbed *Plesianthropus transvaalensis* in 1947, considered at that time to be a middle-aged female, is now generally described as a young male of the species *Australopithecus africanus*. Adult males weighed about 100 pounds, with females half that weight and measuring approximately 3.5 feet tall. Thus far, fossil remains on record do not include any bones from the creature's hands.[9]

If the Tano Giant exists today—or ever did—it remains unidentified.

The *Kooloo-Kamba*

Encyclopedist George Eberhart describes another large, "aggressive" ape reported from Cameroon, Gabon, and the Central African Republic, where it is known by a variety of names including *Kooloo-Kamba*, *Choga*, and *Koula-nguia* ("chimpanzee-gorilla"). Strangely, despite a list of encounters spanning some 140 years, Eberhart's account of the beast mentions no incidents of aggression toward humans.[10]

Paul Belloni du Chaillu, the French-American anthropologist credited with "discovery" of the western gorilla, met a *Kooloo-Kamba* during his four-year exploration of West Africa in 1856-59, sponsored by Philadelphia's Academy of Natural Sciences. As he described the incident in 1868:

> After our camp was arranged we went out to look for gorilla tracks. It was too late to hunt; besides, we were too tired. In the evening Malaouen came in after dark, and said he had heard the cry of the kooloo, and knew where to find it in the morning.

Of course I asked what this kooloo was, for I had not the slightest idea of what he meant. I had never heard the name before. I received, in answer, a description of the animal, which threw me into the greatest excitement; for I saw this was most certainly a new species of ape, or man-like monkey—a new man of the woods, of which I had not even heard as yet. It was called kooloo-kamba by the Goumbi people from its cry or call, "Kooloo," and the Commi word kamba, which means "speak." The Bakalai call it simply koola.

I scarce slept all night, with fidgeting over the morrow's prospects. The Bakalai said the kooloo-kamba was very rare here, and there was only a chance that we should find the one whose call had been heard.

At last the tedious night was gone. At the earliest streak of dawn I had my men up. We had fixed our guns the night before. All was ready, and we set out in two parties. My party had been walking through the forest about an hour by a path which led I knew not where, when suddenly I stepped into a file of Bashikouay ants, whose fierce bites nearly made me scream. The little rascals were infuriated at my disturbance of their progress, and they held on to my legs and to my trowsers till I picked them off. Of course I jumped nimbly out of the way of the great army of which they formed part, but I did not get off without some severe bites.

We had hardly got clear of the Bashikouays when my ears were saluted by the singular cry of the ape I was after. "Koola-kooloo, koola-kooloo," it said several times. Only Gambo and Malaouen were with me. Gambo and I raised our eyes, and saw, high up on a tree-branch, a large ape. It looked almost like a black hairy man. We both fired at once, and the next moment the poor beast fell with a heavy mash to the ground. I rushed up, anxious to see if, indeed, I had a new animal. I saw in a moment that it was neither a nshiego mbouvé, nor a common chimpanzee, nor a gorilla. Again I had a happy day. This kooloo-kamba was undoubtedly a new variety of chimpanzee.

We at once disembowelled the animal, which was a full-grown male. We found in his stomach nothing but berries, nuts, and fruits. He had, no doubt, just begun to take his breakfast.

This kooloo-kamba was four feet three inches high. He was powerfully built, with strong and square shoulders. He had a very round head, with whiskers running quite round the face and below the chin. The face was round; the cheek-bones prominent; the cheeks sunken. The roundness of the head, and the prominence of the cheek-bones, were so great as to remind me of some of the heads of Indians or Chinamen. The hair was black and long on the arms, which, however, were partly bare. His ears were large, and shaped like those of a human being. Of its habits the people could tell me nothing, except that it was found more frequently in the far interior. I brought the skin of this kooloo-kamba to New York, and some years ago many people saw it.[11]

W.C. Osman-Hill named du Chaillu's ape *Pan troglodytes koolokamba*—"gorilla-like chimpanzee"—in 1967, designating it as a fifth subspecies of robust chimpanzee, but most primate taxonomists today reject that classification.[12] As for evidence of the *Kooloo-Kamba*'s aggression toward humans, while certainly possible in light of documented chimp misbehaviour, it remains nonexistent.

Who's Got the *Engôt*?

George Eberhart also mentions another mystery primate from Gabon, allegedly known as the *Engôt* ("ogre"), which he describes as a "giant hominid" that "eats humans" and clomps through the jungle on "feet turned the wrong way around." That said, he finally dismisses the creature as a product of "muddled folk memory of encounters with Gorillas in the remote past"—but Eberhart's tale is more muddled than that.[13]

Plainly stated, Eberhart's primary source—pages 208-11 of a book written by American author Richard Lynch Garner and published two years after his death—makes no mention whatsoever of the *Engôt*. It *does* refer in passing to the "kulu-kamba," however, which may be the source of Eberhart's confusion.[14] There, at least for now, the matter rests.

Congo Conundrums

In the Democratic Republic of Congo, a peculiar biped variously known as *Abamaánji*, *Kikomba*, *Tshingombé*, and *Zaluzúgu* allegedly wreaks havoc with natives and keeps their nerves on edge with wild shrieks and occasional attacks. Though barely five feet tall, the beast leaves twelve-inch footprints on occasion, while strolling through the forest with aid from a walking stick. Despite its relatively modest size, George Eberhart informs us that it "knocks down trees in search of insects." When not so engaged, he writes, the creature is "[s]aid to attack humans either by hitting them with its fists or with an old axe handle or by wrestling."[15]

Two French zoologists, Charles Cordier and Bernard Heuvelmans, proposed Latin names for the *Abamaánji-Kikomba*. In 1963, Cordier dubbed it *Paranthropus congensis*, while Heuvelmans named it *Kikomba leloupi* in 1980.[16] Neither classification is presently recognised by mainstream primate taxonomists.

The wife of Italian explorer and film-maker Attilio Gatti described a larger bipedal primate from the same region, in the following account which treats her husband rather curiously.

> Then there are rumours about strange anthropoids. One is a large ape which is said to live in the Rainy Forest, the pygmy tribes call it the *Muhalu*. Commander Attilio Gatti, the well-known African explorer, has repeatedly declared that he, for one, believes in the existence of the Muhalu and willingly accepts the descriptions of the pygmies who say that it is exceptionally large, walks erect habitually, and is covered with very dark, possibly black, fur, except for the face, where the hairs are

white.

Another again, and the worst of all, is a big animal with a coat of long hair, black on the back, white on the other parts of the body. And it is enough to be seen by this monster, for one to die in the most atrocious agony.

We found awaiting us a man from Soli's to say that the pygmies had been on the trail of a Bongo mother and young one, and that if the Bwana would come they were sure they would capture the little one.

So Tille decided to have one more fling. He also decided to take a group of our own boys with him to act as porters. Before they could start, however, an event occurred which reduced all Kalume's men to panic.

Ever since we had been in the Ituri we had heard repeated tales and rumours of a great animal called by the Bondande, "muhalu." Of all things that could arouse terror, this muhalu was the King Bee. Tille had been extremely interested in the matter and believed that the creature really did exist and was a hitherto unknown fifth anthropoid or subhuman.

At this time, however, he had done no more than talk about it now and then. Now, on this morning, one of our men rushed into the clearing, his face grey with fright, babbling about the dread muhalu. His stories were conflicting. First he said it had knocked him down, and this seemed odd because the natives firmly believed that a muhalu had only to look at a man and that man would instantly die. Then the boy said he had seen the muhalu first and ran away. No matter what had actually happened, the news that a muhalu was in the vicinity nearly paralysed our men.

Tille insisted on going to investigate at the point where the boy claimed to have seen the beast. I don't know how he succeeded in dragging that boy, half-dead with fright, or in flicking the pride of Lamese and two of the other men until they agreed to accompany him.

He did find enormous footprints, and several stiff black hairs in the hollow of a tree where the evidence showed the brute had been sitting. Neither hairs nor print corresponded to any other known ape.

But the panic of our natives had grown so fast that Tille could not stem it. Even Kalume begged us, with all his heart, to leave Tzambehe and come down to his village. All of our natives, though they had no wish to abandon us, were preparing to leave.[17]

Author George Witten spelled the creature's name "Mulahu" in a 1938 article for the magazine *Family Circle*, referring to it as "the real King Kong" and relating the tale of an Australian photographer whom the beast allegedly killed sometime during World War I. Ivan Sanderson speculated that the Tano Giant and *Muhalu* might be one and the same, a hominid on the scale of North America's Sasquatch, but evidence of its existence remains elusive.[18]

Footprints on Kilimanjaro

Our last stop on the Dark Continent takes us eastward to Kenya and Tanzania, where George Eberhart describes a most peculiar giant hominid known to various tribes as *Loldaika*, *Milhoi* ("evil spirit"), and *Ngoloko*. Distinguishing features, aside from its eight-foot height and shaggy coat of three-foot-long grey hair, include "huge ears like an elephant's" and pincer-like hands with only a thumb and one finger. The thumb, at least, sounds lethal, with its 2.5-inch claw. Eberhart describes its feet as having "one prehensile big toe and three small toes," then describes the incongruous discovery of three-toed footprints on Mount Kilimanjaro—which he misplaces in Kenya, rather than Tanzania.[19]

According to Eberhart, this creature subsists on a diet of honey, blood, and buffalo milk. While thus a potential threat to livestock, it apparently has no record of stalking humans. Meanwhile, authors Colin and Janet Bord cite a report filed from Kenya in 1978, by French anthropologist Jacqueline Roumeguère-Eberhardt. Writing to the French National Centre for Scientific Research—and six years later in a book, *The Unidentified Hominids of the African Forest*—Dr. Roumeguère-Eberhardt detailed native encounters with bipedal creatures she dubbed "X." One Kenyan claimed that an "X"-beast had held him captive for an hour, saying of his kidnapper: "His eyes, his mouth were those of a man, and his face was not covered with hair, but his forehead was very low, rather like that of a baboon." Finally, Roumeguère-Eberhardt attempted to describe five separate "X" species. Most were vegetarians, but one group used clubs to kill prey, while members of another carried bows and arrows![20]

Who Ate the Lion? It was Bili!

Before dismissing all reports from Africa as native myths or "travelers' tales," we must consider the case of the Bili or Bondo ape, called "lion killers" by tribal huntsmen of the Bili Forest, situated between the Ubangi and Uele Rivers in Bas-Uele Province, Democratic Republic of the Congo. For decades, natives have described the creatures—ground-dwelling primates larger than chimpanzees, which kill lions either as prey or in self-defence and seem impervious to poisoned arrows.[21]

Scientists pooh-poohed those tales as simple-minded fantasies until 1996, when Swiss photographer and anti-poaching activist Karl Ammann discovered a chimp-sized skull with a prominent sagittal crest resembling a gorilla's. Soon afterward, Ammann found ground nests similar to those made by gorillas, plus scat three times the size of normal chimpanzee droppings and footprints rivalling a gorilla's in size. Finally, he bought a photo snapped by a motion-detecting camera, depicting apes that resembled oversized chimps. Five years later, Ammann led an expedition to find the apes, teamed with George Schaller of the Wildlife Conservation Society and Mike Belliveau from Harvard University, but their search proved fruitless.[22]

Meanwhile, marathon human conflict engulfed the Congo, comprising two barely-separated wars in 1996-97 and 1998-2003. As the latest civil war ran out of steam—still leaving Hema and Lendu tribesmen to kill each other in the Ituri conflict of 1999-2007, while government troops battled Hutu rebels in the Kivu conflict of 2004-2009—more scientists went in search of the Bili/Bondo lion-killers. First to actually see the elusive creatures was primatologist

Shelly Williams, who tagged them as a potentially unknown species. As she described the encounter, "We could hear them in the trees, about 10 meters away, and four suddenly came rushing through the brush towards me. If this had been a mock charge they would have been screaming to intimidate us. These guys were quiet, and they were huge. They were coming in for the kill—but as soon as they saw my face they stopped and disappeared."[23]

Cleve Hicks, from the University of Amsterdam, led another search for the apes in 2004 and emerged from the forest eighteen months later, claiming twenty full hours of close observation. Hicks observed one specimen feeding on the carcass of a leopard, though he could not prove the ape had killed the cat. "How can they get away with sleeping on the ground when there are lions, leopards, [and] golden cats around as well as other dangerous animals like elephants and buffalo?" Hicks asked. "I don't like to paint them as being more aggressive, but maybe they prey on some of these predators and the predators kind of leave them alone."[24]

His final verdict: the Bili apes are simply chimpanzees, though some are "strangely oversize" for reasons still unknown. "I think people are going to be disappointed with the yeti in the forest," Hicks said. As for a new species, "The evidence doesn't point to it. I think what needs to be focused on is the cultural differences. Genetically, they're not even a subspecies. But behaviourally, we may be seeing the beginning of a departure from chimpanzee norms. We could actually be catching evolution in the act. That is, if they're allowed to survive."[25]

A huge "if" in the dark heart of Equatorial Africa, where *Homo sapiens* remains the most savage predator of all.

Chapter 7.
Asia: The Inscrutable

A sia is rife with legends and eyewitness sightings of hairy bipeds unrecognised by science, and a fair percentage of them are said to be hostile toward humans. The basis for those claims shall be examined and evaluated in this chapter, as we tour the Far East in search of man-hunting primates. Beginning in Siberia, we'll make a circuit through Japan, the Philippines and Indonesia, to Sri Lanka, then return to the mainland for a tour of Malaysia, Myanmar, and the states once joined as Indochina, before visiting China itself, then moving on to India. Our final stop, amidst the Himalayas, will include discussion of alleged attacks by Yeti—the "Abominable Snowman."

Stalin's Apes of Wrath

While pushing Russian scientists to fabricate an army of invincible subhumans, Josef Stalin packed an estimated fourteen million adversaries into prison camps across Siberia, where 516,841 died during 1941-43 alone. Another seven or eight million were deported to the vast wasteland without being confined to camps. The final death toll may never be known.[1]

Siberia is more than snow and permafrost, however. At 5.1 million square miles in area, Siberia comprises seventy-seven percent of Russia's total territory and nearly ten percent of Earth's land surface. Vegetation ranges from tundra and taiga in the north to temperate forests in the south, where most of the district's population lives in close proximity to the Trans-Siberian Railway. The climate is likewise varied. On the north coast, summer last barely one month, while in the south a normal-length summer sees occasional temperatures topping 100° Fahrenheit (approximately 40° Centigrade). Precipitation is low, with the yearly maximum rainfall—twenty inches on average—concentrated on the Kamchatka Peninsula. Thirteen major mountain ranges mark Siberia's landscape, from the Urals in the west to the Dzhugdzhur Mountains in the east.[2]

In short, there is ample room for monsters. But if they exist, are they hostile to humans?

In western Siberia's Yamalo-Nenets Autonomous Okrug, villagers reportedly live in fear of an eight-foot-tall manimal called the *Zemlemer* ("land surveyor"), which roams over migratory paths throughout the district's 289,692 square miles. Our only eyewitness account comes from schoolteacher Marfa Senkina, who lived for a time during 1917 with peasants in Puyko village, on the Ob' River. One September night the town dogs raised an uproar, and Senkina saw several confront a tall hairy biped. One dog attacked, and the creature hurled it away, then fled.[3] All in all, hardly a reign of terror.

Most Siberian hominid action is concentrated in the Far East, where three manlike beasts—o one with three names—inspire fear among natives. The mountain-dwelling *Kiltanya* ("goggle eye")—also known as the *Arysa* ("plainsman"), *Dzhulin* ("sharp-head"), *Girkychavyl'ir* ("swift runner"), and *Teryk* ("dawn man")—leaves eighteen-inch humanoid tracks and is relatively harmless, scavenging fish and game from hunters. At the far northeastern limit of Siberia, on the Chukchi Peninsula in Chukotka Autonomous Okrug, the *Mirygdy* ("broad shoulders") likewise robs hunters, ripping chunks of meat from dead game with its powerfu hands. And from neighbouring Magadan Oblast, to the south, come tales of the *Pikelian*— which again steals reindeer meat from hunters, storing it for leaner times.[4]

While an encounter with such creatures might prove frightening, no evidence exists of hairy hominids attacking anyone throughout the vast range of Siberia.

Kamikaze *Kappas*

The *Kappa* ("river child") or *Katawaro* ("river boy") of Japanese folklore bears no true resem blance to Sasquatch, but as a manimal known for its hostile intentions toward humans, it rate: mention here. Typically described as child-sized, three to four feet tall and weighing thirty to fifty pounds, the Kappa is a malicious merbeing said to drown or devour children if the oppor

tunity arises. Most folklorists regard *Kappa* tales as a parental means of warning children away from deep water, and signs found in modern Japan to this day reinforce that notion.[5]

While no modern eyewitness reports alleged *Kappa* aggression, circumstantial evidence of the creatures' existence may be found in Kyūshū's Kumamoto Prefecture, where a shrine contains the supposed mummified hand of a *Kappa*, and at Imagi in Saga Prefecture (also on Kyūshū), where an entire *Kappa* mummy is preserved, found during renovation of the Matsuura Brewery, in the 1950s.[6]

Filipino Phantoms

The Philippines have a long tradition of hairy cannibal giants at large. One of the oldest is the *Bungisngis*, from the Tagalog word *ngisi,* "to giggle," literally translated as "showing his teeth." Fangs, indeed, were the primary attribute of this one-eyed horror, whose upper lip was so large it could be drawn back to hide its cyclopean face. Said to frequent Luzon's Bataan Peninsula, the *Bungisngis* allegedly stalked humans as prey, consuming any who fell into its

OPPOSITE: Early depiction of Japan's *Kappa*.
ABOVE: A *Kappa* warning in present-day Japan.

unbreakable grip.[7]

Some natives of Luzon and neighbouring Samar knew the *Bungisngis* or its one-eyed twin by a different name, as *Kapre* (from the Spanish *kafre,* "Moor"). While sometimes less brutal than the *Bungisngis*—fond of cigars and willing to trade fruit or fish for cooked rice—the *Kapre* still lapsed on occasion by kidnapping women it met in the forest. Still, the *Kapre* might be useful, as when one called Agyo reportedly fought against Miguel López de Legazpi's Spanish conquistadors on Samar in 1565.[8]

Indonesia's Lost World
Despite its long history of colonisation and conquest, spanning some four thousand years, the Indonesian archipelago remains a realm of mystery. Earth's largest known lizard was discovered on Komodo in 1912, with other specimens later found on the nearby islands of Flores, Gili Motang, and Rinca. Between 1994 and 2006, 361 new animals' species were identified on Borneo alone. March 2007 brought word that a previously unknown species of clouded leopard had been found on Borneo and Sumatra. Today, humans inhabit only one-third of Indonesia's 18,000 islands—1,000 of which were discovered for the first time via satellite photography, in February 2003.

But there may be other humanoids at large.

Indonesia's best-known cryptid is the *Orang Pendek* ("short man") or *Orang Gugu,* a hairy biped seen by European travelers and settlers since World War I, whose existence is supported by footprint casts and DNA analysis of hairs collected in the Sumatran jungle.[9] The *Orang Pendek* also appears to be completely inoffensive, which cannot be said for some of its reputed neighbours.

One legendary predator from Java, the *Anjing Ajak,* was said to be a night-prowling werewolf, and while supernatural myths are distinct from reports of Bigfoot-Sasquatch aggression—or should be—similar tales of lycanthropy overlap claims of hairy hominid attacks in parts of mainland Southeast Asia. Meanwhile, the shaggy cannibal giants known as *Reksasi* or *Reksoso* seem to be legendary transplants from India, but we cannot rule out their possible connection to local hominid encounters.[10]

Neither, as it happens, can we document a single incident from modern times involving claims of unknown primates troubling humans. Despite some vague reports of villagers pelted with sticks and stones by the mischievous *Orang Gugu,* the cryptid rap sheet is blank.[11]

Nasty *Nittaewo*
Sri Lanka—formerly Ceylon—reportedly harbours small hominids bearing a strong resemblance to Indonesia's *Orang Pendek,* except in temperament. The Vedda people of Sri Lanka preserve ancient stories of war with the hostile *Nittaewo,* who disembowelled their prey and human enemies alike with long, sharp fingernails. If the stories are true, they still need not concern us, since Vedda storytellers insist that the last *Nittaewos* were trapped in a cave, sometime during the late 18th Century, and asphyxiated by a fire kept burning at the cave's

mouth for three days.[12]

Monstrous Malaysia

Reports of giant hairy humanoids began emerging from Malaya—now the mainland portion of Malaysia—in 1889, when author Aug Daniel Frederickson published an account of his visit to the maharajah of Johor in the early 1870s. Frederickson claimed to have seen a captive wild-man, called *Hantu sakai* by the natives, whom he sketched before it was packed off for study by "a learned society" in Calcutta. Most subsequent authors spell the creature's Malay name *Santu sakai*, with all agreeing that *Hantu* or *Santu* means "devil." As for *sakai*, it complicates matters, being a broad derogatory term for the nomadic Senoi people of Malaya.[13]

What is so "devilish" about the *Hantu/Santu sakai?* According to native tradition, the crea-tures are man-eaters who prefer thin victims over those with more meat on their bones. To explain that curious behaviour, Ivan Sanderson surmised a deficiency in the creatures' diet, wherein "their whole metabolism went haywire. To counterbalance this, their bodies de-manded that they do something; so, overcoming their natural racial fear [of humans], they descended upon their old homelands looking for what they needed—i.e., what we call 'red meat.' And to take this to its end, let us say that, fats nauseating them, they picked the lean—and what easier than thin people?"[14]

What, indeed? But where is the proof?

Fast-forward to Christmas Day 1953, on a plantation owned by Scotsman G.M. Browne in the state of Perak A teenage Chinese girl named Wong Yee Moi was tapping trees that afternoon, when she either felt a hand upon her shoulder or was clutched from behind by powerful arms (accounts differ). In either case, she turned somehow to confront a shaggy, malodorous female creature who bared long fangs. Farther back, Wong Yee Moi saw two male specimens watch-ing from the forest. Before she fled—suggesting that she was not, after all, gripped in a bear-hug—Wong Yee Moi noted that the female creature wore a loincloth. Despite her panic, she also later indicated that the apewoman's grin seemed friendly.[15]

British security forces, already immersed in their twelve-year war with the Malayan Races Liberation Army—modestly dubbed the "Malayan Emergency"—beat the bushes in vain for any trace of the cryptids. Their communist opponents might have told them where to look, if they had been on speaking terms. Author Warren Smith reports that a cadre of cave-dwelling guerrillas lost one of their sentries to night-prowling apemen, sometime in the early 1950s. When found, Smith says, "His neck was broken. Something had eaten almost 20 or 30 pounds of meat from his corpse." One witness, prior to execution by a military firing squad, allegedly blamed the killing on subhuman "mouth men"—a term we shall hear repeated farther east. Smith also briefly describes the case of a young hunter who grappled with a pair of "bristly, black-haired beasts" near Kuala Lumpur, but a dearth of detail makes the incident impossible to document.[16]

Two years after Malaysia achieved independence from Britain, in September 1965, reports of an aggressive "oily monster" emanated from peninsular Malaysia. Sadly, our only sources for the flap are authors "Eric Norman" and Warren Smith—who, as we have seen, may be one and the same. Aside from one specific date—29 September—their very similar accounts of a shaggy manbeast that accosted villagers and military sentries, leaving puddles of an unidentified "dark, oil-like substance" in its wake, offer no substantive details.[17]

"Eric Norman's" next report may solve the riddle of the undated, barely-described attack on a Malayan hunter with his next report, dated 14 June 1967. Norman claims that one Henri van Heerdan was hunting birds near Kuala Lumpur that afternoon, when "two absolute monstrosities" attacked him. "They were tall," van Heerdan said, "very large, and they looked like demons from Hell." Despite their strength and ferocity, van Heerdan—who had dropped his shotgun in a panic—reportedly escaped after clocking one beast in the face with a stone. Brad Steiger, who shared the "Norman" pseudonym with Warren Smith, told the same tale thirty years later, in his *Werewolf Book,* referring to the creatures both as "mouth men" and "*Santu sakai.*" Since he cites Norman as his source, we're left to wonder if the events in question ever occurred.[18]

In 1969-70, while studying orang-utans in Borneo, British zoologist John MacKinnon met a Malay boatman who described a smaller hairy hominid, some four feet tall, known to natives in Sabah State—part of Malaysia since 1963—as *Batutut* or *Ujit.* Described both as a living creature who left footprints and "a type of ghost," the beast was "said to be fond of children, whom it lures away from their villages but does them no harm. To adults, however, it never shows itself, but occasionally men had been found that Batutut had killed and ripped open to feast on their liver (to Malays the seat of all emotions, analogous to the European heart)."[19]

Sightings of Malaysian apemen continue in the 21st Century, sans any claims of aggression toward humans. The score of documented cases: zero.

Mouth-Men of Myanmar
Pushing northward into Myanmar, formerly Burma, we encounter more tales of large and aggressive bipedal cryptids. According to various authors, these creatures congregate primarily along the mountainous border separating Myanmar from China, Laos, and Thailand, with their territory overlapping into those three countries. In Myanmar proper, they are variously known as *Kung-Lu, Taw,* or *Tok,* all translating as "mouth man." Without exception, they are viewed by natives as ferocious man-eaters. Warren Smith and Brad Steiger add a supernatural twist, suggesting that the *Taw* or *Tok* may be werewolves.[20]

American travel writer Hassoldt Davis introduced Western readers to the *Kung-Lu* in 1940. According to Davis, "The *Kung-Lu*...was a monster that resembled a gorilla, a miniature King Kong, about 20 feet tall. It lived on the highest mountains, where its trail of broken trees was often seen, and descended into the villages only when it wanted meat, human meat. We were told also that no one in Kensi [now Kawmayo, Myanmar] had been eaten by the *Kung-Lu* for more years than the eldest could remember."[21]

Brad Steiger blames the *Kung-Lu* for killing a porter employed by "famous mountaineer Huerta" during the "Argentinean Mountaineering Expedition in 1955," but once again his ource is "Eric Norman"—whose book places that untraceable incident in the Himalayas, blaming it on the Yeti.[22]

f the *Kung-Lu* was retired from hunting humans before World War II, the *Taw/Tok* seems to have spent more time at the game. Ivan Sanderson, writing in 1961, related the tale of William Wilson, a young man born to American missionaries in Burma, whose family home was twice invaded by *Toks* during the 1950s. As Sanderson paraphrased Wilson's account, "he actually had a *Tok* in his arms twice and when it broke loose it left handfuls of long, coarse, shiny black hairs in his hands. The occasions were when it broke into his family home which was deep in the hill jungles and some distance from the nearest small, permanent settlement. On both occasions it chose a bright moonlight night and both times it crashed about apparently looking for food. Both times the young man tackled it thinking that it was a native thief or marauder and, being a powerfully built man and an athlete, and since his parents refused to possess any firearms, he did so with his bare hands. On each occasion it did not attempt to attack him in return, but only to flee, and being immensely strong and well over 6 feet tall it easily broke away, once running straight through a screen door."[23]

Brad Steiger offers another report, allegedly filed from eastern Burma's Shan State in 1960, by British colonial official Harold M. Young. While hunting along the Thai border, Young and company spent the night in a Lahu village, where their sleep was interrupted by horrible screams from a nearby hut. Rushing to the scene, Young caught a hairy humanoid in the act of eating a woman alive and fired several shots at the beast. It fled, and Young followed its blood trail at sunrise, discovering a dead man whom the villagers identified as *Taw*—a lycanthrope reverted to its human form in death.[24] Whatever one may think of werewolves, if the tale is true, it certainly exonerates Bigfoot.

According to author John Keel, Burma's "mouth men" continued their antipathy for Red guerillas well into the Vietnam War. In June 1969, Keel says, a pair of ten-foot-tall "monkey men" rampaged along the border shared by Burma, Laos, and Thailand, putting Lahu rebels to flight with a shower of stones. Keel's original source, a Reuters dispatch dated 17 June, remains elusive.[25]

Indochinese Enigmas

Turning eastward from the land of "mouth men," we arrive in the region once known as French Indochina, presently the nations of Cambodia, Laos and Vietnam. Soldiers of East and West, propelled by various philosophies and creeds, have battled over this domain since forces from the Champa kingdom of Aman arrived during the 7th Century C.E. Their blood has drenched the soil for generations, but the fighters that concern us here—if they exist—are something less than human.

Ivan Sanderson supplies our first report, from 1943, when Japanese invaders controlled the region. As he explains:

> It begins way down in the plateau of Kontum, in what used to be north-
> ern Indo-China [now Vietnam]. There, the locals say they have a kind of

enormous *monkey* that walks on its hind legs and which is actually vicious and is quite willing to attack people. They call it the *Kra-Dhan*. In the neighbouring territory of the Jölong it is called the *Bêć-Boć* (Bekk-Bok). The mountain people of the south also insist that it is a *monkey*, and not a man or an ape. This is odd, for there are virtually tailless monkeys thereabouts, the Stump-tailed Macaques (*Lyssodes*). At the same time, the locals are equally insistent that these creatures are not ghosts, departed spirits, demigods, or anything nonmaterial; all of which, though they often speak of them, they most clearly distinguish from real physical beings. There is a report that one of these creatures either committed a murder, or was responsible for a murder near Konturn in 1943. Unfortunately the matter was tried by the local native court, of which no records were sent to the central French authority, while the French Resident of that area at the time is no longer alive, and the native Commune has been dispersed since the retirement of the French. This is not by any means the only report of these *Kra-Dhan* to be made to foreigners, and we have heard of similar entities in areas far to the west of Kontum. There would be nothing unexpected in reports of an unknown *ape* in this area, and I

personally would not be a bit surprised if someone told me of an alleged ABSM thereabouts; and for all the same old reasons—ample, unexplored montane forests; small and isolated human communities; and appropriate geographical position. But, the insistence on the "monkey" theme is novel.[26]

The next homicidal encounter on record, according to author "Eric Norman," occurred in 1951, while French colonial troops struggled to hold their empire from native Viet Minh guerrillas. Untraceable official Jean-Pierre Delaine was visiting a jungle village near the Indochinese border with Thailand, when he encountered murderous humanoids known—once again—as *Taw*. On this occasion, Norman claims, two nine-foot hairy monsters invaded the village by night, dodging spears and bullets to abduct a female victim.[27] Norman quotes Delaine's supposed diary, describing the grim aftermath.

We found the young woman's body about a mile from the village. She had been assaulted viciously during the night. The giant footprints around her body indicated that several of the monsters had gathered for their bestial pleasures. Even more horrible was the appearance of her head. Something had gnawed on her with strong teeth, ripping the flesh from her bones. Her arms were almost bare of flesh, and we presumed that she had tried to cover her face for protection.... Before I left, the old chieftain informed me that a band of werewolf-like apemen lived in the high mountains, in almost inaccessible areas, and no native dared venture into these craggy places."[28]

Fact or fiction? When the author cites no retrievable sources, and himself remains anonymous, we should err on the side of caution.

Encounters with Vietnamese apemen continued after American forces inherited the Indochina

War from France. In what was then North Vietnam, sometime in 1963, zoologist Dao Van Tien claimed that a "wildman" had invaded homes around Thuận Châu, in Sơn La Province, stealing food at night. Four years later and far to the south, at Cam Ranh Bay on the South China Sea, a soldier named Powell fired on a hairy prowler at a U.S. Army supply depot, afterward finding drops of blood and allegedly photographing a footprint "said to be neither human nor ape." Natives called the beast *Nguòi Rùng* ("forest man") or *Khi trâu* ("big monkey" or "buffalo monkey"). [29]

Our last report from Indochina is dated 17 December 1974, and allegedly comes from U.S. troops on patrol beyond the demilitarized zone that separated North and South Vietnam along the 17th parallel. As described by longtime UFO researcher Albert Rosales [syntax uncorrected]:

> A group of heavily armed soldiers had gone out in a search and destroy mission and had gone along a river bank by a heavily wooded area and had reached a clearing, when they began spreading out, their leader sensed something peculiar about the area. There was a strange eerie silence all around with the normal animals sounds totally absent. A scout went ahead and reported finding no tracks of any kind around. The silence continued. Strange faecal deposits were located, then sounds from the nearby brush were heard, several huge figures then came into view just ahead of the soldiers. The figures were almost eight-foot tall and bright yellow in colour, as they came closer, large three digit hands with what appeared to be long claws could be seen on the creatures. They had large eyes, nose slits and flat faces. The figures passed near the men apparently without noticing them. The men then decide to turn back, as they walked into the bushes they began hearing loud crashing noises and realised that the creatures were running behind them. The men all ran towards the river where their boat was located with the creatures in hot pursuit. Several times the men fired their high calibre weapons at the creatures without any apparent effect. At one point one of the men fired several armour piercing rounds at one of the creature's chest area, this also without any apparent effect. The men finally reached their boat and left the area, before leaving they saw a strong powerful glow on the riverbank as if dozens of the creatures had gathered to watch them leave. [30]

The beasts in question bear no resemblance to any apemen previously described from Indochina, and in fact are apparently meant to represent extraterrestrials. Rosales rates the incident "Type E," defined as a case wherein "an entity or humanoid is seen alone, without related UFO activity." [31]

As if that were not confusing enough, Rosales lifts the tale from a 1993 paperback, Natural *or Supernatural?*, written by late author Martin Caidin, a recognised authority on aeronautics and aviation. Before his death in March 1997, Caidin published more than fifty books, roughly divided between military history and speculative fiction. While well respected overall, he may have had some lapses in his later years. Online reviewer Dave Summers complained that in *Natural or Supernatural?* Caidin had "concocted a batch of off-the-wall whoppers that have little relationship to anything in the real world—and passes them off as true....The book has all the charm of the *National Enquirer*, but without the credibility."[32]

Ye-rén Trouble Now!

Vast China spans 3,705,407 to 3,722,029 square miles, depending on how the nation's boundaries are defined. In either case, it encompasses a wide variety of landscapes and animal habitats, from arid deserts and tropical rainforests to some of Earth's tallest mountains. There is room to spare for cryptids and no shortage of reports, from ancient legendry to modern sightings.

The Chinese take their monsters seriously. While they have not followed Josef Stalin's lead in trying to create a race of subhuman super-soldiers (at least, as far as we know), the Chinese Academy of Sciences sought evidence of living "wildmen" from 1977 through the 1990s, and a standing government reward remains in place for presentation of a specimen, alive or dead. Meanwhile, state scientists reportedly have found unclassifiable hair, faeces and footprints, plus the skeleton of a "monkey child" unearthed in Sichuan Province.[33]

While that quest goes on in the 21st Century, we shall confine ourselves to reports of violent contact between Chinese apemen and humans. The problem is compounded by a plethora of local names and varying descriptions for the creatures widely known in China as "wildmen." The many names include *Dà-mao-rén* ("big hairy man"), *Mao-rén* ("hairy man"), *Rén-xióng* ("man-bear"), *Sūet-jùen* ("snowman"), *Xuě-rén* ("snowman") and *Ye-rén* ("wild man"). As with the Yeti of the Himalayas, the creatures reported differ in size, coloration, and temperament.[34]

Despite the large number of "wildman" sightings in China during successive generations, only two cases of physical attacks on humans are recorded—and the first, from 1957, has been definitively purged from Bigfoot's rap sheet. On 23 May of that year, a supposed *Rén-xióng* attacked Wang Congmei while she was tending cattle in the Jiulong Mountains of sparsely-populated Zhejiang Province. Congmei's mother heard her screams and ran to help with other village women, striking the *Rén-xióng* with sticks and driving it into a rice paddy, where it became stuck in mud. Thus trapped, the beast was clubbed unconscious, then beheaded. Its hands were also severed, given with the head to local teacher Zhou Shousong, who permitted government researchers to examine the relics in 1980. Scientific analysis convinced *Ye-rén* hunter Zhou Guoxing that the aggressive beast had been a stump-tailed macaque monkey (*Macaca arctoides*) of unusual size.[35]

The second case, reported seventeen years later, involved a reputed *Ye-rén*. Yin Hongfa was passing through a wooded portion of the Dahei Mountains, in Yunnan Province, when he was (allegedly) attacked on 1 May 1974. The *Ye-rén* clutched him with long arms, but Yin fought

OPPOSITE: Chinese poster offering a reward for the *Yé-ren*.

back with a machete, routing the beast and retaining a handful of long hair ripped from its scalp. DNA profiling was unknown at the time, and nothing suggests that the hair was preserved for subsequent analysis.[36]

There ends the modest case against the Chinese wildman, with one charge tossed out of court and the other necessarily dismissed for lack of evidence.

Monkey-Man, Where Are You?

Despite its egregious overcrowding, with 1.2 billion souls crammed into 1,269,210 square miles, India remains a land of mystery—eight major religions competing for converts; Kali-worshipping *thugee* cultists waylaying hapless pilgrims; fakirs sprawled on beds of nails, walking on coals, or climbing ropes to nowhere. Indeed, for all the news of Bollywood, terrorism and organised crime nationwide, superstitious hysteria still pervades vast tracts of India. Where else on Earth are "temple stampedes" an accepted part of daily life, claiming 700 lives in the first decade of the 21st Century?[37]

In such an atmosphere, monsters abound. In legend, they include the man-eating *Kirata* (half-human, half-tiger), *Loha-mukha* ("iron-faced" giants), and *Rakshasas*. The dog-headed *Kynoképhalos* or *Sunamukha* was smaller, a three-foot cave-dweller who used bows and arrows for hunting.[38] None appear in any modern-day reports.

Of more immediate concern to our inquiry are the *Vanamanushas* ("wicked wild men"), said to terrorise the Chamoli district of northern India's Uttarakhand State, adjoining Tibet. Sadly, the only known reports of *Vanamanusha* activity come from authors "Eric Norman," Warren Smith, and Brad Steiger (citing "Norman," thus perhaps himself).[39] Still, despite those suspect origins, I include the tale here for the sake of completion.

According to Smith, Steiger, and their shared pseudonym, an undated article from the untraceable weekly newspaper *Garhwal Samachar* detailed an attack staged by *Vanamanushas* on the supposed village of Talah Malkoti, sometime in 1965. The apelike beasts allegedly kidnapped a teenage girl and dragged her to a cave where she was "repeatedly assaulted." Lucky enough to escape while two of the monsters battled for ownership of their prize, the girl returned home, but was clapped into a mental institution where, the paper reported, "She sits and stares both day and night. When she is touched by a friendly attendant, she screams in terror and crawls under her bed."[40]

Nor was the anonymous teen the *Vanamanushas'* only victim. The authors assure us that *Vanamanushas* have ravaged Chamoli villages for "hundreds of years." Steiger sounds a more ominous note, reporting in 1999 that the beasts "have become increasingly bolder over the years." As to what they might be, a predictably anonymous "newsman in New Delhi" purportedly told Warren Smith, "They sound suspiciously like an ABSM"—the abbreviation for "Abominable Snowman" coined by Ivan Sanderson in 1961.[41]

An even stranger—though more amply documented—simian terrorist was "Monkey Man," a vicious creature blamed for multiple attacks on humans between April 2001 and February 2002. Before the thing vanished for good, sightings and assaults were logged from Ghaziabad, New Delhi and Noida, in Uttar Pradesh State (adjoining both Nepal and *Vanamanusha* territory in Uttarakhand; at Nalbari in Assam State (also bordering Nepal); far to the northwest, in the Nagaur district of Rajasthan State; and at Ahmadabad in Gujarat State (on the Bay of Bengal).[42]

The first attack supposedly occurred in Ghaziabad, during early April 2001. According to the

Two view of India's Monkey-Man.

Hindustan Times, an auto rickshaw driver told police that he was mauled by a passenger "who changed his appearance midway through the journey and caught [the driver] by the neck." By 30 April the panic had engulfed New Delhi and Noida, prompting vigilante patrols and promiscuous gunfire. *Two* apelike creatures attacked victim Om Veer, then "ran away when they saw the headlights of an approaching car." Some witnesses described an ape with glowing red eyes; others a "masked man" who verbally threatened their lives. The thing seen by a doctor's wife in Noida was "dressed in white. He seemed to be covered in bandages like a mummy. Only the large, frightening eyes were visible." Other specimens wore jumpsuits and helmets, while slashing victims with metallic claws.[43]

By 19 May police had logged 328 calls reporting monstrous encounters; they rated 257 as hoaxes. Sixty persons claimed injuries from the beast now called Monkey Man, and police in Delhi offered a reward of 50,000 rupees (£769) for information leading to apprehension of "a group of mischief makers." A dozen suspects were arrested, and reports of Monkey Man bites subsided when local physicians began prescribing painful rabies vaccinations at a cost of 1,800 rupees per patient.[44]

The prowler morphed again by 26 May, when twenty residents of Nalbari claimed injuries inflicted by a savage "bear-man." Sixteen local witnesses, interviewed by members of the Assam Science Society, admitted they were half-asleep when they "heard a noise on the tin roof of their houses, following which they felt that something was trying to clutch them with sharp nails." Residents of Nagaur, in Rajasthan, described their assailant as "a cross between a huge monkey and a computerised robot," while police blamed "a wild cat." On 23 and 24 May, in the Moulvibazar district of Bangladesh, two women and a girl claimed they were attacked by a three-foot-tall "oddly-shaped animal" sporting the face of a man. Monkey Man's last incarnation, reported from Ahmadabad in early February 2002, was a roof-hopping humanoid figure dressed all in black, with curly hair sprouting above the mask that covered its face.[45]

There the madness ended—almost. In August 2002, Uttar Pradesh State spawned another monster, this one dubbed *Muhnochwa* ("face-scratcher"). Variously described as a flying insect, a blue ray of light, a huge man armed with tiger's claws, a dog-human hybrid, a mutated cat or bear, *Muhnochwa* left its victims plastered with bandages—some masking wounds which police described as self-inflicted. Victim Ramji Pal reportedly died with his stomach slashed open. A female neighbour displayed forearms blistered by burns. Unable to corral the nocturnal prowler(s), frightened villagers lynched at least a dozen human suspects before the mass hysteria ran its course.[46]

In retrospect, what can we say about such monsters of the mind? Whatever sparked the rampant fear of 2001-02, there is no reason whatsoever to blame any flesh-and-blood cryptids.

Abominable Snowjobs

The Himalayan Yeti, or "Abominable Snowman," stands with Bigfoot and the Loch Ness Monster as a superstar within the global panoply of cryptids. First introduced to the West in 1832 by Brian Hodgson, Britain's minister to Nepal, the Himalayan hominid is known by many names, including (but by no means limited to) *Ban-manush* ("forest man"), *Chelovek mishka* ("bear man"), *Chu-mung* ("spirit of the glaciers"), *Dre-mo* ("brown bear"), *Dzu-teh* ("bear-animal"), *Gérésun bamburshé* ("wild man"), *Jungli-admi* ("wild man"), *Metoh-kangmi* ("snow man"), *Mi-chen-po* ("big man"), *Mi-gö* ("wild man"), *Mi-teh* ("man-animal"), *Nyalmo* (translation unknown), *Rakshi-bompo* ("powerful demon"), *Samdja* ("man-animal"), and *Snezhniy chelovek* ("snowman"). It's most common name—*Yeh-teh* or Yeti—translates as "snowy mountain animal."[47]

As elsewhere, some Yetis are regarded as a threat to humans and their property. The *Ban-manush* is rumoured to abduct both men and women. The *Chu-mong* (or *Chemo*) only slaughters men who "startle" it, and then devours them. The *Dre-mo* and *Gérésun bamburshé* lob stones at humans, while the *Dzuh-teh* eats cattle and yaks after breaking their necks. The *Mi-teh* is "shy unless provoked," whereupon it turns savage. The *Nyalmo* is branded a "possible" man-eater. None of those claims is supported by any concrete reports.[48]

There are, however, more specific claims against the Yeti. First, in 1917, it is alleged that a female hominid snatched a teenage boy from Keronja village, near Dhāding, Nepal, and held him captive as a sex slave, producing offspring said to still inhabit the vicinity in the late 1970s. That story is a neat reversal of the tale surrounding "Zana," a female cryptid supposedly snared in the western Caucasus during the late 19th Century, who bore four children or a sort to human fathers in the village of Tkhina.[49]

The Yeti grabs a snack.

Tokyo tackles the Abominable Snowman.

Our next case dates from 1938, when authors "Eric Norman" and Warren Smith claim that shrieking, unseen creatures lobbed stones at members of the first American Karakoram expedition on K2, Earth's second-tallest mountain after Everest. Strangely, the definitive published account of that mountaineering adventure mentions no such incident.[50]

Ten years later, Norwegian uranium prospectors Jan Frostis and Aage Thorberg claimed that they had survived a close encounter with two vicious Yetis at the Zemu Gap—the scene of three other reported Yeti encounters in 1928 and 1938. Located at the head of the Zemu Glacier, found at the base of Kangchenjunga (Earth's third-highest mountain, in the Sikkim Himalayas), the Zemu Gap leads to the Tongshyong Glacier on Kangchenjunga's east side. There, Frostis and Thorberg said, they spotted two man-sized bipedal creatures and lassoed one with a rope, whereupon it turned and tackled Frostis, injuring his shoulder. Only shots from Thorberg's pistol spared them both from further injury, though Frostis required treatment at a hospital in Darjeeling, West Bengal. Ivan Sanderson branded the report a "suspected fabrication,"

Half Human's Yeti finds a mate.

while other critics were less tactful.[51]

Author John Keel, himself a Himalayan traveller, provides our next case, from 1949. Sometime in that year, he says, a Sherpa herdsman named Lakhpa Tensing was "reportedly torn apart" by a Yeti on Nanga Parbat, in the western Himalayas—Pakistan's second-highest mountain, and the world's ninth-tallest. Sadly, no further information is available.[52]

As noted earlier, writers "Eric Norman" and Brad Steiger claim another Yeti slaying during 1955, citing their source as "famous mountaineer Huerta" of the "Argentinean Mountaineering Expedition," but Steiger places the incident in Burma, while Norman offers no location at all. The victim, we are told, was an anonymous porter. The rest is highly dubious silence.[53]

The best-documented case on record reportedly occurred on 11 July 1974, when a young Sherpa woman named Lhakpa Dolma (or Lakpa Sherpani) was tending her family's yaks near Machermo, Pheriche, or Tengboche, Nepal (reports differ). As she later told the story, a five-foot-tall manbeast scooped her up and carried her to a nearby stream, then went back to kill some of her yaks (various versions of the tale say two, three or five), first punching them senseless, then breaking their necks before eating the brains from their skulls. The girl escaped, meanwhile, to summon help. Police arrived several days later, allegedly sketching and photographing the creature's footprints. That said, no photos of the tracks or slaughtered yaks have yet been published.[54]

Tyrolean mountaineer Reinhold Messner serves up our last three cases. The first, from 1977, describes a pig-abduction by a *Chu-mung* or *Chemo* near Lhasa, in Tibet. The beast was also said to prey on goats. Another vague tale, related to Messner in the 1980s by the "town drunk" in Laya, Nepal, refers to hairy "forest people" who "broke the spines of sheep and then dragged shepherd girls off to their caves." Finally, in 1992, Messner visited Solo Khumbu, near Mount Everest, where "a rumour was going round that a young woman had been raped by a yeti." Messner finally concluded that the Yeti is, in fact, a bear—perhaps a species yet unrecognised by science, but a simple bruin nonetheless.[55]

Perhaps. What we *can* say, with reasonable certainty, is that no evidence exists sufficient to support a charge of homicide or any other crime against the Yeti, under any of its many names. If it exists, it may have killed or injured humans, or their livestock, at some point in time, and should be shown the same respect as any other large wild animal. The case, however, still remains unproved.

Chapter 8.
Oceania: Dreamtime Demons

Oceania is one of Earth's eight terrestrial ecozones, generally considered to include Australia, its external territories (Christmas Island, Norfolk Island, the Cocos Islands and Coral Sea Islands), with various proximate Pacific islands, including New Zealand and the countless island-states of Melanesia, Micronesia and Polynesia. None are known to harbour any recognised great apes, and most will not concern us here, but there are still reports aplenty of predatory manimals demanding our attention. We begin Down Under, where aboriginal legends sometimes take on a life of their own.

Outback Oddities

Long before Dutch navigator Willem Janszoon first set foot on Australian soil in February 1606, generations before Captain James Cook claimed New South Wales for Britain in 1788, aboriginal tribesmen spun tales of their resident cannibal giants. As usual, they went by many names: *Barmi bigroo*, *Illankanpanka* and *Quinkin* in Queensland; *Jimbra*, *Jingra*, *Jinka*, and *Togung* in Western Australia; *Pankalanka* in the Northern Territory; *Kraitbull* or *Tjangara* in South Australia; *Lo-an* in Victoria. Descriptions were consistent, all referring to hairy bipeds seven to ten feet tall, sometimes armed with crude clubs, prone to picking off solitary hunters or raiding aboriginal villages by night.[1]

At the other end of the scale dwelt hairy, often-hostile "little people," known throughout the island continent as *Bitarr*, Brown Jack, *Burgingin*, *Dinderi*, *Junjadee*, *Net-net*, *Nimbunj*, *Nyol*, *Waaki*, *Winambuu* or *Yuuri*. They left child-sized footprints—sometimes three-toed, in defiance of the scientific rule that all primates boast five digits—and were prone to attack human beings. Our first report of such violence comes from one Nathan Moilan, who claimed that his father and uncle suffered a harrowing encounter with a night-prowling *Junjadee* while logging in the Kirrama Range near Tully, Queensland. One of the creatures invaded their hut and mauled Moilan's uncle before the two men managed to eject it. Sadly, no published account of the skirmish provides a date or any other details.[2]

George Gray reportedly suffered a similar assault in 1968, at Kempsey, New South Wales. He was sleeping when a four-foot-tall "*mannikin*" covered in grey hair tried to drag him from his bed and out the door. The beast's hair was bristly, like a pig's, while its copper-coloured face was hairless, with a flattened nose. Despite its evident aggression, Gray observed that his assailant did not seem angry and made no sound, hardly seeming to breathe. After grappling on the floor "for many minutes," the creature released Gray and fled.[3]

There ends our record of attacks by "little people" in Australia, but a more substantial history exists for the continent's best-known bipedal cryptid, commonly called the Yahoo ("devil") or Yowie ("dream spirit").[4] While British colonists published their first report of a Yahoo encounter in 1789, hearsay hostility toward humans only reared its head seven decades later.[5]

On 19 July 1861, while exploring the south-western portion of Western Australia, three men remembered only as Clarkson, Dempster and Harper interviewed a tribe of natives at Lake Grace. The aborigines regaled them with tales of the *Jimbra* or *Jingra*, a large apelike creature that preyed on hapless travellers. Specifically, the tribesmen referred to three previous, unnamed white explorers and their native guide Boodjin, who "were either killed by the *jimbras* or perished from want of water" after fleeing from the monsters.[6]

Our next report comes from adventurer Arthur Bicknell. Sometime in the latter 1880s, while hunting along the Einasleigh River in Queensland, Bicknell met an aged settler who reported seeing a hairy, bipedal "wood devil" prowling by night. The old man blamed it for snatching several of his dogs, and Bicknell promptly stationed himself in a handy tree, armed with a pistol. As he later told the tale, in 1895:

> I had not been long in the tree when I heard the peculiar moaning noise...and also the crashing and breaking of the brushwood...[I]t was nearly dark and the moon only just rising. I could see nothing. The noise had an unearthly ring about it...[S]lipping down from my perch...I waited a moment to fire two or three shots...in the direction the sounds came from, and then turned and bolted for the house. If the devil himself were after me I could not have made better time.

> When the old man appeared [next morning] we got him to go with us to the place...There sure enough he [the creature] lay, as dead as any stone, shot through the heart...He was nothing but a big monkey, one of the largest I have ever seen, with long arms and big hands, as the old man had described. These huge monkeys or apes are common in Nicaragua, but this one was certainly the largest I ever came across.[7]

Authors Paul Cropper and Tony Healy rightly note that Central American primates have no place Down Under, regardless of size, and they treat Bicknell's failure to preserve some relic of the beast as "highly suspicious," dismissing the tale as a probable hoax.[8]

On 27 February 1932, Melbourne's *Argus* ran a story from Myrtleford, Victoria, headlined "Strange Animal at Large. Man Attacked in Paddock." The victim was William Nuttall, who suffered the assault on Friday night, 26 February. Returning to his ranch from a nearby railroad station, Nuttall was dismounting from his horse when a seven-foot bipedal beast with a 'round head and four tusks" rushed out of the shadows, ripping his shirt to ribbons. Nuttall fled on foot until a fence frustrated his pursuer and the apelike thing retreated. The *Argus* speculated that it was "an animal which escaped from a travelling circus when it was at Yackandandah some time ago." No species was suggested, although the creature was "said to resemble an ape." Search parties scoured the countryside in vain, although "its tracks were plainly discernable."[9]

Three years later, horseman Walter Beddoe was travelling from Stanthorpe, Queensland, to Mount Tully, when he "struck a hairy man" on the open road. The beast "made a grab at the bridle," and failing to grasp it, "strode over the fence" along one side of the road. A relative of Beddoe's later said, "It was apparently tall enough to stride over the top wire."[10]

Author Warren Smith presents our next case, allegedly occurring sometime in the late 1930s. His witnesses are "Bill Donovan" and "Jerry Flynn," both apparently unknown to veteran Yowie researchers Paul Cropper, Tony Healy and Malcolm Smith (no relation to Warren). According to Warren Smith, Donovan and Flynn were searching for "Lasseter's Reef"—a fabulous vein of gold supposedly found, then lost in 1897, somewhere near the border of Western Australia and the Northern Territory—when they encountered "a tribe of monkey men" who "threw stones and rolled boulders down on us." Barely escaping with their lives, Donovan and Flynn supposedly told their tale to reporters, but the resultant news articles remain as elusive as the Yowie itself.[11]

Three decades passed before the next alleged clash between Yowie and human, occurring near Mount Butler, Victoria, sometime in 1965. Cattleman John Lovick woke near midnight in his bunk, to find "this bloody heavy thing pressing on my chest. It had its hands around my throat, trying to strangle me. It had a strong animal smell like you'd run across in a zoo. Its hair felt coarse and I could feel its hot breath in my face. I yelled and screamed and tried to throw it off, and we fell onto the floor." The creature fled past howling ranch dogs and escaped, while Lovick bore the bruises from his near-miss with death. He speculated that the prowler was accustomed to sleeping in the bunkhouse during off-seasons, when it was empty, and flew into a rage when it found the building occupied by snoring drovers.[12]

Domestic pets were the Yowie's victims at Woodenbong, New South Wales, on 10 August 1977. Jean Maloney woke in bed that night, to the yapping of her terrier and wails of panic from her Siamese cat. Rushing outside, she turned on a light and beheld a squatting apelike beast, squeezing the dog in its arms. At sight of Maloney, the Yowie dropped its intended prey and fled, leaving behind a foul odour and humanoid footprints. Maloney blamed her dog for the fight, noting in retrospect that the bipedal prowler "didn't seem vicious" and may have been acting in self-defence.[13]

Sometime in 1977 or '78, teenager John MacLean and several unnamed friends were fishing at Toonumbar Dam, twelve miles west of Kyogle, New South Wales, when large stones began falling into the water. Startled, they turned to see a hulking figure twelve or thirteen feet tall, winding up for its next pitch from thirty feet away, whereupon the boys turned tail and fled.[14]

The next report, from nineteen-year-old Michael Mangan, harks back to the *Junjadee* but may—if it occurred at all—involve a juvenile Yowie. According to Mangan's story, he and a girlfriend were parked on Towers Hill, Queensland, enjoying themselves one night in October 1978, when a smallish "half-man, half-ape" crashed the party and punched out the passenger-side window of his car. The couple escaped unharmed, and kept the incident secret until February 1979, when they led a party of friends to search for the beast and one youth became separated from the rest. At the sound of his screams in the dark, Mangan went for police, arriving at the Charter Towers station house "ashen-faced and visibly upset."[15]

The officers listened, then followed Mangan back to Towers Hill, where they found Mangan's friend jogging down a rural road, one leg streaked with blood. The anonymous youth described an attack by an apelike creature, which he had repulsed in a brawl, using stones. No sign of said creature was found, but Sergeant Gill Engler reported that the blood found on the boy's leg was not his own. (Whether it matched another human being is unknown.) Despite storms of ridicule, Michael Mangan defended his story until his suicide, some years later.[16]

In June 1983, residents of Bonnyrigg, New South Wales (a Sydney suburb), reported losing ducks and chickens to a nocturnal predator they dubbed a "phantom dog." Canids were absolved, however, on the night one local responded to sounds from a creek near his home and caught some unknown creature in the act of drowning several ducks. Furious, the man rushed forward, flailing at the figure with an iron bar, whereupon it rose to seven feet on its hind legs and snarled at him, long arms extended. In his haste to flee, the man first thought he had surprised a bear—odd in itself, since Australia has none—but later recognised the prowler as a Yowie.[17]

Another encounter reminiscent of Sasquatch reportedly occurred in 1987, while Queenslanders Michael Beran and Lloyd Madison were camped on Henry River, eighteen miles southeast of Glen Innes, New South Wales. One night, they were disturbed by "grumbling roars" from an "immense furry brown creature—half-man, half-ape and at least two and a half meters [eight feet] tall." The intruder fled when they opened fire with rifles, but returned the next night to steal a cooked rabbit while leaving its wrap of aluminium foil by the fire.[18]

A rambunctious "little hairy man" surfaced near Brewarrina, New South Wales, one night in 1991. Young brothers Bill and Ron Gibson were camped with a third white companion and several aboriginal boys, when a strange creature leaped from a nearby tree to surprise them. It was roughly five feet tall and "very thickset." One of the group's pig dogs pursued it, but returned from the skirmish with a broken shoulder and "never really came good again."[19]

Nine years later, a further example of Yowie aggression was reported from Queensland. On 11 March 2000, in another case that sounds like Bigfoot, a hairy biped allegedly rocked a campervan occupied by two elderly tourists. The report comes from Dean Harrison—cofounder (with wife Lissa) of Australian Yowie Research, unrelated to Rex Gilroy's Australian Yowie Research Centre—who placed the attack at "a rugged, undisclosed location" somewhere west of Gympie. According to Harrison, the van's male owner "opened the door and this thing ran off through the bush. He didn't get a good look at it, but he heard the foliage

19th-century depiction of Austalia's Yowie.

breaking and the footsteps." Its sixteen-inch footprints were "definitely not human," Harrison said, while adding, "We are over the moon, we are so excited."[20]

In April 2009, researcher Andrew McGinn told a telejournalist from Sydney's Channel 9 that a Yowie "may have killed" a puppy found decapitated in a rural district south of Darwin, in the Northern Territory. No monster was caught in the act, but McGinn declared, "The way the guy's dog was killed was typical of a Yowie. I know it sounds fanciful but over the past 100 years, dogs get killed or decapitated and people report feeling watched, having goats stolen or seeing some tall hairy thing in the days beforehand."[21]

Barely one month later, Dean Harrison himself claimed to be the victim of an unprovoked Yowie attack. While prowling the bush near Gympie—scene of the March 2000 camper incident—for a suspected female Yowie and her young at 3:00 A.M., Harrison says that he was "rugby tackled" and sent sprawling by a shaggy biped. Harrison subsequently emailed the following account to Loren Coleman's Cryptomundo blog online:

> The event was one that I shall never forget. Unfortunately I had a first timer [with me], who wasn't present during the attack..., who is trying to call the entire incident a hoax....It was certainly not. The bruising I received he says was caused by a rock that I repetitively struck myself with. The rest of the crew tailed the creature for quite some time. I got hit hard enough to send me back landing in a rock pool. I've been around too long to make things up. I have no need to. All I can say is that it was bloody scary. Especially the way it ran at me.[22]

Harrison supported his tale with photos of his nude, bruised body, posted on the Internet, and while his injuries seem genuine enough, the Yowie element—contested by a member of his team—remains unsettled.[23]

There ends our chronicle of Yowie violence, at least for now, and nothing from the rest of Oceania can rival it. Still, there are stories to be told, and I present them in a bid to leave no stone unturned.

New Zealand

Like Australia's aborigines, Maori natives of New Zealand preserve tales of giants abroad in the land. One, the huge kidnapper called *Matau*, surrounds itself with magic trappings and may be entirely mythical. The other—commonly known as *Maeroero* ("wild man"), but also known as *Maero* on the North Island, or *Ngatimamaero* on the South Island—may be a more substantial creature.[24]

Tribal tales of the *Maeroero* claim that hairy wildmen not only eat birds, but also snatch humans and stab them to death with the long claws. No specific attacks are detailed, but discoveries of Bigfoot-type humanoid footprints were logged from the South Island's Fiordland National Park in 1974 (near Dusky Sound), and again in 1993 (near Lake Manapouri).[25]

Melanesia

The first alleged apelike predator reported from this sprawling realm of islands is known in myth as the *Abere*, a "wild woman"—or tribe of wild women—said to inhabit marshes and devour human beings who fall within the creatures' grasp. The published tales refer to no specific island, nor are any modern-day attacks alleged.[26]

Papua New Guinea is a land of mystery and danger, even though authorities insist that "open cannibalism" had "almost entirely ceased" by the 1950s. Police turned out to hunt a living dinosaur on East New Britain in March 2004, and while that beast eluded pursuers, members of Conservation International discovered a mountainous "lost world" in September 2009, cataloguing more than fifty new species. Many more doubtless remain undiscovered.[27]

But are there any hostile hominids at large? The closest thing to evidence among the island's tribesmen is an antiquated legend of an ogre known as *Kewanambo*, said to feed on children. No reports of modern sightings are available, and we are safe, it seems, in relegating the monster to mythology.[28]

Which brings us to the Solomons, an archipelago lying east of New Guinea, consisting of nearly one thousand islands with a total land mass of 10,965 square miles. The nation's capital, Honiara, is found on Guadalcanal, scene of protracted bloody combat during World War II. Guadalcanal also claims one-fifth of the archipelago's estimated 523,000 inhabitants, significantly reducing the average population density of forty-seven persons per square mile.[29]

Guadalcanal and neighbouring Makira (formerly San Cristobal) also are said to harbour a malicious race of "little people," the *Kakamora* or *Mumulou*, described as foul-smelling man-eaters. Explorer Charles Elliot Fox claimed a near-miss with the creatures, in the early 1920s, when he found small humanoid footprints surrounding half-eaten raw fish on a Makira riverbank. A quarter-century later, writing for *Pacific Islands Monthly,* author A.H. Wilson dismissed the *Kakamora* as "just another tall tale."[30] Whether they were mythical creatures, or they fell prey to the war of 1941-45, no trace of them remains today.

Thus ends our tour of Oceania, with anecdotes suggesting possible aggression against humans by some unknown hominid, still unsupported by hard evidence. If the vast Pacific hides a modern King Kong with a taste for native maidens, we have yet to find the island where he dwells.

Chapter 9.
Kidnapped!

T hroughout recorded history, from every settled continent, tales have emerged of apes or apelike monsters snatching human beings. Details vary, but in cases where the victims are not instantly devoured, sexual motives are frequently suggested. French sculptor Emmanuel Frémiet scandalised Paris in 1859, with his piece titled *Gorilla Carrying Off a Woman.* Four decades later, ape-hunter Robert von Beringe wrote of "ape monsters that abducted the native women and, in passionate lust, crushed them to death." His first gorilla trophy convinced many Europeans that the stories were true.[1]

Closer study did little to dispel such florid myths, at least in the popular mind. Various Tarzan films and others, such as *Bride of the Gorilla* (1951), reinforced the stereotype of libidinous primates at large. Cold War-era "men's adventure" magazines such as *Man's Life, Rage for Men,* and *True Men Stories* cheerfully climbed aboard the ape-rape bandwagon during 1956-58, then shifted to stories of sex-crazed Yetis, cavemen, and "Hairy Ainu" during 1959-61. Lurid cover art depicted almost-human bipeds stripping damsels in distress and bludgeoning their brave-but-hapless male escorts in various exotic settings. Although billed as "true reports," they were entirely fictional.[2] Modern supermarket tabloids have no better proof for their front-page stories of "Bigfoot love slaves."

That said, the extant literature on unknown hominids offers a range of cases spanning two centuries, in which dates and various other details are offered to support claims that Bigfoot, Yeti, and similar creatures habitually kidnap men, women, and children. They deserve examination here, as we complete our survey of alleged hominid aggression.

The Nineteenth Century

Reverend Elkanah Walker, a Protestant missionary to the Pacific Northwest's Spokane Indians, penned an early account of Sasquatch-type creatures in April 1840. He wrote that the Spokane "believe in the existence of a race of giants which inhabit a certain mountain, off to the west of us....They hunt and do all their work in the night. They are men stealers. They come to people's lodges in the night, when the people are asleep and take them and put them under their skins and take them to their place of abode without their even awakening....They say their track is about a foot and a half long....They frequently come in the night and steal their salmon from their nets and eat them raw. If the people are awake they always know when they are coming very near by the smell which is most intolerable."[3]

Sixteen years later, Smithsonian Institution spokesman George Gibbs wrote of a Bigfoot-type beast called *Tsiatko* or *Skoo-kum* among the Nisqually people of Washington State. It was described as being "of gigantic size, their feet eighteen inches long and shaped like a bear's. They wear no clothes, but the body is covered with hair like that of a dog, only not so thick...they are said to live in the mountains, in holes underground, and to smell badly. They come down chiefly in the fishing season, at which time the Indians are excessively afraid of them....They are visible only at night, at which time they approach the houses, steal salmon, carry off young girls and smother children. Their voices are like that of an owl, and they possess the power of charming, so that those hearing them become demented, or fall down in a swoon."[4]

Such fear was justified, Gibbs said, by abductions of tribal women. According to Gibbs, "One Indian woman who lived at Fort Vancouver on the Columbia River told of having been captured by a group of Tsiatkos and taken into the woods. She lived to tell the tale of her adventure." Another tribesman "reported having shot at and wounding a Tsiatko while the beast was carrying off a young girl. Ke-kai-simi-loot, daughter of To-wus-tan, a former chief, and a Nisqually woman, claimed she was descended from four generations of what she called 'skookums.'"[5]

We owe our next tale to author Sidney Warren, who brought it to public attention in 1949. According to Warren, an unspecified issue of the *Oregon Statesman* carried a front-page account of a Bigfoot abduction sometime during 1857. Warren himself brands the tale a fabrication, but it bears repeating here for its avid reception in certain "Bigfooter" circles. According to the article, a man and his son were camped in Marion County, Oregon, when a plaintive cry woke the youth at midnight. Thereupon—

> He observed an object approaching him that appeared like a man about twelve or fifteen feet high ...with glaring eyes which had the appearance of equal balls of fire. The monster drew near to the boy who was unable from fright, to move a single step, and seizing him by the arm, dragged him forcibly away towards the mountains, over logs, underbrush, swamps, rivers and land with a velocity that seemed to our hero like flying.

> They had travelled in this manner perhaps an hour, when the monster sunk upon the earth apparently exhausted. Our hero then became aware that this creature was indeed a wild man, whose body was completely covered with shaggy brown hair, about four inches in length; some of his teeth protruded from his mouth like tuskes [sic], his hands were armed with formidable claws instead of fingers, but his feet, singular to relate, appeared natural, being clothed with moccasins similar to those worn by Indians.

Emmanuel Frémiet's 1859 sculpture, *Gorilla Carrying Off a Woman*.

Our hero had scarcely made these observations when the "wild man" suddenly started onward as before, never for a moment relaxing his grip on the boy's arm....They had not proceeded far before they entered an almost impenetrable thicket of logs and undergrowth, when the "wild man" stopped, reclined upon a log, and gave one shriek, terrific and prolonged, the reverberations of which seemed to continue for the space of five minutes; immediately after which the earth opened at their feet, as if a trap door, ingeniously contrived, had just been raised.

Entering at once this subterranean abode by a ladder rudely constructed of hazel brush, they proceeded downward, perhaps 150 or 200 feet, when they reached the bottom of a vast cave, which was brilliantly illumined with a peculiar phosphorescent light, and water trickled from the sides of the cave in minute jets. Above, the cave seemed slightly arched, the ceiling apparently composed of sea shells. The bottom was thickly strewn with the bones of many kinds of animals.

As our hero thus closely observed the interior of this awful cave, the "wild man" left him. Presently the huge monster returned by a side door, leading gently by the hand a young and delicate female of almost miraculous grace and beauty, who had doubtless been immured in this dreadful dungeon for years. The young lady fell upon her knees, and in some unknown language seemed to plead for the privilege of remaining forever in the cave.

This singular conduct caused our hero to imagine that the "wild man" conscience stricken, had resolved to set at liberty his lovely victim, by placing her in charge of our hero, whom he had evidently captured for that purpose. As this thought passed through his mind his ears were greeted with the strains of the most unearthly music.

The "wild man" wept piteously; and sobbing like a child, his handkerchief moist with grief, he raised her very carefully from her recumbent posture, and led her gently away as they had come.

A moment afterwards, the damsel returned alone, and advanced toward our hero with lady-like modesty and grace, placed in his hands a beautifully embossed card, upon which appeared the following words, traced in the most exquisite hand evidently the lady's own, "Boy, depart hence, forthwith, or remain and be devoured."

Our hero looked up, but the lady had vanished. He acted at once upon the hint and commenced retracing his steps towards the "ladder of hazel brush" which he shortly reached and commenced the ascent. Upon arriving at the top, his horror may be imagined when he found the aperture closed! The cold sweat stood on his brow, his frame quivered with mental

Hollywood takes up the theme.

ASHER SMALL ROGERS
THE GORILLA
with
Charlie Murray
An ALFRED SANTELL PRODUCTION
ALFRED SANTELL
A FIRST NATIONAL PICTURE

agony, when he bethought himself of a small barlow knife with which he instantly commenced picking the earth.

After labouring in this manner, he was rejoiced to see daylight through the earth, and he was not much longer in working a hole large enough through which he was enabled to crawl.[6]

In 1871 a Sasquatch supposedly kidnapped an unidentified Amerindian teenager in British Columbia, forced her to swim across the Harrison River, then carried her to a rock shelter which the abductor shared with its parents. The girl remained in captivity for a year, then was released because she "aggravated it so much." Later, she told Indian agent J.W. Burns that the beasts had treated her kindly.[7]

In 1992, anthropologist Ed Fusch of Riverside, Washington, published a paper on "the interaction of large bipedal hominids with American Indians" on Washington's Colville and Spokane reservations, where the beasts were known by various names, including *Choanito, S'cwene'y'ti*, and "stick Indians." The report includes three incidents of kidnapping by beasts that "like the smell of virgins," described as follows:

- Date unknown: An unnamed girl was snatched and held captive until her return as an adult. Fusch writes that "[w]hen returned she was found asleep along the banks of a stream and upon being awakened could not remember where she had been during the long period of time that she had been missing."[8]

- Date unknown: After another teenaged virgin vanished, tribesmen mounted the usual fruitless search. Two or three years later, the girl reappeared, wearing unfamiliar clothes, and "smelled so strongly of S'cwene'y'ti that the people could hardly get near her." Scorned by tribal bachelors, she lived outdoors, and displayed symptoms of mental illness. According to Fusch, she "appeared to be more animal than human. She was not viscous [*sic*], was able to give some account of where she had been, and had not been molested."[9]

- "Turn of the century": Victim "Laura" was abducted from a fishing camp near Keller, on the Sanpoil River, and impregnated during her captivity by a hominid she called *Skanicum*. She bore a son called Patrick, described as simian and "very ugly" in appearance, although gentle and "extremely intelligent." Before his death at age thirty, Patrick married and fathered five children. Two sons and one daughter died young, while two daughters lived into their sixties. Fusch says that Laura died in 1987, at age eighty-five, clearly negating his estimate that she was kidnapped sometime between 1885 and 1900.[10]

Author Warren Smith published the next report in 1970, without providing a specific date for its supposed occurrence. He says that seventeen-year-old "Indian maiden" Seraphine Long was camped near Harrison Lake, in British Columbia, when a Sasquatch carried her off to the mountains. An unnamed "elderly resident of the area" takes up the narrative, telling Smith that

OPPOSITE: Another cinematic take lust-crazed primates.

THE
"GORILLA
WOMAN"
GIANT MONSTERS
ENTHRONED AS LOVE GODS!
STARTLING IN IT'S
WEIRD ACTION!

Simian seduction, coming to a theatre near you...

"[s]he was kidnapped to be the ape-man's bride. I understand that she was treated very well She was not harmed physically in any way." Unless, of course, we count her pregnancy. Becoming homesick, she somehow persuaded her captor to release her. The Sasquatch, teary-eyed, led Seraphine back to her village and left her there, where their half-human child was stillborn. Long subsequently died at age eighty-three, in the early 1940s, placing her supposed abduction sometime in the latter 1880s.[11]

Modern Claims
The first known 20th Century case of hominid abduction supposedly occurred in Nepal around 1910, belatedly aired in 1968 by the surviving victim, a then-elderly Buddhist nun named Noma Dima. The daughter of a Sherpa family, living at Khumbu Himal near Mount Everest Dima claimed she was abducted by a "ghastly" hominid at age seventeen, subsisting on a diet of fruit and small frogs over the next year, until she became pregnant. Three months into her confinement, Dima's rapist left the cave they shared, returning with "an aged she-yeti" who examined Dima's body. The male yeti then led her back to her village, where Dima gave birth

to a half-human boy with "the face of a monkey." Her "husband" visited from time to time, bringing gifts of fruit, until a mob pursued him and drove him over a cliff. Though badly injured, the Yeti returned two weeks later to slaughter its son. Dima subsequently found shelter in a local monastery.[12]

Our next case, posted online by John Lewis of San Francisco, California, offers more vague dates, falling somewhere between 1916 and 1921. Lewis's grandfather was employed by the Southern Pacific Railroad, maintaining tracks along the Oregon-California border, when another crew member disappeared. After a brief search of the woods, the team moved on. "Some

In Happier Times

...and played for laughs on greeting cards.

weeks later," Lewis says, they found the missing man: "[H]e was naked and hysterical/crazed, and apparently died soon after he was found. He told of being abducted by a female ape that kept him in a large open pit. During the time he was in the pit the man told of being forced to have sexual contact with the ape many times and said that the ape kept him in the hole or pit by licking his hands and feet raw, so that he was not able to escape from the pit. Apparently my grandfather saw this man's hands and feet and said that they were completely raw."[13]

George Eberhart offers a similar tale from the same time frame, occurring halfway around the world. That story reads, in its entirety: "In 1917, a female Yeti captured a boy from Keronja village, near Dhālding, Nepal. According to a story told sixty years later, their descendants are said to still live there."[14]

The best-known tale of alleged Sasquatch abduction involves Albert Ostman, supposedly kidnapped while logging near Toba Inlet, British Columbia, during summer 1924. Despite the remarkable nature of his supposed adventure, Ostman kept it secret until 1957, when he shared the details with Canadian researcher John Green.[15]

Ostman's story has been widely published, by Green and others. To summarise it briefly, he was snatched from camp one night, inside his sleeping bag, and carried to "a small valley or basin," where he found himself held captive by a Sasquatch family consisting of an "old man, old lady and two young ones, a boy and a girl. The boy and the girl seem to be scared of me. The old lady did not seem too pleased about what the old man dragged home. But the old man was waving his arms and telling them all what he had in mind." Ostman deduced that he had been kidnapped as a potential mate for the "girl," but he remained unmolested for several days, until he fed the "old man" a can of snuff that sickened him, then frightened the "old lady" with a gunshot and escaped on foot.[16]

Green accepted the story as true, noting that Ostman survived interrogation by "a magistrate, a zoologist, a physical anthropologist, and a veterinarian" without contradicting himself or making any plainly false statements. Half a century later, Loren Coleman opined that Ostman's story "stands the litmus test of time."[17] Skeptics, as expected, disagree.

Four years after Ostman's strange adventure, a similar fate allegedly befell Nootka tribesman Muchalat Harry on Vancouver Island, B.C. Like Ostman, Harry was fast asleep when a Sasquatch grabbed him, blanket and all, from a camp on the Conuma River. Deposited under a rock shelf, he found himself surrounded by twenty-odd hominids—and an ominous pile of bones.

Harry feared that the creatures meant to devour him, but they lost interest in their prize by the next afternoon, permitting him to flee unnoticed from the tribe. A priest, Father Anthony Terhaar of Oregon's Mt. Angel Abbey, later told the story to Bigfoot-hunter Peter Byrne, who searched the area in 1972 and predictably found no trace of Harry's camp from forty-four years earlier.[18]

OPPOSITE: Bigfoot battles bikers...and "breeds with anything."

The greatest
monster since
"KING KONG"

COLOR

"BIG FOOT"

breeds with anything...

CHRIS MITCHUM · JOHN CARRADINE · JOI LANSING · LINDSAY CROSBY

Bigfoot's baby-bump exposed.

Pseudonymous author "Eric Norman" presents the next alleged case of abduction, occurring sometime during World War II, subsequently recorded by Soviet researchers tracking Yeti reports in Tibet. According to Norman, Chinese merchant Ling Chee fled Japanese invaders during their occupation of his homeland, transporting his family to Tibet. Alas, they had barely arrived when Ling's wife disappeared without a trace. She returned, Norman says, a year later, "gaunt-faced and smelling like an animal."

She was also expecting a child, sired by the Yeti that abducted her. Enraged, Ling beat his wife to death, faced trial for murder, and received a light sentence after pleading temporary insanity. An untraceable "Dr. Samuel Morton (not his real name)" assured Norman that "there are hundreds of stories such as this in every part of Asia"—presumably too many to report.[19]

A marginal case from May 1956 comes to us courtesy of author John Keel. He reports that three young men were hunting near Marshall, Michigan, when a Sasquatch grabbed two of them—Otto Collins and Philip Williams—clutching one under each arm. Philip's brother Henry grabbed a gun, whereupon the beast dropped its captives and "ambled off" into the forest, leaving them with an impression of green eyes "as big as light bulbs."[20]

Another foiled abduction reportedly occurred one year later, in May 1957, near Zhejiang, China. Villager Xu Fudi sent her daughter to tend the family's cattle, then heard her screaming and ran to investigate. She found the girl struggling in a Yeti's arms and grabbed a handy club, bludgeoning the would-be kidnapper to death with help from several other women. Rather than report the incident, they cut up the carcass and hid it, reporting "eerie cries of mourning" from the nearby hills, next day.[21]

Before its disappearance from the Internet, Ray Crowe's International Bigfoot Society website reported several cases of Sasquatch abduction. One from 1959 involves a victim known only as "Carol," who experienced the traumatic event near Estacada, Oregon. Carol was relieving herself in the woods when a small-breasted female Sasquatch grabbed her and carried her up a mountainside, then dropped her on the ground, inflicting several bruises. Despite that rough introduction, Carol—who professed herself "able to commune with animals by picking up their vibrations"—spent time "talking" to her simian captor, a self-described spokeswoman for "The Ancient People." They found common ground in love of peaches, which Carol left at the site from time to time, following her release.[22]

Three years later, once again near Estacada, photographer Ellen English was snapping woodland pictures, but took a break for naptime with her two-year-old daughter. Like Albert Ostman and Muchalat Harry before her, English was literally snatched from sleep by "something large, hairy, and very smelly, like someone who never took a bath." Her poodle saved the day, yapping until the Sasquatch dropped her and fled through the trees.[23]

A four-year-old child was the supposed victim in July 1968, grabbed from his own backyard in Kinloch, a suburb of St. Louis, Missouri. The child's aunt screamed, while the family dog rushed to attack the hairy biped. Bigfoot dropped its victim and escaped, leaving no tracks or other evidence for police who were summoned to investigate.[24]

A third-hand account, devoid of any supporting evidence, dates from 1971, reported to the IBS by one Don Peterson, who in turn heard it from "witness" Mike Machheid. Interviewed at a tavern in Toledo, Washington, Macheid described an unnamed girl being "drug off, scratched and released" by a Sasquatch at Brinson Hollow, near Vader, Washington. No other details are available.[25]

Another bungled child-abduction was reported from Flintville, Tennessee, on 26 April 1976. Jennie Robertson claimed that a foul-smelling bipedal creature seven to eight feet tall invaded her yard that afternoon and "came within a few inches" of grabbing her four-year-old son before she saved the child and rushed back to her house. "Swarms" of police and armed civilians scoured the surrounding woods, "resolved to track down and kill the creature," but failed to locate it, despite being screamed at and pelted with stones "on at least two occasions." Oddly, the incident went unreported for twenty-one years.[26]

While mountaineering in Bhutan, during 1991, adventurer Reinhold Messner heard a tale dating "a few years back." Residents of Laya blamed a Yeti for the disappearance of a local woman, whereupon King Jigme Singye Wangchuck ordered a full-scale search by "gamekeepers, shepherds, and soldiers." No traces were found, but the woman returned to her village months later, presumably unharmed.[27]

Peter Byrne supplies our next highly speculative case, reporting that an unnamed hiker vanished from Cathedral Ridge, near Mount Hood, Oregon, on 25 September 1995. A search was mounted, then abandoned on 3 October, while Byrne reports a Bigfoot sighting in the same area on 24 October. Any link between the events—assuming they ever occurred—is pure supposition.[28]

Beyond Belief?

Five other cases still remain, in each case lacking dates or other details necessary for corroboration. Two were furnished by a hoaxer who could scarcely be believed if asked the time of day, but all are offered here for what—if anything—they may be worth.

In 1990, Oregon State University published a volume of *Nehalem Tillamook Tales*, told by full-blood tribeswoman Clara Pearson (1861-1948) and edited by Melville Jacobs. One story relates the abduction of an Indian woman by a "wild man" who cooked her on a spit and devoured part of her corpse, before her husband arrived and killed him with arrows. Since the monster carried a club and wore a quiver made of animal hide, we may rightly question both the story and the "wild man's" Sasquatchian identity.[29]

David Childress, writing in 2010, relates the story of a Yeti abduction occurring "many years ago" at Hushe, among the Karakoram Mountains in the Ghanche District of northern Pakistan. The victim was a girl, recovered by her brothers after six or seven years, at which time she "had two yeti babies and didn't want to go back to the village." Her brothers compelled her, dropping both infants into a river along the way, while their sister wept hysterically. Her yeti lover returned to the village days later, whereupon Hushe's residents shot and killed it. The woman reportedly died soon thereafter.[30]

And gay Sasquatch gets equal time.

04?6-04?0-? • $1.?5 • A BERKLEY MEDALLION BOOK

AN EXPLOSIVE ORDEAL OF
RAPE AND REVENGE BEYOND
ANY WOMAN'S EXPERIENCE

NIGHTS WITH SASQUATCH

JOHN COTTER & JUDITH FRANKLE

In 1997, Bangkok's White Lotus Press published a 165-page volume titled *Bhutanese Tales of the Yeti*, compiled by author Kunzang Choden in a bid "to document a vital tradition before it is wiped out entirely." Whether the tales are advanced as nonfiction is open to question, but several describe native women abducted by Yetis to serve as their mates.[31]

Our last two cases come from inveterate hoaxer Ray Wallace, and risk dismissal as fiction on those grounds alone. One cites statements made in February 1954 by "Chief Stokes" and a California Indian named Tuffy Dowd, alleging that hairy apelike creatures "carry many girls away at night-time that we never see again." Those abductions supposedly happened along Blue Creek, but since California boasts six Blue Creeks in five counties, no corroboration is possible.[32]

Wallace's other tale again quotes "Chief Stokes," this time describing the abduction of a full grown Indian woman in Klamath County, Oregon. The victim later returned with a child "covered with fine soft fur all over his whole body," but schoolmates teased him so unmercifully that the boy, aged ten, returned to "our home in the woods with my dad."[33]

Lights, Camera, Fiction!

On 22 May 1976, sheriff's officers in Humboldt County, California, received a complaint that Bigfoot had kidnapped a female member of a five-person expedition organised to film Sasquatch in the flesh. Team leader Ed Bush and his teenage daughter, Kathleen, claimed they were walking with the victim along a creek bed when "a large furry animal" knocked Kathleen to the ground and seized their twenty-three-year-old companion, variously known as Cherie Darvell and Cherie Nelson. Darvell-Nelson's family in Redding, California, professed ignorance of her whereabouts, one cousin describing the circumstances of Cherie's disappearance as "pretty weird."[34]

It was all that, and then some. More than 150 rescue workers scoured the landscape in search of the missing woman, until she surfaced at a resort near Eureka, on 24 May. Humboldt County's sheriff told reporters, "She's not in too bad a shape," adding his personal suspicion that the incident might be a hoax. Such proved to be the case, in fact, after Ed Bush and cohort Terry Gaston screened an amateurish film pretending to depict Cherie's abduction by a lumbering figure in an ill-fitting ape suit. A welter of lawsuits resulted, with Miss Darvell ultimately forced to pay a share of the $11,613 search costs, while Humboldt County bore the rest of the burden. Humboldt's effort to recoup expenses from neighbouring Shasta County failed when Judge Frank Peterson dismissed Bigfoot-hunting as "an exercise in futility."[35]

Cheeky Monkeys

Most tales of Sasquatch-Yeti kidnappings expressly state—or, at the very least, strongly imply—a sexual motivation. If Bigfoot and its shaggy kin exist, what is the likelihood that unknown hominids might seek to mate with human beings?

At least among orang-utans, there seems to be strong evidence of sexual aggression against

---

OPPOSITE: Bigfoot porn, billed as "nonfiction."

human females. Dutch primatologist Herman Rijksen, specialising in orangs, writes that "Th red ape behaves like the classic satyr. On first encounter with a female (human or orang), a attempt at rape is a fully normal way of advertisement for an orang-utan male wanting to es tablish a relationship....Recurrent stories in the Indonesian newspapers of women who claim t have been abducted by orang-utan males seem to corroborate the legends....Mawas (orang males have reliably been reported to go after women to try to wrestle them down for intromis sion."[36]

One firsthand account of such an attack comes from German primatologist Birutė Marija File mena Galdikas, in her book *Reflections of Eden: My Years with the Orangutans of Borne* (1995). Galdikas relates the tale of a female research assistant who was, in fact, raped by male orang who physically overpowered her in the jungle.[37]

More recently, in September 2007, a French tourist at Borneo's Semenggoh Wildlife Centr lost her clothing to a male orang that "got bored of being photographed and tried to take th tourist's bag." The victim told reporters, "He took my shoes and socks off, and then tried t take off my trousers. As he couldn't manage it with his hands only, he tried with his teeth, an that's when I got bitten. As soon as he got my trousers he went away."[38] Had she been alon the story might have had a rather different ending.

Six months later, in March 2008, a videotape was posted to YouTube from somewhere in Ai rica, depicting a relatively small baboon in the act of ripping off a woman's blouse. Althoug the clip is brief, the incident appears to be unprovoked.[39]

On a lighter note, we have the scene from *Tarzan, the Ape Man* (1981), in which an amorou chimpanzee gets carried away with a nude Bo Derek. The sequence of the ape mouthing he nipple somehow passed muster with the normally strait-laced Motion Picture Association c America and remained in the final print.[40]

Assuming that Bigfoot/Yeti-type creatures exist, it plausible that that male specimens migh sometimes be attracted to human females. With no case on record of a female ape or monke displaying sexual aggression toward male humans, the opposite case—à la Albert Ostman an John Lewis's anonymous railroad worker—seems far-fetched. But even if our hypothetica unknown hominids have abducted women on occasion, could procreation result?

Species are broadly defined as groups of organisms capable of interbreeding and producin fertile offspring. Members of different species may interbreed in artificially confined situa tions, such as zoos and laboratories, producing offspring like the hybrid big cats dubbed liger tigons, pumapards, jaglions, etc. In such cases the hybrid males are normally infertile, bu some of the female offspring are fertile.[41]

Hybrid primates are sometimes produced in the exotic pet trade, including combinations o various macaques, "rheboons" (a rhesus macaque/hamadryas baboon hybrid), and sterile hy brids spawned by mating Bornean and Sumatran orang-utans. As seen in Chapter 5, Russia attempts to cross-breed chimpanzees and human beings failed across the board. A suppose humanzee" known as Oliver, caught in Zaire during 1960 and famed for its habitual bipedal style of locomotion (until stricken with arthritis), supposedly tried to mate with owner Janet Berger on several occasions, prompting her to sell Oliver in the 1970s. DNA testing performed in 1996 tagged Oliver as a common chimpanzee, although he possessed forty-eight chromosomes, rather than the forty-seven found in other chimps.[42]

Finally, we have the tale of "Zana," a supposed female Yeti or *abnauayu* allegedly captured by peasants in the Caucasus Mountains, somewhere in Abkhazia, during the 1880s or 1890s. Following a brief course of domestication, Zana supposedly welcomed—or was coerced into accepting—the sexual attentions of various male villagers. In due time, we are told, she bore two sons (Dzhanda and Khwit) and two daughters (Kodzhanar and Gamasa). Each in turn had children of their own, with Khwit surviving until 1954.[43]

Various Soviet scientists explored the tale of Zana, discovering some "probable" bones from Gamasa in 1965, which presented "slight, but definite paleoanthropic features." Igor Bourtsev ultimately found a skull supposed to be Khwit's, submitting it for study by anthropologists M.A. Kolodieva and M.M.Gerasimova, whose results were published in 1987.[44]

According to Dr. Kolodieva,

> The Tkhina skull exhibits an original combination of modem and ancient features ... The facial section of the skull is significantly larger in comparison with the mean Abkhaz type....All the measurements and indices of the superciliary cranial contour are greater not only than those of the mean Abkhaz series, but also than those of maximum size of some fossil skulls studied (or rather were comparable with the latter). The Tkhina skull approaches closest the Neolithic Vovnigi II skulls of the fossil series.[45]

Dr. Gerasimova, meanwhile, reported that "The skull discloses a great deal of peculiarity, a certain disharmony disequilibrium in its features, very large dimensions of the facial skeleton, increased development of the contour of the skull, specificity of the non-metric features (the two foramina mentale in the lower jaw, the intrusive bones in the sagittal suture, and the Inca bone). The skull merits further extended study."[46]

Still, obvious questions remained. In 2006, while refusing to release the actual relics, Bourtsev sent computed tomography (CT) scans of two skulls—Khwit's and one he thought "might be" Zana's—to New York University's Centre for the Study of Human Origins. Also included were hair samples and teeth extracted from both skulls. While Zana's supposed skull differed greatly from Khwit's, with a jutting lower jaw, large orbits and a wide nose, the CT scans revealed that both skulls had internal cranial contours within the modern human range of variation. Zana, in other words, was no Neanderthal throwback. DNA extracted from the teeth belonged to modern humans, and a match proved that the two skull donors were related.[47]
Speculation persists on the possibility of Neanderthals cross-breeding with *Homo sapiens,* but the question remains unanswered.[48] Pending resolution of that enigma, *and* discovery of still-elusive evidence that giant Bigfoot-Yeti creatures are in fact Neanderthals capable of such

pairing, we leave this case with a hung jury. Unknown hominids *might* be moved to snatc humans on occasion, for sexual reasons, but nothing suggests that any such incident has prc duced "Yeti babies."

NXP177359/XBP052501-5/26/76-EUREKA, CALIF.: Police officials 5/26 are trying to determine if charges should be brought against Sherie Darvell (L, '71 photo), 23, alleged kidnap victim of "Big Foot," the legendary ape-man of the Pacific Northwest. A party of Big Foot fans, who were making a film about the hairy monster, reported Miss Darvell was carried off by the creature 5/22. A massive search was launched and she turned up 5/24 not far from where she was reported missing. Humboldt County Sheriff Gene Cox said Miss Darvell smelled too pretty when she returned and the abduction has been labeled a hoax. The alleged "Big Foot" is shown (R) in photo made somewhere northeast of Spokane, Wash., in a 1973 photo.
(BIGFOOT)   UPI -hmr-

Media coverage of a 1976 kidnapping hoax.

Conclusion:
Summing Up

The question of potential danger from a meeting with Bigfoot, Yeti or Yowie matters only if such creatures truly exist. Today, professional nay-sayers notwithstanding, we may say that substantial evidence has been gathered to support the ongoing existence of large unknown hominids on several continents. As detailed by Jeffrey Meldrum, Gordon Krantz and many other researchers, that evidence includes:

- Eyewitness sightings in the tens of thousands, spanning centuries. Despite some notorious hoaxes and tales that strain credulity beyond the breaking point, many encounters have been logged by witnesses of substantial experience (veteran hunters, naturalists, outdoorsmen) and individuals in positions of responsibility (law enforcement officers at all levels, forestry officials, active-duty military personnel) who report such encounters at risk to their credibility and careers.

- Striking similarities between the actions of unknown hominids reported worldwide and the conduct of recognised primate species, including acts of mimicry, vocalisation, nest-building, drumming on trees, selection of foods, and throwing of various objects.

- Thousands of unexplained and unidentified footprints. Again, in spite of well-publicised frauds, many track casts reveal physical details—dermal ridges, scars, deformities—beyond the scope of any common prankster's scientific knowledge, expertise, or budget for special-effects. Faking so many tracks worldwide, spanning centuries, demands acceptance of a vast—and frankly ludicrous—conspiracy.

- Audio recordings of vocalisations by unidentified animals, analysis of which suggests the source to be a primate substantially larger than *Homo sapiens* or any known great ape.

- Hair and faecal samples collected from North America and Asia, which have produced DNA analyses indicating donors from an unknown primate species.

- Photographic evidence, perhaps the most suspect in light of modern technology, but still producing several examples that have not been persuasively debunked.

If we conclude that Bigfoot-Yeti-Yowie creatures do exist in fact, we must acknowledge them for what they are: large wild animals beyond our present scientific knowledge. Any creature of substantial size may pose a threat to humans—the Centres for Disease Control reports an average of twenty persons killed by cows each year in the United States[1]—and that risk is increased if the animals are carnivorous.

Many eyewitness accounts describe Bigfoot-Yeti creatures as omnivores, consuming both vegetable matter and meat from a wide variety of sources: fish, small rodents, deer, domestic fowl and livestock, dogs—and human beings. As seen in the preceding chapters, no specific case of man-eating can be substantiated, but humans *have been* killed and devoured by various other large mammals in the wild, including bears, big cats, and known primates. It is no great stretch of the imagination, therefore, to suppose that someone has been killed by a Sasquatch or Yeti, somewhere, at some time. We simply cannot prove it, and until such time as solid evidence presents itself, we must acquit the suspects *in absentia.*

Does this mean that a hiker fortunate enough to sight an unknown hominid should rush to greet it, much less try to capture it? Of course not. Adult specimens are often described as rivalling or exceeding adult bears in size. Only a suicidal fool would try to restrain such a creature. The end result, we must suspect, would be a swift and lonely death. That said, bears have slain only ninety-three persons in all of North America since 1908.[2] Domestic dogs, by contrast, killed 156 Americans between 1994 and 2003.[3] On balance, we may be safer with our possible distant cousins in some trackless forest, than with man's best friend in our own backyard.

Notes

Introduction

.	Carthaginian Exploration: The Voyages of Hanno and Himlico, http://www.barca.fsnet.co.uk/hanno-voyage.htm.
.	Quoted in Thomas Huxley, Man's Place in Nature (London: Modern Library, 2001).
.	Quoted in Heuvelmans, p 26.
.	Ibid.
.	Gorillas Online, http://staff.washington.edu/timk/gorillas/.
.	Quoted in James Clarke, Man is the Prey (New York: Stein and Day, 1969), pp. 163-4.
.	Roger Caras, Dangerous to Man (New York: Holt, Rinehart and Winston, 1975), p. 94.
.	Clarke, p. 165.
.	Jordi Sabater Pi, "Gorilla Attacks against Humans in Rio Muni, West Africa," Journal of Mammalogy 47 (February 1966): 123-4.
0.	"Gorilla at Dallas Zoo raids kitchen, injures keeper." CNN News (28 November 1998).
1.	Brian MacQuarrie and Douglas Belkin. "Franklin Park gorilla escapes, attacks 2." Boston Globe (29 September 2003).
2.	David Flick, "Gorilla's escape still a mystery." Dallas Morning News (19 March 2004); Katie Menzer, "Charging gorilla killed by police after hurting 4." Dallas Morning News (19 March 2004); Lisa Falkenberg, "Zoo officials say gorilla escaped enclosure by leaping over trench, wall." Associated Press (15 June 2004).
3.	Robert Kittle, "Gorilla Escapes at Riverbanks Zoo, Attacks Worker," WJBF-TV, Channel 6 (Augusta, GA), 16 June 2009.
4.	Caras, p. 92.
5.	Clarke, p. 167.
6.	Ibid.
7.	"Extreme measures take." Sky News (6 January 2004), http://www.sky.com/skynews/article/0,,30000-12967943,00.html.
8.	Rich Shapiro, "The Worst Story I Ever Heard," Esquire (17 February 2009), http://www.esquire.com/features/chimpanzee-attack-0409.

19. Stephanie Gallman, "Chimp attack 911 call: 'He's ripping her apart,'" CNN, 17 February 2009; Stephanie Gallman, "Victim of chimp attack in 'critical but stable' condition," CNN, 18 February 2009.
20. Caras, p. 91.
21. Clarke, p. 170.
22. Ibid., p. 169.
23. Ibid., p. 168.
24. Ibid., p. 169.
25. "Aggressive baboons eliminated." (26 September 1999) Ultimate Africa Safaris, http://www.ultimateafrica.com/sept99.htm.
26. Marlise Scheepers and Jo Prins, "Baboon attacks 'not isolated.'" (20 November 2002) News24.com, http://www.news24.com/News24/South_Africa/News/0,,2-7-1442_1287190,00.html.
27. Bhekie Matsebula, "Swazi baboons attack toddlers," *The Star* (Johannesburg), 12 June 2001.
28. "Baboons 'on the rampage' in Saudi Arabia." *Ananova* (14 August 2001).
29. Scheepers and Prins, "Baboon attacks 'not isolated.'"
30. "Baboons go bad." *Fortean Times* 174 (October 2003), p. 16.
31. Ibid.
32. Brian Hayward, "Brutal baboon attacks raise concern," *Cape Argus* (Cape Town), 12 February 2006.
33. Mariam Al Hakeem, "Saudi town under attack by baboons," Gulf News, http://www.gulfnews.com/news/gulf/saudi_arabia/10203592.html.
34. Caras, pp. 91-2.
35. "Monkey attack puts man in hospital." *Mainichi Shimbun* (15 July 2000).
36. "Rogue monkey attacks 23 women." *Ananova* (12 March 2002).
37. "Escaped monkey attacks two in Japan." *Ananova* (31 March 2002).
38. "Monkeys destroy library, stall classes in girls' college." Indo-Asian News Service (2 April 2003).
39. "Berserk monkey attacks 3 women in Quepem." Goa (India) *Herald* (2 July 2003).
40. "Monkeys go ape." *News 24,* South Africa (19 August 2004).
41. "Orang utan attacks sisters at centre," *The Star* (Bayan Lepas, Penang, Malaysia), 3 June 2005.

Chapter 1

1. Russell Annabel, "Long hunter—Alaskan style." *Sports Afield* 150 (July 1963) 34-6, 102-8; Scott DeLancey, "Alaskan ABSM's?" *INFO Journal* 44 (May 1984): 16-17; Grant Keddie, "On creating un-humans," in Vladimir Markotic and Grover Krantz (eds.), *The Sasquatch and Other Unknown Hominids* (Calgary, Alberta: Western Publishers, 1984), pp. 22-9; Kyle Mizokami, Bigfoot-like Figures in North American Folklore and Tradition, http://www.rain.org/campinternet/ bigfoot/bigfoot-folklore.html; Cornelius Osgood, "The ethnography of the Tanaina." *Publications in Anthropology,*

Yale University 16 (1937): 171-3; Polaris, "Alaskan mythology." *San Francisco Chronicle* (27 February 1876), p. 1; John Swanton, "Tlingit myths and texts." *Bulletin of the Bureau of American Ethnology* 39 (1909): 86.

2. Ellen Basso, "The enemy of every tribe: 'Bushman' images in northern Athapaskan narratives." *American Ethnologist* 5 (1978): 690-709; Franz Boas, "Traditions of the Tsetsaut." *Journal of American Folklore* 10 (1897): 44-6; Franz Boas and George Hunt, "Kwakiutl texts." *Memoirs of the American Museum of Natural History* 5 (1902): 431-6; Diamond Jenness, "Myths of the Carrier Indians of British Columbia." *Journal of American Folklore* 47 (1943): 97, 220-22; Aert Kuipers, *The Squamish Language* (The Hague, Netherlands: Mouton, 1969); José Mariano Maziño, *Noticias de Nutka: An Account of Nootka Sound in 1792* (Seattle: University of Washington Press, 1970), p. 25; Mary Moon, *Ogopogo* (Vancouver, B.C.: J.J. Douglas, 1977), pp. 144-5; Richard Nelson, *Make Prayers to the Raven: A Koyukon View of the Northern Forest* (Chicago: University of Chicago Press, 1983); Ronald Olson, "The Quinault Indians." *University of Washington Publications in Anthropology* 6 (1936): 170; Bruce Rigsby, "Some Pacific Northwest native names for the Sasquatch phenomenon." *Northwest Anthropological Research Notes* 5 (1971): 153-6; Susanne Storie and Jennifer Gould, *Bella Coola Stories* (Victoria, B.C.: British Columbia Indian Advisory Committee Project, 1971), pp. 1, 44, 101; Wayne Suttles, "On the cultural track of the Sasquatch." *Northwest Anthropological Research Notes* 6 (Spring 1972): 65-90; James Teit, "Kaska tales." *Journal of American Folklore* 30 (1917): 427, 438; Joseph Wherry, *Indian Masks and Myths of the West* (New York: Funk and Wagnalls, 1969), pp. 121-3.

3. Ellen Clark, *Indian Legends of the Pacific Northwest* (Berkeley, CA: University of California Press, 1958), pp. 109-110; Walter Cline, "Religion and world vies, in Leslie Spier (ed.), *The Sinkaietk or Southern Okanagon of Washington* (Menasha, WI: George Banta, 1938), pp. 170-1; Alice Ernst, *The Wolf Ritual of the Northwest Coast* (Eugene, OR: University of Oregon Press), p. 74; George Gibbs, "Tribes of western Washington and northwestern Oregon." *Contributions to North American Ethnology* 1 (1877): 308; Hermann Haeberlin and Erna Gunther, "The Indians of Puget Sound." *University of Washington Publications in Anthropology*, vol. 4, no. 1; R. James Holton, *Chinook Jargon: The Hidden Language of the Pacific Northwest* (San Leandro, CA: Adisoft, 2000); Kyle Mizokami, Bigfoot-like Figures in North American Folklore and Tradition; Ronald Olson, "The Quinault Indians"; Bruce Rigsby, "Some Pacific Northwest native language names for the Sasquatch phenomenon"; Wayne Suttles, "On the cultural track of the Sasquatch."

4. Mick and Ruth Gidley, "Plateau and basin," in Colin Taylor (ed.), *Native American Myths and Legends* (New York: Smithmark, 1994), p. 61; Kyle Mizokami, Bigfoot-like Figures in North American Folklore and Tradition.

5. Craig Bates, "California," in Taylor, *Native American Myths and Legends,* pp. 72-3; Jaime de Angulo, "Pomo creation myth." *Journal of American Folklore* 48 (1935): 230-62; Kyle Mizokami, Bigfoot-like Figures in North American Folklore and Tradition; Marion Place, *On the Track of Bigfoot* (New York: Dodd, Mead, 1974), pp. 48-52; Sanderson, *Abominable Snowmen*, pp. 47, 119.

6. C.M. Barbeau, "Supernatural beings of the Huron and Wyandot." *American Anthropologist* 16 (1914): 288-313; Michael Bradley, "Quebec Sasquatches, a brief note."

Pursuit 35 (Summer 1976): 66; John Colombo (ed.), *Windigo: An Anthology of Fact and Fantastic Fiction* (Saskatoon, Sask.: Western Produce Prairie Books, 1982); D.S. Davidson, "Folktales from Grand Lake Victoria, Quebec." *Journal of American Folklore* 14 (1928): 275-7; James Dorsey, "Siouan folk-lore and mythologic notes." *American Antiquarian* 7 (1885): 105-8; James Dorsey, "Teton folk-lore." *American Anthropologist* 2 (1889): 143, 155; Mary Eastman, *Dacotah* (New York: John A. Wiley, 1849), pp. 208-11; Peter Matthiessen, *In the Spirit of Crazy Horse* (New York: Viking, 1991), pp. 149, 558-9; Marvin Rapp, "Legend of the stone giants." *New York Folklore Quarterly* 12 (1956): 280-2

7. Loren Coleman and Mark Hall, "Some Bigfoot traditions of the North American tribes," in Jacques Bergier (ed.), *Extraterrestrial Intervention: The Evidence* (New York: Signet Books, 1974), pp. 73-83; Jean-Claude Dupont, *Le légendaire de la Beauce* (Montréal, Queb.: Leméac, 1978); Mark Harrington, *Religion and Ceremonies of the Lenape* (New York: Museum of the American Indian, 1921); William McSherry (ed.), *A Relation of the Colony of the Lord Baron of Baltimore, in Maryland, near Virginia* (Washington, D.C.: W.Q. Force, 1846), pp. 18-24; Kyle Mizokami, Bigfoot-like Figures in North American Folklore; James Mooney, "Myths of the Cherokee." *Annual Report of the Bureau of American Ethnology* 19 (1900): 3-575; Elsie Parsons, "Micmac folklore." *Journal of American Folklore* 38 (1925): 55-133; Frank Speck, "Penobscot tales and religious beliefs." *Journal of American Folklore* 48 (1935): 81-2; Bruce Wright, "The Gougou: The Bigfoot of the East." *Bigfoot Bulletin* no. 25 (1971).

8. Russell Bates, "Legends of the Kiowa." *INFO Journal* 52 (May 1987): 4-10; David Bushnell Jr., "The Choctaw of Bayou Lacomb." *Bulletin of the Bureau of American Ethnology* 48 (1909): 31; James Dorsey, "Siouan folk-lore and mythologic notes"; Mick and Ruth Gidley, "Plateau and basin"; Don Hunter and René Dahinden, *Sasquatch* (New York: Signet Books, 1973), p. 33; David Jones, *Sanapia, Comanche Medicine Woman* (New York: Holt Rinehart Winston, 1972); Kyle Mizokami, Bigfoot-like Figures in North American Folklore and Tradition.

9. Sarah Hopkins, *Life Among the Piutes: Their Wrongs and Claims* (Reno: University of Nevada Press, 1994); Smith, *Strange Abominable Snowmen*, pp. 57-9.

10. Smith, *Strange Abominable Snowmen*, p. 59.

11. Heuvelmans, pp. 93-6, 121.

12. Jack Clayton, "The giants of Minnesota." *Doubt* 35 (1952): 120-2; Dorothy Dansie, "John T. Reid's case for the redheaded giants." *Nevada Historical Society Quarterly* 18 (1975): 152-67; "Giant skeletons." *Pursuit* 23 (July 1973): 69-70; Ross Hamilton and Patricia Mason, "A tradition of giants and ancient North American warfare." *Ancient American* 36 (December 2000): 6-13; "A nine-foot skeleton." *Scientific American* 124 (1921): 203; Phyla Phillips, "Giants in ancient America." *Fate* 1 (Spring 1948): 126-7; Sanderson, *More "Things,"* pp. 79-88; Henry Splitter, "The impossible fossils." *Fate* 7 (January 1954): 65-6; Edward Wood, *Giants and Dwarfs* (London: R. Bentley, 1868).

13. Coleman and Huyghe; Mark Hall, *The Yeti, Bigfoot and True Giants* (Minneapolis: The Author, 1997); Sanderson, *Abominable Snowmen*.

14. Eric Pettifor, "From the teeth of the dragon—*Gigantopithecus blacki*," http://www.wynja.com/arch/gigantopithecus.html.

Chapter 2

1. Bobbie Short, "The Bauman Story," http://www.bigfootencounters.com/classics/bauman.htm; The Fur Trade, http://xroads.virginia.edu/~HYPER/HNS/mtmen/furtrade.html.
2. Theodore Roosevelt, *The Wilderness Hunter* (New York: P.F. Collier, 1893), pp 441-447.
3. "Chetco River," http://en.wikipedia.org/wiki/Chetco_River.
4. Sanderson, *Abominable Snowmen*, p. 116.
5. Ibid.
6. Ibid.; Green, *Sasquatch*, pp. 45, 334.
7. "Nahanni National Park Reserve," http://en.wikipedia.org/wiki/Nahanni_National_Park_Reserve; "Canada: Northwest Territories: Home of Devils?" *Time* (January 20, 1947), http://www.time.com/time/magazine/article/0,9171,854301,00.html; "South Nahanni River," http://en.wikipedia.org/wiki/South_Nahanni_River.
8. R.M. Patterson, "The Dangerous River," http://www.oldjimbo.com/Outdoors-Magazine/The-Dangerous-River-RM-Patterson.pdf.
9. "Canada: Northwest Territories: Home of Devils?"
10. Ibid.
11. Ibid.
12. The Headless Valley Expedition, http://marina.fortunecity.com/reach/361/berton.htm.
13. Mangiacopra and Smith, p. 14; "Fortean Society," http://en.wikipedia.org/wiki/Fortean_Society.
14. Sanderson, *Abominable Snowmen*, pp. 42-3.
15. Ibid., p. 43.
16. Graves, p. 45.
17. Dave Wolfe, http://marina.fortunecity.com/reach/361/dave_wolfe.htm; Mike Eliseuson, http://marina.fortunecity.com/reach/361/eliseuson.htm.
18. Eliseuson; Graves, p. 45; Loren Coleman, "Dire wolves, Shunka Warak'ins, and Waheelas," (6 December 2007), http://www.cryptomundo.com/cryptozoo-news/dire-waheela.
19. Graves; "Society for the Investigation of the Unexplained," http://www.answers.com/topic/society-for-the-investigation-of-the-unexplained.
20. Graves; Loren Coleman, "Random reports of Bigfoot wearing clothes," (4 May 2009), http://www.cryptomundo.com/cryptozoo-news/bushman; Coleman, "Dire wolves, Shunka Warak'ins, and Waheelas."
21. Brad Steiger, http://www.bradandsherry.com/brad.htm; Norman, pp. 120-1; Smith, *Strange Abominable Snowmen*, pp. 77-80.
22. North, pp. 99-107; Internet Movie Database, http://www.imdb.com/title/tt0082247.
23. North, pp. 99-101, 103; Mangiacopra and Smith, p. 12.
24. Mangiacopra and Smith.
25. Rachel Wills, "About the Mystery of the Deadmen Valley of the Northwest Territories," http://geography.suite101.com/article.cfm/the_haunted_nahanni_national_park_of_canada.

26. Great Canadian Parks, http://www.greatcanadianparks.com/northwest/nahninp/page2.htm.
27. "Fight with big apes reported by miners," *The Oregonian*, July 13, 1924.
28. Green, *Sasquatch*, p. 90.
29. Ibid.
30. Ibid.
31. Byrne, pp. 22-5.
32. Beck, http://www.bigfootencounters.com/classics/beck.htm.
33. Ibid.
34. Ibid.
35. "Logger says his big mouth is responsible for Bigfoot," Associated Press, April 4, 1982.
36. Bord, *Bigfoot*, p. 176.
37. Hunter and Dahinden, p. 25.
38. Ibid., p. 26.
39. Bigfoot Field Researchers Organization (hereafter "BFRO"), Media Article #236, http://www.bfro.net/GDB/show_article.asp?id=236.
40. Bigfoot Encounters, http://www.bigfootencounters.com/articles/seattlemag70.htm and http://www.bigfootencounters.com/articles/spiritlake.htm.
41. "Oregon Journal," http://en.wikipedia.org/wiki/Oregon_Journal.
42. "Seattle youth is missing on Mt. St. Helens," *Longview Daily News*, May 22, 1950; "Ski patrol to hunt youth," *Longview Daily News*, May 23, 1950; *The Columbian*, May 22, 1950; "Search for skier goes into third day," "Mt. St. Helens hunt for lost man grows," *The Columbian*, May 23, 1950; "St. Helens climber still unfound; fears mounting," *The Columbian*, May 24, 1950.
43. "Hopes rise that Carter may get out," *Longview Daily News* (May 24, 1950); "Hunt center moved to Cougar vicinity," *Longview Daily News* (May 25, 1950); "Focal point shifts in search for lost man," *The Columbia*, (May 25, 1950); "Hopes for lost Seattle skier are dwindling," *Longview Daily News* (May 26, 1950); "Hope waning for man lost on St. Helens," *The Columbian* (May 26, 1950); "Search center shifted back," *The Columbian* (May 29, 1950); "Last search effort slated," *The Columbian* (1 June 1950); "Hunt for lost skier ended," *The Columbian* (5 June 1950); "Search for missing Seattlite halted," *Longview Daily News* (6 June 1950).
44. The Minnesota Iceman, http://www.angelfire.com/mn2/mnbf/iceman.html; The Minnesota Iceman, http://www.bigfootencounters.com/articles/translation.htm.
45. The Missing Link? http://www.bigfootencounters.com/articles/argosy2.htm; Ivan Sanderson, "Preliminary description of the external morphology of what appeared to be the fresh corpse of a hitherto unknown form of living hominid," *Genus* 25 (1969): 259-78; Bernard Heuvelmans and Boris Porshnev, *L'homme de Néanderthal est toujours vivant* (Paris: Plon, 1974).
46. The Minnesota Iceman, http://www.angelfire.com/mn2/mnbf/iceman.html; Sanderson, "Preliminary description...," *Genus* 25 (1969): 259-78.
47. The Minnesota Iceman, http://www.angelfire.com/mn2/mnbf/iceman.html.
48. Ibid.
49. Frank Hansen, "I killed the ape-man creature of Whiteface," *Saga* (July 1970), pp. 8-

11, 55-6, 58, 60.

0. Ibid., pp. 55-6.
1. Ibid., p. 56.
2. Ibid. pp. 56, 58.
3. Ibid., p. 60.
4. Ian Simmons, "The abominable showman," http://www.bigfootencounters.com/ articles/showman_hansen.htm; Dmitri Bayanov, "Updating the Minnesota Iceman 2005," http://www.bigfootencounters.com/articles/iceman_update2005.htm.

Chapter 3

.   Green, *Sasquatch,* p. 6.
.   Berry, back cover.
.   Murphy, p. 8.
.   IBS website.
.   SIS website.
.   BFRO website
.   Oregon Bigfoot website.
.   Arment, pp. 127-30.
.   Bigfoot Encounters; "Curry County, Oregon," http://en.wikipedia.org/wiki/ Curry_County,_Oregon.
0. Norman, pp. 104-5; Smith, *Strange Abominable Snowmen,* pp. 127-8; Tim Banse, "Warren Smith: UFO Investigator or Hoaxer?" A Different Perspective, http:// kevinrandle.blogspot.com/2007/05/warren-smith-ufo-investigator-or.html.
1. Green, *Sasquatch,* p. 334; "The Monster of Deadman's Hole," Museum of Hoaxes, http://www.museumofhoaxes.com/hoax/af_database/permalink/ the_monster_of_deadmans_hole.
2. Norman, p. 89; IBS #1329; USA Place Names, http://www.placenames.com/us.
3. Norman, p. 89; IBS #1329.
4. Green, *Sasquatch,* p. 335.
5. IBS #40 and #2098.
6. Green, *Sasquatch,* p. 335.
7. Ibid., pp. 335-6.
8. Ibid., p. 336.
9. Ibid.; Book Trail, http://www.booktrail.com/hunting_alaska/Return%20to% 20Toonaklut%20-%20The%20Russell%20Annabel%20Story.asp.
0. IBS #2921.
1. IBS #2487.
2. IBS #1365.
3. Coleman, *Bigfoot!* pp. 181-2.
4. IBS #1642,
5. Bigfoot Encounters, http://www.bigfootencounters.com/stories/inyo_county.htm.
6. IBS #2478.
7. "Prehistoric and historic volcanic eruptions in Oregon," Oregon Department of Geol-

ogy and Mineral Industries, http://www.oregongeology.org/sub/earthquakes/volcanoeshist.htm.

28. IBS #1432.
29. Jan Thompson, "The Beast of LBL," http://www.guardiantales.freewebspace.com/JAN-Beast.html.
30. IBS #2429; Portland Mountain Rescue Mission Summaries, http://www.pmru.org/pressroom/summaries_95to01.html.
31. IBS #2918.
32. Arment, pp. 50-1.
33. Murphy, pp. 56-7.
34. BFRO Media Article #420.
35. Murphy, p. 40.
36. Arment, p. 138.
37. Ibid., pp. 219-20.
38. Ibid., pp. 153-4.
39. Berry, p. 128.
40. Green, *Sasquatch,* pp. 411-16.
41. Kentucky Bigfoot, http://www.kentuckybigfoot.com/reports.htm.
42. Ibid., pp. 215-16.
43. Bord, *Bigfoot,* pp. 61-2; Clark and Coleman, pp. 52-3.
44. Bord, *Bigfoot,* p. 66; Smith, *Strange Abominable Snowmen,* pp. 72-4.
45. IBS #1713.
46. Bigfoot Encounters, http://www.bigfootencounters.com/articles/spiritlake.
47. Berry, p. 39.
48. Green, *Sasquatch,* p. 308.
49. Bord, *Bigfoot,* p. 245.
50. Berry, p. 78.
51. Bord, *Bigfoot,* p. 249.
52. Green, *Sasquatch,* p. 339.
53. IBS #1822.
54. Green, *Sasquatch,* p. 186.
55. Ibid., pp. 340-1.
56. Berry, p. 79.
57. BFRO #3472.
58. BFRO #447.
59. Berry, p. 46.
60. BFRO #3385.
61. Berry, p. 89.
62. Bord, *Bigfoot,* p. 295; BFRO Media Articles #74 and 75.
63. Berry, p. 91.
64. Bord, *Bigfoot,* p. 296; Berry, p. 91.
65. Ibid., p. 299; USA Place Names, http://www.placenames.com/us.
66. IBS #531.
67. BFRO Media Article #130.
68. IBS #2658.

69. Kentucky Bigfoot.
70. GCBRO.
71. IBS #2010.
72. IBS #1390.
73. GCBRO.
74. Ibid.
75. Green, *Sasquatch,* p. 339;
76. Berry, p. 135; Green, *Sasquatch,* p. 370; USA Place Names, http://www.placenames.com/us.
77. Keel, p. 120; Green, *Sasquatch,* p. 370; USA Place Names.
78. Bord, *Bigfoot,* p. 231; Green, *Sasquatch,* p. 194; USA Place Names; Piney Ridge Center, http://www.amicarebehavioral.com/piney_mo.htm.
79. Arment, p. 272; IBS #188, 314, 322, 815, 1336, 1846, 2181, 2393, 2400, 3261.
80. IBS #1618 and 1691; GCBRO; BFRO #4885.
81. Arment, p. 281; Bord, *Bigfoot,* p. 245; GCBRO; IBS #1424.
82. IBS #361, 1484, 1557, 1784, 3434; BFRO #2590, 2909, 3535; Murphy, pp. 102-4, 107, 109; GCBRO.
83. Quoted in Arment, p. 188.
84. IBS #1546.
85. GCBRO.
86. Ibid.
87. IBS #1463.
88. GCBRO.
89. IBS #1853.
90. Bord, *Bigfoot,* p. 296.
91. Oregonbigfoot.com File #00473.
92. IBS #1808.
93. Bord, *Bigfoot,* p. 248; BFRO #7399, 10114.
94. BS #1335.
95. RO #3086; Oregonbigfoot.com File #00473.
96. Green, *Sasquatch,* p. 201,
97. Ibid., p. 308.
98. Ibid., pp. 306-7.
99. Ian Sample, "Chimp who threw stones at zoo visitors showed human trait, scientist says," *The Guardian* (London), 9 March 2009; "Chimpanzee's plan to attack zoo visitors shows evidence of premeditated thought," *The Times* (London), 10 March 2009.
100. IBS #1796.
101. IBS #2062, 2720; "Deaths at Crater Lake National Park," Crater Lake Institute, http://www.craterlakeinstitute.com/cultural-history/smith-brothers-chronology/b-deaths.htm.
102. *MonsterQuest,* History.com, http://www.history.com/content/monsterquest.
103. *Lost Tapes,* Animal Planet, http://animal.discovery.com/tv/lost-tapes.
104. Loren Coleman, "Blair Dog Project: Gable Film Fakery?" Cryptomundo (29 September 2007), http://www.cryptomundo.com/cryptozoo-news/gable-film.
105. Autumn Williams, "Investigating the Gable Film," Oregon Bigfoot Blog (29 July 2009), http://www.oregonbigfoot.com/blog/bigfoot/gable-film-research; "The Gable

Film #2" (21 July 2009), http://www.oregonbigfoot.com/blog/bigfoot/the-gable-film-2-michigan-dogman-or-persistent-hoax; "More thoughts on the Gable Attack Film" (28 July 2009), http://www.oregonbigfoot.com/blog/general-updates-from-autumn/more-thoughts-on-the-gable-attack-film.

Chapter 4

1. Sanderson, *Abominable Snowmen,* pp. 157-60.
2. Eberhart, p. 16.
3. Martin Morita, "Alleged wolfwoman has killed hundreds of farm birds in this county," *Reforma* (2 February 2004).
4. Eberhart, pp. 502-3.
5. Ibid.
6. Quoted in Sanderson, *Abominable Snowmen,* pp. 160-1.
7. Ibid., p. 162.
8. Edward Jonathan Hoyt, *Buckskin Joe: A Memoir* (Lincoln, NE: Bison Books, 1966), p. 177.
9. Green, *Sasquatch,* p. 133.
10. Richard Oglesby Marsh, *White Indians of Darien* (New York: G.P. Putnam's Sons, 1934), pp. 19-21.
11. John Gardiner, "Alligators in the Bahamas," *Science* 8 (1886): 369; Michel Raynal, "Yahoos in the Bahamas," *Cryptozoology* 4 (1985): 106.
12. "South America," http://en.wikipedia.org/wiki/South_America; "Amazon Basin," http://en.wikipedia.org/wiki/Amazon_Basin; "List of Cities in South America," http://en.wikipedia.org/wiki/List_of_cities_in_South_America.
13. Keel, p. 137.
14. Eberhart, pp. 345, 351-2.
15. Heuvelmans, p. 369.
16. Sanderson, *Abominable Snowmen,* pp. 169-70; Heuvelmans, p. 372; Loren Coleman and Michel Raynal, "De Loys's Photograph: A Short Tale of Apes in Green Hell, Spider Monkeys, and *Ameranthropoides loysi* as Tools of Racism." *The Anomalist* 4 (Autumn 1996): 84-93.
17. Childress, pp. 84-7; Simon Chapman, *The Monster of the Madidi* (London: Aurum, 2001).
18. Eberhart, pp. 471, 571.
19. Heuvelmans, p. 366; Coleman and Huyghe, p. 78.
20. Coral and Jim Lorenzen, *Encounters with UFO Occupants* (New York: Berkley Medallion Books, 1976), p. 144.
21. Eberhart, pp. 131-2; Heuvelmans, p. 386.
22. Heuvelmans, pp. 387-8; Eberhart, p. 131.
23. "Brazil," http://en.wikipedia.org/wiki/Brazil; "Amazon Basin"; "Mato Grosso," http://en.wikipedia.org/wiki/Mato_Grosso.
24. Eberhart, p. 118.
25. "Kuru-Pira," The Spiders Den, http://ladyofspiders.wordpress.com/2007/12/07/kuru-

pira.

26. Percy Fawcett, *Exploration Fawcett* (London: Hutchinson, 1953), pp. 200-202.
27. Norman, p. 57; "Xingu National Park," http://en.wikipedia.org/wiki/ Xingu_National_Park.
28. Eberhart, pp. 318-19, 425.
29. Coleman and Huyghe, p. 74; Heuvelmans, p. 393; Sanderson, *Abominable Snowmen,* p. 177; Marguerite Holloway, "Beasts in the Mist: David Oren searches for giant sloth in Brazilian rainforest," *Discover* 20 (September 1999): 57-65.
30. Heuvelmans, pp. 391-2.
31. Ibid., pp. 392-3; "Primate Factsheets: Gorilla," Primate Info Net, http:// pin.primate.wisc.edu/factsheets/entry/gorilla/behav.
32. "Bigfoot in Latin America," *Fortean Times* 173 (September 2003): 6-7; "Strange hominid sighted again in Argentina," UFO Roundup (30 April 2003), http:// www.ufoinfo.com/roundup/v08/rnd0817.shtml.
33. "Strange hominid sighted again in Argentina."
34. Eberhart, p. 161.
35. Ibid., p. 251; Coleman and Huyghe, p. 76.
36. Eberhart, p. 537; Dmitri Bayanov, *In the Footsteps of the Russian Snowman* (Moscow: Crypto-Logos, 1996), pp. 46-52.
37. "Antonio Pigafetta," http://en.wikipedia.org/wiki/Antonio_Pigafetta; Smith, *Strange Monsters and Madmen,* p. 113; "Patagon," http://en.wikipedia.org/wiki/Patagon.
38. "Patagon"; Smith, *Strange Monsters and Madmen,* p. 113.
39. "Patagon"; "Jacques Mahu and Simon de Cordes," http://www.win.tue.nl/~engels/ discovery/mahucordes.html.
40. "Patagon"; "The Patagonian Giants," Museum of Hoaxes, http:// www.museumofhoaxes.com/patagonia.html.
41. "Patagon"; "The Patagonian Giants"; "Tehuelche," http://en.wikipedia.org/wiki/ Tehuelche42.
42. "Central and South America," Miranda's Temple of Trash, http://rhandi.tripod.com/ samerica.html.
43. Keel, p. 137.
44. Coleman and Huyghe, pp. 82-3.
45. Ibid.; "Presidente Roque Sáenz Peña," http://en.wikipedia.org/wiki/ Presidente_Roque_S%C3%A1enz_Pe%C3%B1a.

Chapter 5

1. Eberhart, pp. 215, 558; Rose, pp. 84, 274-76.
2. Eberhart, p. 474; Rose, pp. 119, 321-22; "Goatman (Maryland)," http:// en.wikipedia.org/wiki/Goatman_(Maryland).
3. Rose, p. 73.
4. Eberhart, pp. 593-6.
5. Garden, pp. 62-73; Rose, pp. 391-3; Steiger, pp. 124, 265-8.
6. "Werewolf and Vampire Reports from the Paranormal Database," http://

www.paranormaldatabase.com/reports/vampdata.php.

7. Norman, p. 71.
8. "Beast of Gévaudan," http://en.wikipedia.org/wiki/Beast_of_G%C3%A9vaudan.
9. J.D.H. Temme, *Die Volkssagen von Pommern und Rügen* (Berlin: In der Nicolaischen Buchhandlung, 1840), p. 308.
10. Norman, p. 69; Steiger, pp. 33-4; Michael Speidel, "Berserks: A History of Indo-European 'Mad Warriors,'" *Journal of World History* 13 (2002): 253-290; "Eaters of the Dead," http://en.wikipedia.org/wiki/Eaters_of_the_Dead.
11. Redfern, pp. 10, 15.
12. Ibid., pp. 57, 60, 87-8, 107-11.
13. Nick Redfern, "British Bigfoot Controversy Grows," http://www.bigfootencounters.com/articles/britishbf.htm; Andy Lloyd, "I've seen the Beast of Bolam, says hunt man," *Evening Chronicle* (Newcastle), 23 January 2003
14. "Ben Macdui," http://en.wikipedia.org/wiki/Ben_Macdhui_(Scotland).
15. Ron Halliday, *The A-Z of Paranormal Scotland* (Edinburgh: B&W Publishing, 2000), p. 128.
16. Ibid., pp. 128-9; "Brocken spectre," http://en.wikipedia.org/wiki/Brocken_spectre.
17. Eberhart, p. 32; Scott Corrales, "Bigfoot Beyond Our Borders," Inexplicata, http://inexplicata.blogspot.com/2009/08/bigfoot-beyond-our-borders.html.
18. Eberhart, p. 32, citing the Spanish national newspaper *ABC,* for 16 May 1979.
19. "Wild Men in Spain," Bigfoot Encounters, http://www.bigfootencounters.com/articles/spain.htm.
20. Ibid.
21. Corrales, "Bigfoot Beyond Our Borders."
22. Eberhart, p. 418, citing Bernard Heuvelmans and Boris Porshnev, *L'homme de Néanderthal est toujours vivant* (Paris: Plon, 1974), pp. 109, 119.
23. Childress, pp. 208-10.
24. Kiril Rossiianov, "Beyond species: Il'ya Ivanov and his experiments on cross-breeding humans and anthropoid apes," Science in Context 15 (June 2002): 277–316.
25. Ibid; Roger Williams, "Attack of the Super Soviet Apemen!" Dictators of the World, http://authoritarianism.blogspot.com/2007/10/attack-of-super-soviet-apemen.html
26. Rossiianov.
27. Ibid.; Williams.
28. Rossiianov.
29. Sanderson, *Abominable Snowmen,* pp. 295-6.
30. "Vargen Karapetyan's Captive Alma," Anomalies, http://anomalyinfo.com/articles/sa00080.php.
31. Eberhart, p. 221; "Absheron Rayon," http://en.wikipedia.org/wiki/Absheron_Rayon.
32. Eberhart, pp. 212, 220, 371-2.
33. Dmitri Bayanov, *In the Footsteps of the Russian Snowman* (Moscow: Crypto-Logos, 1996), pp. 190-206.

Chapter 6

1. "Hominidae," http://en.wikipedia.org/wiki/Hominidae.
2. "Gorilla," http://en.wikipedia.org/wiki/Gorilla.
3. "Congo Basin," http://en.wikipedia.org/wiki/Congo_Basin; "Wildlife of the Congo," World Wildlife Fund, http://wwf.panda.org/what_we_do/where_we_work/congo_basin_forests/the_area/wildlife.
4. Eberhart, p. 165.
5. Ibid.; "Cercopithecus cephus," IUCN Red List of Threatened Species, http://www.iucnredlist.org/apps/redlist/details/4214/0.
6. "Moustached guenon," Animal Encyclopedia, http://www.answers.com/topic/moustached-guenon.
7. Louis Bowler, *Gold Coast Palaver* (London: John Long, 1911), pp. 99-100.
8. Sanderson, *Abominable Snowmen,* p. 205.
9. *"Australopithecus africanus,"* http://en.wikipedia.org/wiki/Australopithecus_africanus; Prominent Hominid Fossils, http://www.talkorigins.org/faqs/homs/specimen.html.
10. Eberhart, p. 281.
11. Paul du Chaillu, *Stories of the Gorilla Country* (NY: Harper, 1868), pp. 272-3.
12. Rebecca Kormos, et al. (eds.), *West African Chimpanzees: Status Survey and Conservation Action Plan* (Gland, Switzerland: World Conservation Union, 2003): 6.
13. Eberhart, pp. 165-6.
14. Richard Garner, *Gorillas and Chimpanzees* (London: Osgood, McIlvaine, 1896), pp. 208-11, viewable online at http://www.archive.org/stream/gorillaschimpanz00garniala#page/208/mode/2up.
15. Eberhart, p. 274.
16. Ibid.
17. Ellen Gatti, *Exploring We Would Go* (London: Robert Hale, 1950), pp. 282-3.
18. George Witten, "He's after the real King Kong: a Mulahu?" *Family Circle* (16 September 1938), pp. 10-11, 18; Sanderson, *Abominable Snowmen,* p. 207.
19. Eberhart, pp. 385-6.
20. Bord and Bord, *Unexplained Mysteries,* p. 198.
21. "Bili Ape," http://en.wikipedia.org/wiki/Bili_Ape.
22. Ibid.
23. Emma Young, "The beast with no name," *New Scientist,* (9 October 2004).
24. James Randerson, "Found: the giant lion-eating chimps of the magic forest," *The Guardian* (London), 14 July 2007.
25. Stephan Faris, "Lost apes of the Congo," Time Magazine (9 January 2005), http://www.time.com/time/magazine/article/0,9171,1015856-3,00.html.

Chapter 7

1. Anne Applebaum, Gulag: A History of the Soviet Camps, http://www.arlindo-correia.com/041003.html.

2.   "Siberia," http://en.wikipedia.org/wiki/Siberia.

3.   Eberhart, p. 621.

4.   Ibid., pp. 275-6, 340, 434.

5.   Ibid., p. 265; "Kappa (folklore)," http://en.wikipedia.org/wiki/Kappa_(folklore); Rose, p. 203.

6.   Eberhart, p. 265.

7.   "Bungisngis," http://en.wikipedia.org/wiki/Bungisngis; Rose, p. 61.

8.   Eberhart, p. 266.

9.   Deborah Martyr, "An investigation of the *Orang-Pendek*, the 'short man' of Sumatra," *Cruptozoology* 9 (1990): 57-65; Mark Henderson, "Team 'find traces of Sumatran Yeti,'" *The Times* (London), 27 October 2001.

10.   Rose, pp. 19, 310.

11.   Eberhart, p. 409.

12.   Heuvelmans, pp. 87-10

13.   Eberhart, p. 230; Sanderson, *Abominable Snowmen, p. 227.*

14.   Sanderson, *Abominable Snowmen, pp. 228-9.*

15.   *Cousins; Sanderson, Abominable Snowmen, pp. 229-30.*

16.   Sanderson, *Abominable Snowmen, p. 230; Smith, Strange Abominable Snowmen, pp. 114-16.*

17.   Norman, pp. 93-6; Smith, *Strange Monsters and Madmen*, pp. 61-3.

18.   Norman, pp. 99-102; Steiger, pp. 235-6.

19.   John MacKinnon, *In Search of the Red Ape* (New York: Ballantine, 1974), pp. 100-102.

20.   Eberhart, pp. 286, 552; Sanderson, *Abominable Snowmen, pp. 241-3; Smith, Strange Abominable Snowmen, p. 116; Steiger, pp. 272-4.*

21.   *Hassoldt Davis, Land of the Eye (New York: Henry Holt, 1940), p. 111.*

22.   Steiger, pp. 167-8; Norman, p. 36.

23.   Sanderson, *Abominable Snowmen, p. 243.*

24.   Steiger, pp. 272-4.

25.   Keel, pp. 134-5.

26.   Sanderson, *Abominable Snowmen, Pp. 244-5.*

27.   *Norman, pp. 96-8.*

28.   *bid., pp. 98-9.*

29.   *Eberhart, p. 387.*

30.   Albert Rosales, "1974 Humanoid Reports," http://www.ufoinfo.com/humanoid/humanoid1974.shtml

31.   Ibid.; Albert Rosales, "Humanoid Sighting Reports & Journal of Humanoid Studies," http://www.ufoinfo.com/humanoid/index.shtml.

32.   "Martin Caidin," http://en.wikipedia.org/wiki/Martin_Caidin; Amazon.com, http://www.amazon.com/Natural-Supernatural-Casebook-Unexplained-Mysteries/dp/0809238047/ref=sr_1_1?s=books&ie=UTF8&qid=1281439342&sr=1-1.

33.   Eberhart, pp. 606-7.

34.   Ibid., pp. 318, 457, 605.

35.   Ibid., p. 457.

36.   Ibid., p. 606

37. "Temple stampedes claimed 700 lives in 8 years," *Times of India*, 4 March 2010.
38. Rose, pp. 210, 227, 307.Eberhart, pp. 286-7.
39. Norman, pp. 40-1; Smith, p. 97; Steiger, pp. 300-1.
40. Ibid.
41. Ibid.
42. Eberhart, p. 351; "Man, Myth or Monkey?" *Fortean Times* 148 (August 2001): 8-9; "Monkey Madness," *Fortean Times* 149 (September 2001): 7.
43. "Man, Myth or Monkey?"
44. "Monkey Madness."
45. Ibid.
46. "The Face-Scratcher," *Fortean Times* 164 (December 2002): 6-7.
47. Eberhart, pp. 31, 188, 395, 611.
48. Ibid., pp. 31, 148-9, 151-2, 188, 341, 395; Messner, p. 141.
49. Eberhart, p. 611; Igor Bourtsev, "A skeleton still buried and a skull unearthed: the story of Zana," Bigfoot Encounters, http://www.bigfootencounters.com/articles/zana.htm.
50. Norman, p. 35; Smith, p. 23; Robert Bates and Charles Houston, *Five Miles High: The Thrilling True Story of the First American Karakoram Expedition to K2.* Guilford, CT: Lyons Press, 2000.
51. Messner, pp. 46-7; Norman, p. 35; Sanderson, *Abominable Snowmen,* p. 262.
52. Keel, p. 67.
53. Norman, p. 36; Steiger, pp. 167-8.
54. Bord, *Alien Animals,* pp. 146-8; Bord, *Unexplained Mysteries,* p. 199; Childress, pp. 170-1; Eberhart, p. 612; Messner, p. 62.
55. Messner, pp. 104, 119, 136, 149-65.

Chapter 8

1. Eberhart, pp. 259, 454.
2. Ibid., p. 261.
3. Smith, *Bunyips & Bigfoots,* pp. 164-5.
4. Eberhart, pp. 602, 616.
5. Healy and Cropper, p. 204.
6. Smith, *Bunyips & Bigfoots,* p. 143.
7. Arthur Bickell, *Travel and Adventure in Northern Queensland* (New York: Longmans, Green and Co., 1895), pp. 173-8 (quoted in Healy and Cropper, pp. 212-13).
8. Healy and Cropper, p. 213.
9. Ibid., pp. 219-20.
10. Ibid., p. 220.
11. Smith, *Strange Abominable Snowmen,* p. 126.
12. Healy and Cropper, p. 296.
13. Ibid., pp. 239-40; Smith, *Bunyips & Bigfoots,* pp. 154-5.
14. Healy and Cropper, p. 241.
15. Smith, *Bunyips & Bigfoots,* p. 165.
16. Ibid; Healy and Cropper, p. 243; "Charter Towers 1979," Australia Yowie Research,

http://www.yowiehunters.com/index.php?
option=com_content&task=view&id=26&Itemid=131.

17. Healy and Cropper, p. 253.
18. Ibid., p. 259.
19. Ibid., p. 267.
20. "Yowie Attacks Campervan," Bigfoot Encounters, http://www.bigfootencounters.com/sbs/attacks.htm.
21. "Yowie 'may have killed puppy,'" Channel 9, Sydney (21 April 2009), http://news.ninemsn.com.au/national/804059/yowie-may-have-killed-puppy.
22. "Yowie attacks researcher?" GhostTheory, http://www.ghosttheory.com/2009/05/28/yowie-attacks-researcher.
23. Jason Clarke, "Result of a Yowie attack," The Morningstarr (1 June 2009), http://www.themorningstarr.co.uk/2009/06/01/result-of-a-yowie-attack.
24. Rose, p. 238; Eberhart, pp. 306-7.
25. Eberhart, p. 307.
26. Rose, p. 2.
27. "Papua New Guinea," http://en.wikipedia.org/wiki/Papua_New_Guinea; "Police hunt 'dinosaur' in PNG," The Age (Melbourne, Australia), 12 March 2004; "More than 50 new species found in New Guinea," http://www.msnbc.msn.com/id/29875909.
28. Rose, p. 207.
29. "Solomon Islands," http://en.wikipedia.org/wiki/Solomon_Islands.
30. Eberhart, p. 363.

Chapter 9

1. Meldrum, p. 78; Messner, p. 94.
2. Max Allan Collins and George Hagenauer, Men's Adventure Magazines in Postwar America (Köln, Germany: Taschen, 2004), pp. 74-7, 104-5.
3. IBS #3821; Michael Schmeltzer, "Bigfoot lives," Washington Magazine (30 September 1988).
4. IBS #3329.
5. Ibid.
6. Sidney Warren, Farthest Frontier: The Pacific Northwest (New York: Macmillan, 1949), pp. 159-62.
7. Sanderson, Abominable Snowmen, p. 68.
8. Ed Fusch, S'cwene'y'ti and the Stick Indians of the Colvilles (Riverside, WA: The Author, 1992), p. 7, http://www.bigfootencounters.com/biology/fusch.htm.
9. Ibid.
10. Ibid., pp. 9-10.
11. Smith, Strange Abominable Snowmen, pp. 43-4.
12. Childress, pp. 162-9.
13. John Lewis, "Strange Tale of Bigfoot," Bigfoot Encounters, http://www.bigfootencounters.com/stories/n_california1900s.htm.
14. Eberhart, p. 611.

15. Green, *Sasquatch,* p. 97.
16. Ibid., pp. 103-110.
17. Ibid., p. 110; Loren Coleman, "Ostman abduction story stands up," Cryptomundo (29 June 2010), http://www.cryptomundo.com/bigfoot/ostman2010.
18. Peter Byrne, "The Story of Muchalat Harry," The Bigfoot Classics, http://www.bigfootencounters.com/classics/muchalat.htm.
19. Norman, pp. 23, 28-30.
20. Keel, p. 115.
21. Stephen Wagner, "When Bigfoot Attacks," About.com http://paranormal.about.com/cs/bigfootsasquatch/a/aa033103.htm.
22. IBS #1706.
23. IBS #1419
24. Green, *Sasquatch,* p. 339; Keel, p. 120.
25. IBS #1993.
26. E. Randall Floyd, "Tennessee bigfoot a disagreeable fellow," *Augusta* (GA) *Chronicle* (6 April 1997).
27. Messner, p. 101.
28. IBS #359.
29. IBS #3870.
30. Childress, pp. 204-5.
31. White Lotus Press, http://www.whitelotuspress.com/bookdetail.php?id=E21947; Childress, p. 191.
32. IBS #2198; USA Place Names, http://www.placenames.com/us.
33. IBS #2198.
34. "Kidnapped by Bigfoot? Search Continues," *Spokesman-Review* (Spokane, WA), 25 May 1976.
35. "'Bigfoot hostage' turns up unharmed," *St. Petersburg* (FL) *Times* (26 May 1976); "Bride of Bigfoot," Museum of Hoaxes, http://www.museumofhoaxes.com/hoax/archive/display/category/abduction; "Bigfoot Analysis," http://galearning.com/help/fun-analysis/analyzing-bigfoot-sightings-and-stories; "Bigfoot search costs Humboldt County," *Record-Searchlight* (Redding, CA), 8 February 1978.
36. Meldrum, p. 78.
37. Ibid.
38. "French tourist stripped by orangutan," Sky News, http://news.sky.com/skynews/Home/Sky-News-Archive/Article/20080641285681.
39. YouTube, http://www.youtube.com/watch?v=UrKyyhSymHc,
40. "That time that Bo Derek nursed a chimp," http://fourfour.typepad.com/fourfour/2010/01/that-time-that-bo-derek-nursed-a-chimp.html.
41. "What Are Hybrid Big Cats?" Hybrid and Mutant Animals, http://www.messybeast.com/genetics/hyb-bigcats-whatare.htm.
42. "Hybrid Primates," Hybrid and Mutant Animals, http://www.messybeast.com/genetics/hybrid-primates.htm; "Oliver (chimpanzee)," http://en.wikipedia.org/wiki/Oliver_(chimpanzee).
43. Dmitri Bayanov, *In the Footsteps of the Russian* Snowman (Moscow: Crypto-Logos, 1996), pp. 46-52.

44. Ibid.
45. Ibid.
46. Ibid.
47. "Zana," http://www.squatchopedia.com/index.php/Zana#Examination_of_Skulls.
48. John Wilford, "Did Neanderthals and Homo sapiens mate?" *San diego Union-Tribune,* 23 February 2005; "To mate, or not to mate: the Neanderthal question," BBC News, 11 May 2010.

Conclusion

1. Denise Grady, "Dangerous cows," *New York Times* (31 July 2009).
2. "List of fatal bear attacks in North America," http://en.wikipedia.org/wiki/List_of_fatal_bear_attacks_in_North_America.
3. "Fatal Dog Attacks," American Canine Foundation, http://www.americancaninefoundation.com/fataldogattacks.html.

Bibliography

Arnold, Neil. *Monster!* Bideford, North Devon, UK: CFZ Press, 2007.

Arment, Chad. *The Historical Bigfoot.* Landisville, PA: Coachwhip Books, 2006.

Beck, Fred. *I Fought the Apemen of Mount St. Helens, Wa.* Kelso, WA: The author, 1967.

Berry, Rick. *Bigfoot on the East Coast.* Harrisonburg, VA: The Author, 1993.

Bord, Janet, and Colin Bord. *Alien Animals.* Harrisburg, PA: Stackpole, 1981.

—. *Bigfoot Casebook Updated.* Enumclaw, WA: Pine Winds Press, 2006.

—. *Unexplained Mysteries of the 20th Century.* Chicago: Contemporary Books, 1989.

Byrne, Peter. *The Search for Bigfoot.* New York: Pocket Books, 1975.

Childress, David. *Yetis, Sasquatch & Hairy Giants.* Kempton, IL: Adventures Unlimited Press, 2010.

Clark, Jerome. *Unnatural Phenomena.* Santa Barbara: ABC-CLIO, 2005.

Clark, Jerome, and Loren Coleman. *Creatures of the Outer Edge.* New York: Warner, 1978.

Coghlan, Ronan. *Cryptosup.* Bangor, No. Ireland: Xiphos, 2005.

—. *A Dictionary of Cryptozoology.* Bangor, No. Ireland: Xiphos, 2004.

—. *Further Cryptozoology.* Bangor, No. Ireland: Xiphos, 2007.

Coleman, Loren. *Bigfoot!* New York: Paraview, 2003.

—. *Mothman and Other Curious Encounters.* New York: Paraview, 2002.

—. *Mysterious America.* New York: Paraview, 2001.

Coleman, Loren, and Patrick Huyghe, *The Field Guide to Bigfoot, Yeti, and Other Mystery Primates Worldwide.* New York: Avon Books, 1999.

Cousins, Don. "Malaya's ape people." *Fortean Times* 196 (May 2005): 52-3.

Garden, Nancy. *Werewolves.* New York: Bantam, 1973.

Garner, Betty. *Monster! Monster!* Blaine, WA: Hancock House, 1995.

Graves, Frank. "The Valley Without a Head." *North American BioFortean Review* 6 (October 2004): 45-50.

Green, John. *On the Track of the Sasquatch.* New York: Ballantine, 1973.

—. *Sasquatch: The Apes Among Us.* Blaine, WA: Hancock House, 1978.

Guenette, Robert, and Frances Guenette. *The Mysterious Monsters.* Los Angeles: Schick Sun, 1975.

Guiley, Rosemary. *Atlas of the Mysterious in North America.* New York: Facts on File,

1995.

Healy, Tony, and Paul Cropper. *The Yowie: In Search of Australia's Bigfoot.* San Antonio, TX: Anomalist Books, 2006.

Heuvelmans, Bernard. On the Track of Unknown Animals. London: Kegan Paul, 1995.

Hunter, Don, and René Dahinden. *Sasquatch.* New York: Signet Books, 1973.

Keel, John. *The Complete Guide to Mysterious Beings.* New York: Main Street Books, 1994.

Krantz, Grover. *Bigfoot Sasquatch Evidence.* Blaine, WA: Hancock House, 1999.

"Malaysian man-ape seen." *Fortean Times* 207 (April 2006): 4-5.

Mangiacopra, Gary, and Dwight Smith. "Canada's Headless Valley Revisited." *North American BioFortean Review* 8 (January 2006): 8-14.

Meldrum, Jeff. *Sasquatch: Legend Meets Science.* New York: Forge, 2006.

Messner, Reinhold. *My Quest for the Yeti: Confronting the Himalayas' Deepest Mystery.* New York: St. Martin's Press, 2000.

Murphy, Christopher. *Bigfoot Encounters in Ohio.* Blaine, WA: Hancock House, 2006.

Newton, Michael. *Encyclopedia of Cryptozoology.* Jefferson, NC: McFarland, 2005.

Norman, Eric. *The Abominable Snowmen.* New York: Award, 1969.

North, Dick. *The Mad Trapper of Rat River: A True Story of Canada's Biggest Manhunt.* Guilford, CT: Lyons Press, 2005.

Redfern, Nick. *Man-Monkey: In Search of the British Bigfoot.* Bideford, North Devon, England: CFZ Press, 2007.

Sanderson, Ivan. *Abominable Snowmen: Legend Come to Life.* Philadelphia: Chilton, 1961.

—. *More "Things."* New York: Pyramid Books, 1969.

Slate, Ann, and Alan Berry. *Bigfoot.* New York: Bantam, 1976.

Smith, Malcolm. *Bunyips & Bigfoots.* Alexandria, NSW: Millennium Books, 1996.

Smith, Warren. *Strange Abominable Snowmen.* New York: Popular Library, 1970.

—. *Strange Monsters and Madmen.* New York: Popular Library, 1969.

Steiger, Brad. *The Werewolf Book.* Detroit: Visible Ink, 1999.

Internet Sources

Bigfoot Encounters, http://www.bigfootencounters.com/sbs/ebbetts.htm.

Bigfoot Field Researchers Organization, http://www.bfro.net.

British Centre for Bigfoot Research, http://british-bigfoot.tripod.com/britishbigfootresearchcenter/id7.html.

Cryptomundo, http://www.cryptomundo.com.

Gulf Coast Bigfoot Research Organization, http://www.gcbro.com.

The Haunted Nahanni National Park of Canada, http://geography.suite101.com/article.cfm the_haunted_nahanni_national_park_of_canada.

OregonBigfoot.com, http://www.oregonbigfoot.com.

Sasquatch Information Society, http://www.bigfootinfo.org.

Washington Bigfoot Sightings, http://www.spacepub.com/users/data/bigfoot/was/was.htm.

APPENDIX:
ADDITIONAL MYSTERY APE /
HOMINID ATTACKS FROM THE
CFZ FILES
by Richard Freeman

ASIA

YETI

In 1949 a Sherpa called Lakmpa Tenzing was said to have been torn to shreds by a yeti at a remote pass in Nanga Parbat, but there were no witnesses and his attacker may well have been a bear.

Canadian adventurer Robert A Hutchison explored Nepal in search of the yeti in 1988. Though he didn't see the beast himself he unearthed some interesting information.

His Sherpa guide Gyalzen informed him that in April of 1986 a Sherpa girl called Ang Dahki went looking for her family's yaks, which had not returned from their pasture at Chukhung. Where the valley narrowed between the moraine and the mountain she claimed to have heard several yetis screaming. When she stopped to listen several large rocks were hurled down, narrowly missing her. She ran home and sat in mute terror by the fire. It was hours before her parents could coax out of her what had happened.

In 1902 some workmen, posting telegraph lines between Lhasa, in Tibet, and Kalimpong, in Bengal, began to vanish. Some soldiers sent to investigate found and killed a Yeti they took to be responsible. John A. Keel wrote that an old Indian soldier, who saw it, said it was 3 metres in height with hairs from 7 to 8 cm length, and that it had an alarming face without hairs, yellow and sharp-edged teeth, and red and cold eyes. The body was supposedly sent off to British officials but vanished.

In 1832 *The Journal of the Asiatic Society of Bengal* published an account of B. H. Hodgson, who wrote that while trekking in northern Nepal, his locally based guides spotted a tall, bipedal creature covered with long dark hair, and his staff then fled in fear. Hodgson did not see the creature, but concluded it was an orang-utan. B.H Hodgson, a representative of the UK in Nepal, claimed his servant told him that a hirsute creature had attacked his servants, and that the locals called this creature the Rakshas, or demon.

In the 1950s the *Kathmandu Chronicle* reported the head of a yeti was kept in a monastery in Chilunka, 50 miles north of Kathmandu, and was supposedly that of one killed by Nepali soldiers, a number of whom had been killed by the creature.

YEREN
In May 1975, in Shennongjia, Gan Minzing saw a six foot yeren. He raised his stick to hit it but it grabbed the stick and trod on one of his feet. It opened its mouth in a threatening grimace but then backed away into the forest.

ORANG-PENDEK
On my third expedition to Sumatra in 2009 I met a man called Tarib. He was the supreme chief of the Kubu, the aboriginal people of the island. Most of the Kubu were away hunting but he had made a special effort to visit us. He had an amazing story to tell.

Five years ago he had seen an orang-pendek as he was walking in the forest. It was four feet tall, with black hair that shaded into blonde and grey in places. Its face looked like a monkey's but it walked upright like a man. He took the creature by surprise and it became aggressive. It raised its arms above its head and charged at him. He fled and hid behind a tangle of rattan vines. He watched as it looked for him, turning its head from side to side. Finally it moved away.

Whilst in a hotel in Padang, the famed explorer Benedict Allen met an American businessman called Swartz, who was on a six country development project tour. Swartz told him that there were stories doing the rounds among workers on the Trans-Sumatran Highway, of groups of 'monkey-men' hurling sticks at the machinery. Benedict recalls this in his book *Hunting the GuGu*.

In the early 1930s, a group of Kubu are said to have stumbled across a group of orang-pendek in a cave near the boundary of Ogan Ulu and Komering Ulu. The apes attacked the humans killing all but one of them. This was said to have occurred on a mountain called Bukit Nanti.

AMOMONGO

The Amomongo of The Philippines is said to resemble a gorilla with sharp claws. As recently as June 2008 one of these creatures was supposedly killing livestock and attacking humans in Brgy Sag-ang in La Castellana near the foot of Mt. Kanlaon. It was thought to inhabit a network of caves in the area. Elias Galvez and Salvador Aguilar reported to Mayor Alberto Nicor and the police that a "hairy creature with long nails" separately attacked them on the nights of 9th and 10th June. Aguilar, who was able to escape from the creature, was treated at the La Castellana Emergency Clinic for scratches on different parts of his body, police said. Galvez, who was also attacked by the creature, was rescued by his companions.

ALMASTY

Ukrainian biologist Grigory Panchenko has files on the almasty that are extensive, and he shared some of the more unusual stories with me whilst I was hunting the almasty with him in Russia in 2008. One story involved an adult almasty that approached a house and was attacked by a big dog. The almasty used a club to bludgeon the dog to death. It then entered the house and stole a large Balkarian cheese.

One man saw an almasty close to his house and worried about it stealing food so he threw a stone at it. The almasty retreated behind the house and soon after a huge rock was hurled right over the house narrowly missing the man. In the morning it took two large men to lift it.

Another man struck an almasty that had entered his house. The creature hit him back and knocked him fully 15 feet.

BAR-MANU

In 2003, in a village in the Indian controlled Jammu and Kashmir area, a 20-year-old man named Raju Wasim was attacked by an upright walking, hair-covered creature. The man came out of his uncle's home to feed cattle at a cowshed, and heard a strange noise. When he turned around a 4-foot-tall monster, covered with dense, dark, black hair all over was looking menacingly him.

He said:

> "There is no mistake about what I saw. The monster had the face of a man with monkey-like features. It was four feet tall, but extremely sturdy. It was the Snowman. It pounced at me and I jumped back on the veranda, shouting for help. My uncle and his family rushed to my rescue and the monster lazily walked away. It was hardly frightened by the commotion."

Raju's uncle, Muhammad Shafi, (47) saw the creature as well:

> "After the initial appearance, we burnt fires to scare the visitor and he rushed out of the hedges and crossed to the other

side of an apple orchard. I saw it myself. The description matches Raju's. In addition, the animal made a shrill whistle when frightened. Perhaps scared by the fires, it whistled while running away".

Another villager Rehman Magray, 89, said:

"In our youth there used to be very heavy snowfall. We had five metres deep snow on the ground. There was no electricity. The only lighting we had was from oil lamps or resin-wood fire torches that we carried while moving about in the dark.

Almost regularly, the Snowman would visit this village and others close to the mountains where heavy snow made feeding difficult for them during harsh winters."

During January 1987, in Northern Kashmir, workers on a sheep farm encountered a 4-foot tall, ape-like beast that attacked one of them. The victim, a boy, drove it off by smashing a pot over its head. The details are scant.

NGUOI-RUNG

During the war between Vietnam and the US there were many reports of sightings, and even attacks, by creatures that the GIs referred to as 'rock apes' due to their habit of hurling rocks when annoyed. Their description sounds not unlike the Russian almasty.

Michael Kelly was part of the 101 Airborne Division in 1969 /1970. He encountered some of rock apes:

"We ran into them frequently and I have a friend whose Recon position on Dong Den was overrun one night by hundreds of them. They made a noise that sounded just like a dog barking. In fact, you'd swear it was a dog. One time on a ridge of Nui Mo Tau, about 15 km S of Hue, about eight of them came walking up a trail and surprised a squad of our platoon while it was stopped for lunch. All hell broke loose because they looked very much like NVA soldiers in khaki (same height, size and colour) as they came around a bend in the trail about 10 meters from the unsuspecting GI's.

I was with the other two squads of the platoon eating our lunch on the far side of a clearing about 50 meters wide that separated the two elements. The trails wound up the ridge and then through the clearing. All of a sudden and without any warning, the lone squad opened up with everything they had...M-16's, M-79's and hand grenades. I grabbed about 300 rounds of gun ammo and my M-60, then ran across the clearing with the platoon Sgt. (everyone else stayed home!) to the cover of a huge, toppled tree that was lying on the far side and close to the point of contact. The Sgt. and I looked at one another, nodded and then came up over the top ready to blast away but what we saw instead blew us away. The firing had been non-stop and we fully expected to engage a sizeable enemy force, but instead, we found ourselves looking at our men, some seated, some standing, some kneeling, and firing at these ghostly images swooshing around in brush and trees (some off the ground by that point) in all directions. All except one was light brown to reddish brown in colour, and about 5 ½- four feet tall. One dark, almost black, male remained fighting to protect the others retreat and he was flying through the branches and rushing the men with his teeth bared. He was one very brave animal, I'll tell you that.

Then, as if someone had snapped their fingers, they all just seemed to disappear. Zip, the male turned and flashed into the trees and was out of site in a second.

This may sound very strange to you, but although I had no or little concern about killing the enemy, the killing of innocent animals turned my stomach and could enrage me if done without being a necessity. But I searched the site and but found not a drop of blood, which totally amazed me given the amount of firing that had gone on. I wonder to this day if the men were shooting just to scare the Rock Apes away or whether they were really just poor marksman!

The men who'd suffered the surprise looked a bit worse for wear, and I'm sure a few had to wash their shorts out as a result of the unwelcome visit. It really scared the crap out of them, I kid you not! We, on the other hand, did suffer one casualty. A trooper had an eardrum blown out by the muzzle blast of the first shot fired because the trooper who first saw the apes just picked up his M-16 and fired without saying a word, and the muzzle was right next to this poor fellow's ear when he did."

n 1970, GI Steve Canyon was out testing a new flash and noise suppressor for the AK-47 automatic rifle. Steven and a friend took their position for the test then saw a rock ape looking down at them. It made a noise like the bark of a dog. Steve's friend threw a rock at the crea ture but it picked it up and threw it back harder. Then twenty or so of the creatures emerge from the jungle, hurling rocks and making barking noises. Steve and his friend ran back to th camp.

In 1966, the most infamous event was alleged to have happened in Quang Nam Province. Hi 868, or Dong Den Mountain in Vietnamese, was supposedly inhabited by rock apes. The Thir Marines created a Divisional Outpost and Landing zone by blowing the top off the hill. Th Marines on the hill had radioed their captain telling him they heard movement in the foliag and thought it was the Viet Cong. As the captain was listening, a group of rock apes emerge and attacked the Marines with rocks. They answered with gunfire. The captain could not get response from the radio and dispatched a squad over to investigate. When they got there the found the area strewn with dead apes and wounded soldiers. Four men needed serious medic attention.

SOUTH AMERICA

DI-DI
During my 2006 expedition to hunt the giant anaconda in Guyana, I heard several stories abou the di-di, a yeti like beast. Some included violent interaction.

Whilst in the native village of Pakuri we were told of a di-di encounter that occurred only tw years before. It happened in another Amarindian village some 30 miles north of Pakuri. Tw children, a boy and a girl of about 12, were walking home from school across the savannah What the boy described as a 'huge hairy man' stepped out of a stand of trees and grabbed th girl. She was never seen again. There was no police investigation, but this is unsurprising a the government of Guyana seems to care very little for its native peoples.

A local hunter named Kenard Davis told us that in the 1940s a girl was kidnapped by a di-d and was taken deep into the jungle. It took her as its mate and together they had a hybrid chil - half human, half di-di. The girl stayed with the di-di against her will until one day she saw hunter in a canoe. She shouted him over to the bank and leapt aboard. As the hunter paddle off , the di-di emerged from the jungle and stood on the bank gesticulating for the girl to re turn. When she did not the monster picked up their half-breed offspring and tore it to shred like a doll.

Another story told of a group of men boating down the Essequibo River. At one point, the had stopped and disembarked when they saw one of their colleagues grabbed from behind by massive hairy arm. A huge ape-like figure carried him into the jungle. The other men pursue shooting at the shaggy giant till it let the man drop.

Italian archaeologist Pino Turolla was told a bloody story by an Indian guide in Venezuel Antonio, the man in question , had gone with his two sons to the Pacaraima Range. As the approached the savannah three lumbering, ape-like beasts with smallish heads and long arms attacked them with clubs, killing his younger son. Some six months later Turolla persuaded Antonio and some other Indians to show him the area in question. They heard shrill roars and the natives would go no further. Turolla himself claimed to have glimpsed an 8-foot, ape-like, lumbering form.

NORTH AMERICA

FOUKE MONSTER

In 1971, a skunk ape christened by the media as the Fouke Monster terrorised a house belonging to Bobby and Elizabeth Ford near Fouke, Miller County, Arkansas. It reached through a screen window and grabbed at Elizabeth. Later that night it grabbed Bobby by the shoulders and threw him to the floor, who was later treated in St. Michael Hospital, Texarkana, for scratches and shock.

AUSTRALIA

YOWIE

According to Rex Gilroy, in 1910 two men were walking in the Victoria Falls area of the Blue Mountains when a ten foot gorilla-like creature emerged from the bush and attacked them. It hurled a large rock, smashing the skull of one man as his friend fled. When the survivor returned with a party of armed men and dogs, the body was gone with only bloodstains remaining. Sadly we have not been able to substantiate this story from any other source.

Tony Healy and Paul Cropper recount a disturbingly suggestive tale in their excellent book *The Yowie: In Search of Australia's Bigfoot.* They heard it from fellow yowie investigator Neil Frost. In the 1990s Neil interviewed a Blue Mountains based lawyer who in the 1970s had discovered a decapitated body in the bush behind the Warrimoo Bush Fire Station. The police said the man's head had not been cut off, but had been literally torn from his body and was found fifty feet away! Was it a yowie? We shall probably never know, but such a creature would certainly be capable of ripping off a man's head.

In 1996, Dean Harrison was jogging one night near Ormeau, Queensland ,when he began to get the feeling he was being followed by something that stayed hidden by the bush. The thing brought a horrid sensation with it.

> "I just had an indescribable chill that ran from my head to my toes. The unfamiliar and hugely terrifying sensation just overtook my entire body...I simply could not understand why I suddenly felt so uneasy and so vulnerable as I did but I knew something was terribly wrong and it had something to do with whoever or whatever was behind me."

Turning round he saw a 7-foot, hulking silhouette behind the trees. Dean felt paralyzed and had to force himself to move. The creature pursued him with a blood chilling roar. He narrowly escaped its grasp as it lunged for him from the bush line and he dodged into the light of a street lamp.

On the 10th August 1977 Jean Maloney was awoken at 2.30 am by her Australian terrier yelping. Its barks were intermingled with a weird high-pitched screaming sound. On investigation she found an ap- like beast squatting in her garden only 6-feet away from her. It was clutching the dog to its chest. It was over 6-feet tall with big, dark eyes, a heavy brow and no chin. It head sat directly on the shoulders with no neck. It was covered with ginger hair. The creature had a pungent odour like a ferret.

Dropping the dog, it backed away towards the fence making grunting sounds. When several stray dogs arrived, it ran off into the night.

Jean's dog had wounds to the chest and neck and had a greasy residue on her fur. She died shortly afterwards. Jean thought that the yowie was feeding from a bucket of fruit in the back yard when the dog attacked it. Three distinct footprints were found alongside the house. Gary Buchanan, a reporter for the *Northern Star* examined and photographed one. It was 9-inches long and 4- inches across, and showed five distinct toes.

STILL ON THE TRACK OF UNKNOWN ANIMALS

The Centre for Fortean Zoology, or CFZ, is a non profit-making organisation founded in 1992 with the aim of being a clearing house for information, and coordinating research into mystery animals around the world.

We also study out of place animals, rare and aberrant animal behaviour, and Zooform Phenomena; little-understood "things" that appear to be animals, but which are in fact nothing of the sort, and not even alive (at least in the way we understand the term).

Not only are we the biggest organisation of our type in the world, but - or so we like to think - we are the best. We are certainly the only truly global cryptozoological research organisation, and we carry out our investigations using a strictly scientific set of guidelines. We are expanding all the time and looking to recruit new members to help us in our research into mysterious animals and strange creatures across the globe.

Why should you join us? Because, if you are genuinely interested in trying to solve the last great mysteries of Mother Nature, there is nobody better than us with whom to do it.

Members get a four-issue sub
scription to our journal *Animal.
& Men*. Each issue contain:
nearly 100 pages packed with
news, articles, letters, research
papers, field reports, and even a
gossip column! The magazine is
Royal Octavo in format with a
full colour cover. You also have
access to one of the world's
largest collections of resource
material dealing with cryptozo
ology and allied disciplines, and
people from the CFZ member
ship regularly take part in field
work and expeditions around
the world.

The CFZ is managed by a three-man board of trustees, with a non-profit making trust regis
tered with HM Government Stamp Office. The board of trustees is supported by a Permanen
Directorate of full and part-time staff, and advised by a Consultancy Board of specialists -
many of whom are world-renowned experts in their particular field. We have regional repre
sentatives across the UK, the USA, and many other parts of the world, and are affiliated with
other organisations whose aims and protocols mirror our own.

You'll find that the people at the CFZ are friendly and approachable. We have a thriving forum on the website which is the hub of an ever-growing electronic community. You will soon find your feet. Many members of the CFZ Permanent Directorate started off as ordinary members, and now work full-time chasing monsters around the world.

Write to us, e-mail us, or telephone us. The list of future projects on the website is not exhaustive. If you have a good idea for an investigation, please tell us. We may well be able to help.

We are always looking for volunteers to join us. If you see a project that interests you, do not hesitate to get in touch with us. Under certain circumstances we can help provide funding for your trip. If you look on the future projects section of the website, you can see some of the projects that we have pencilled in for the next few years.

In 2003 and 2004 we sent three-man expeditions to Sumatra looking for Orang-Pendek - a semi-legendary bipedal ape. The same three went to Mongolia in 2005. All three members started off merely subscribers to the CFZ magazine. Next time it could be you!

We have no magic sources of income. All our funds come from donations, membership fees, and sales of our publications and merchandise. We are always looking for corporate sponsorship, and other sources of revenue. If you have any ideas for fund-raising please let us know.

However, unlike other cryptozoological organisations in the past, we do not live in an intellectual ivory tower. We are not afraid to get our hands dirty, and furthermore we are not one of those organisations where the membership have to raise money so that a privileged few can go on expensive foreign trips. Our research teams, both in the UK and abroad, consist of a mixture of experienced and inexperienced personnel. We are truly a community, and work on the premise that the benefits of CFZ membership are open to all.

Reports of our investigations are published on our website as soon as they are available. Preliminary reports are posted within days of the project finishing.

Each year we publish a 200 page yearbook containing research papers and expedition reports too long to be printed in the journal. We freely circulate our information to anybody who asks for it.

We have a thriving YouTube channel, CFZtv, which has well over two hundred self-made documentaries, lecture appearances, and episodes of our monthly webTV show. We have a daily online magazine, which has over a million hits each year.

Each year since 2000 we have held our annual convention - the Weird Weekend. It is three days of lectures, workshops, and excursions. But most importantly it is a chance for members of the CFZ to meet each other, and to talk with the members of the permanent directorate in a relaxed and informal setting and preferably with a pint of beer in one hand. Since 2006 - the Weird Weekend has been bigger and better and held on the third weekend in August in the idyllic rural location of Woolsery in North Devon.

Since relocating to North Devon in 2005 we have become ever more closely involved with other community organisations, and we hope that this trend will continue. We have also worked closely

with Police Forces across the UK as consultants for animal mutilation cases, and we intend t forge closer links with the coastguard and other community services. We want to work closel with those who regularly travel into the Bristol Channel, so that if the recent trend of exoti animal visitors to our coastal waters continues, we can be out there as soon as possible.

Apart from having been th only Fortean Zoological o ganisation in the world to hav consistently published materi on all aspects of the subject f over a decade, we hav achieved the following con crete results:

• Disproved the myt relating to the headless s called sea-serpent carcass Durgan beach in Cornwa 1975

• Disproved the story the 1988 puma skull

Lustleigh Cleave
Carried out the only in-depth research ever into the mythos of the Cornish Owlman.
Made the first records of a tropical species of lamprey
Made the first records of a luminous cave gnat larva in Thailand
Discovered a possible new species of British mammal - the beech marten
In 1994-6 carried out the first archival fortean zoological survey of Hong Kong
In the year 2000, CFZ theories were confirmed when a new species of lizard was added to the British List
Identified the monster of Martin Mere in Lancashire as a giant wels catfish
Expanded the known range of Armitage's skink in the Gambia by 80%
Obtained photographic evidence of the remains of Europe's largest known pike
Carried out the first ever in-depth study of the ninki-nanka
Carried out the first attempt to breed Puerto Rican cave snails in captivity
Were the first European explorers to visit the `lost valley` in Sumatra
Published the first ever evidence for a new tribe of pygmies in Guyana
Published the first evidence for a new species of caiman in Guyana
Filmed unknown creatures

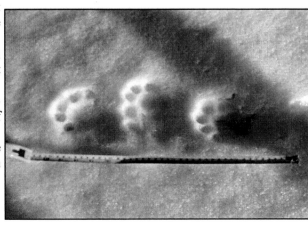

on a monster-haunted lake in Ireland fc the first time

- Had a sighting of orang pende in Sumatra in 2009
- Found leopard hair, subsequentl identified by DNA analysis, from rura North Devon in 2010
- Brought back hairs which appea to be from an unknown primate in Su matra
- Published some of the best evi dence ever for the almasty in souther Russia

CFZ Expeditions and Investigations include:

- 1998 Puerto Rico, Florida, Mexico (Chupacabras)
- 1999 Nevada (Bigfoot)
- 2000 Thailand (Naga)
- 2002 Martin Mere (Giant catfish)
- 2002 Cleveland (Wallaby mutilation)

- 2003 Bolam Lake (BHM Reports)
- 2003 Sumatra (Orang Pendek)
- 2003 Texas (Bigfoot; giant snapping turtles)
- 2004 Sumatra (Orang Pendek; cigau, a sabre-toothed cat)
- 2004 Illinois (Black panthers; cicada swarm)
- 2004 Texas (Mystery blue dog)
- Loch Morar (Monster)
- 2004 Puerto Rico (Chupacabras; carnivorous cave snails)
- 2005 Belize (Affiliate expedition for hairy dwarfs)
- 2005 Loch Ness (Monster)
- 2005 Mongolia (Allghoi Khorkhoi aka Mongolian death worm)

- 2006 Gambia (Gambo - Gambian sea monster , Ninki Nanka and Armitage's skink
- 2006 Llangorse Lake (Giant pike, giant eels)
- 2006 Windermere (Giant eels)
- 2007 Coniston Water (Giant eels)
- 2007 Guyana (Giant anaconda, didi, water tiger)
- 2008 Russia (Almasty)
- 2009 Sumatra (Orang pendek)
- 2009 Republic of Ireland (Lake Monster)
- 2010 Texas (Blue Dogs)
- 2010 India (Mande Burung)

For details of current membership fees, current expeditions and investigations, and voluntary posts within the CFZ that need your help, please do not hesitate to contact us.

The Centre for Fortean Zoology,
Myrtle Cottage,
Woolfardisworthy,
Bideford, North Devon
EX39 5QR

Telephone 01237 431413
Fax+44 (0)7006-074-925
eMail info@cfz.org.uk

Websites:

www.cfz.org.uk
www.weirdweekend.org

THE WORLD'S WEIRDEST PUBLISHING COMPANY

HOW TO START A PUBLISHING EMPIRE

Unlike most mainstream publishers, we have a non-commercial remit, and our mission state
ment claims that "we publish books because they deserve to be published, not because w
think that we can make money out of them". Our motto is the Latin Tag *Pro bona caus*
facimus (we do it for good reason), a slogan taken from a children's book *The Case of the Si*
ver Egg by the late Desmond Skirrow.

WIKIPEDIA: "The first book published was in 1988. *Take this Brother may it Serv*
you Well was a guide to Beatles bootlegs by Jonathan Downes. It sold quite well, bu
was hampered by very poor production values, being photocopied, and held togethe
by a plastic clip binder. In 1988 A5 clip binders were hard to get hold of, so the pub
lishers took A4 binders and cut them in half with a hacksaw. It now reaches surpris
ingly high prices second hand.

The production quality improved slightly over the years, and after 1999 all the book
produced were ringbound with laminated colour covers. In 2004, however, the
signed an agreement with Lightning Source, and all books are now produced perfec
bound, with full colour covers."

Until 2010 all our books, the majority of which are/were on the subject of mystery anima
and allied disciplines, were published by `CFZ Press`, the publishing arm of the Centre fc
Fortean Zoology (CFZ), and we urged our readers and followers to draw a discreet veil ove
the books that we published that were completely off topic to the CFZ.

However, in 2010 we decided that enough was enough and launched a second imprin
`Fortean Words` which aims to cover a wide range of non animal-related esoteric subject
Other imprints will be launched as and when we feel like it, however the basic ethos of th
company remains the same: Our job is to publish books and magazines that we feel are wort
publishing, whether or not they are going to sell. Money is, after all - as my dear old Mam
once told me - a rather vulgar subject, and she would be rolling in her grave if she thought tha
her eldest son was somehow in `trade`.

Luckily, so far our tastes have turned out ne
to be that rarified after all, and we have sol
far more books than anyone ever thought tha
we would, so there is a moral in there some
where…

Jon Downes,
Woolsery, North Devon
July 2010

CFZ PRESS

Other Books in Print

When Bigfoot Attacks by Michael Newton

Mystery Animals of the British Isles: Gloucestershire and Worcestershire by Paul Williams

Weird Waters – The Mystery Animals of Scandinavia: Lake and Sea Monsters by Lars Thomas

Monstrum! By Tony `Doc` Shiels

CFZ Yearbook 2011 edited by Jonathan Downes

Karl Shuker's Alien Zoo by Shuker, Dr Karl P.N

Tetrapod Zoology Book One by Naish, Dr Darren

The Mystery Animals of Ireland by Gary Cunningham and Ronan Coghlan

Monsters of Texas by Gerhard, Ken

The Great Yokai Encyclopaedia by Freeman, Richard

NEW HORIZONS: Animals & Men issues 16-20 Collected Editions Vol. 4 by Downes, Jonathan

A Daintree Diary -
Tales from Travels to the Daintree Rainforest in tropical north Queensland, Australia
by Portman, Carl

Strangely Strange but Oddly Normal by Roberts, Andy

Centre for Fortean Zoology Yearbook 2010 by Downes, Jonathan

Predator Deathmatch by Molloy, Nick

Star Steeds and other Dreams by Shuker, Karl

CHINA: A Yellow Peril? by Muirhead, Richard

Mystery Animals of the British Isles: The Western Isles by Vaudrey, Glen

Giant Snakes - Unravelling the coils of mystery by Newton, Michael

Mystery Animals of the British Isles: Kent by Arnold, Neil

Centre for Fortean Zoology Yearbook 2009 by Downes, Jonathan

CFZ EXPEDITION REPORT: Russia 2008 by Richard Freeman et al, Shuker, Karl (fwd)

Dinosaurs and other Prehistoric Animals on Stamps - A Worldwide catalogue by Shuker, Karl P. N

Dr Shuker's Casebook by Shuker, Karl P.N

The Island of Paradise - chupacabra UFO crash retrievals,
and accelerated evolution on the island of Puerto Rico by Downes, Jonathan

The Mystery Animals of the British Isles: Northumberland and Tyneside by Hallowell, Michael J

Centre for Fortean Zoology Yearbook 1997 by Downes, Jonathan (Ed)

Centre for Fortean Zoology Yearbook 2002 by Downes, Jonathan (Ed)
Centre for Fortean Zoology Yearbook 2000/1 by Downes, Jonathan (Ed)
Centre for Fortean Zoology Yearbook 1998 by Downes, Jonathan (Ed)
Centre for Fortean Zoology Yearbook 2003 by Downes, Jonathan (Ed)
In the wake of Bernard Heuvelmans by Woodley, Michael A
CFZ EXPEDITION REPORT: Guyana 2007 by Richard Freeman *et al*, Shuker, Karl (fwd)
Centre for Fortean Zoology Yearbook 1999 by Downes, Jonathan (Ed)
Big Cats in Britain Yearbook 2008 by Fraser, Mark (Ed)
Centre for Fortean Zoology Yearbook 1996 by Downes, Jonathan (Ed)
THE CALL OF THE WILD - Animals & Men issues 11-15
Collected Editions Vol. 3 by Downes, Jonathan (ed)
Ethna's Journal by Downes, C N
Centre for Fortean Zoology Yearbook 2008 by Downes, J (Ed)
DARK DORSET - Calendar Custome by Newland, Robert J
Extraordinary Animals Revisited by Shuker, Karl
MAN-MONKEY - In Search of the British Bigfoot by Redfern, Nick
Dark Dorset Tales of Mystery, Wonder and Terror by Newland, Robert J and Mark North
Big Cats Loose in Britain by Matthews, Marcus
MONSTER! - The A-Z of Zooform Phenomena by Arnold, Neil
The Centre for Fortean Zoology 2004 Yearbook by Downes, Jonathan (Ed)
The Centre for Fortean Zoology 2007 Yearbook by Downes, Jonathan (Ed)
CAT FLAPS! Northern Mystery Cats by Roberts, Andy
Big Cats in Britain Yearbook 2007 by Fraser, Mark (Ed)
BIG BIRD! - Modern sightings of Flying Monsters by Gerhard, Ken
THE NUMBER OF THE BEAST - Animals & Men issues 6-10
Collected Editions Vol. 1 by Downes, Jonathan (Ed)
IN THE BEGINNING - Animals & Men issues 1-5 Collected Editions Vol. 1 by Downes, Jonathan
STRENGTH THROUGH KOI - They saved Hitler's Koi and other stories by Downes, Jonathan
The Smaller Mystery Carnivores of the Westcountry by Downes, Jonathan
CFZ EXPEDITION REPORT: Gambia 2006 by Richard Freeman *et al*, Shuker, Karl (fwd)
The Owlman and Others by Jonathan Downes
The Blackdown Mystery by Downes, Jonathan
Big Cats in Britain Yearbook 2006 by Fraser, Mark (Ed)
Fragrant Harbours - Distant Rivers by Downes, John T
Only Fools and Goatsuckers by Downes, Jonathan
Monster of the Mere by Jonathan Downes
Dragons:More than a Myth by Freeman, Richard Alan
Granfer's Bible Stories by Downes, John Tweddell
Monster Hunter by Downes, Jonathan

Fortean Words

The Centre for Fortean Zoology has for several years led the field in Fortean publishing. CFZ Press is the only publishing company specialising in books on monsters and mystery animals. CFZ Press has published more books on this subject than any other company in history and has attracted such well known authors as Andy Roberts, Nick Redfern, Mihael Newton, Dr Karl Shuker, Neil Arnold, Dr Darren Naish, Jon Downes, Ken Gerhard and Richard Freeman.

Now CFZ Press are launching a new imprint. Fortean Words is a new line of books dealing with Fortean subjects other than cryptozoology, which is - after all - the subject the CFZ are best known for. Fortean Words is being launched with a spectacular multi-volume series called *Haunted Skies* which covers British UFO sightings between 1940 and 2010. Former policeman John Hanson and his long-suffering partner Dawn Holloway have compiled a peerless library of sighting reports, many that have not been made public before.

Other books include a look at the Berwyn Mountains UFO case by renowned Fortean Andy Roberts and a series of forthcoming books by transatlantic researcher Nick Redfern.

CFZ Press are dedicated to maintaining the fine quality of their works with Fortean Words. New authors tackling new subjects will always be encouraged, and we hope that our books will continue to be as ground-breaking and popular as ever.

Haunted Skies Volume One 1940-1959 by John Hanson and Dawn Holloway
Haunted Skies Volume Two 1960-1965 by John Hanson and Dawn Holloway
Space Girl Dead on Spaghetti Junction - an anthology by Nick Redfern
Fort the Lore - an anthology by Paul Screeton
UFO Down - the Berwyn Mountains UFO Crash by Andy Roberts

CPSIA information can be obtained at www.ICGtesting.com
Printed in the USA
LVOW081518031111

253400LV00002BA/8/P